Employment for Individuals with Asperger Syndrome or Non-Verbal Learning Disability

of related interest

Asperger Syndrome Employment Workbook
An Employment Workbook for Adults with Asperger Syndrome
Roger N. Meyer
Foreword by Tony Attwood
ISBN 1 85302 796 0

How to Find Work that Works for People with Asperger Syndrome
The Ultimate Guide for Getting People with Asperger Syndrome
into the Workplace (and Keeping Them There!)
Gail Hawkins
ISBN 1 84310 151 3

Succeeding in College with Asperger Syndrome
A Student Guide
John Harpur, Maria Lawlor and Michael Fitzgerald
ISBN 1 84310 201 3

Autism, Advocates, and Law Enforcement Professionals
Recognizing and Reducing Risk Situations for People
with Autism Spectrum Disorders
Dennis Debbaudt
ISBN 1 85302 980 7

Asperger's Syndrome
A Guide for Parents and Professionals
Tony Attwood
Foreword by Lorna Wing
ISBN 1 85302 577 1

Build Your Own Life
A Self-Help Guide for Individuals with Asperger Syndrome
Wendy Lawson
Foreword by Dr Dinah Murray
ISBN 1 84310 114 9

Employment for Individuals with Asperger Syndrome or Non-Verbal Learning Disability

Stories and Strategies

Yvona Fast and others

Jessica Kingsley Publishers
London and New York

First published in the United Kingdom in 2004
by Jessica Kingsley Publishers Ltd
116 Pentonville Road
London N1 9JB, England
and
29 West 35th Street, 10th fl.
New York, NY 10001-2299, USA
www.jkp.com

Library of Congress Cataloging in Publication Data

Fast, Yvona, 1955-
  Employment for individuals with Asperger syndrome or non-verbal learning disability : stories and strategies / Yvona Fast and others.
1st American pbk. ed.
    p. cm.
Includes bibliographical references and index.
  ISBN 1-84310-766-X (pbk.)
  1. People with mental disabilities Vocational guidance. 2. Learning disabled Vocational guidance. 3. Asperger's syndrome Patients Vocational guidance. 4. People with mental disabilities Employment. 5. Nonverbal learning disabilities. I. Title.
  HV3005.F37 2004
  331.702'087'5 dc22

                                        2003026448

British Library Cataloguing in Publication Data
A CIP catalogue record for this book is available from the British Library

ISBN 1 84310 766 X

Printed and Bound in Great Britain by
Athenaeum Press, Gateshead, Tyne and Wear

Contents

Part I Career Voices

NLD Voices

AS Voices

Part II Career Strategies

Planning for a Career

Finding a Job

Maintaining a Career

Part III Resources

Tables

Acknowledgements

I'm indebted to many people for the ideas in this book. I have learned much from folks with AS and NLD whom I've come to know. A few I've met in person. Some I've spoken with on the telephone. Many more I know only as online friends from e-mail lists and Internet forums. All have contributed their advice and perspective indirectly to this book.

Many friends were congenial and helpful, providing suggestions and encouragement along the way. Some read and re-read various chapters, offering insight and corrections. My mother's support, encouragement, and patience is and has always been a great blessing.

Disclaimer

This book does not constitute legal or professional advice. I have tried to correctly cite sources of information and to credit contributors. Examples given are hypothetical and fictitious. Some names have been changed, and alterations have been made in descriptive material to ensure confidentiality. Any resemblance to real persons, living or dead, is wholly coincidental. Readers agree to indemnify the authors from any errors or omissions and/or from any misunderstandings or interpretations arising from the information contained herein.

This book is not an endorsement for any resources or publications that are mentioned. Readers should exercise judgment in researching information and making decisions about their respective situations.

Introduction

Why this book is needed

As individuals with Non-Verbal Learning Disability (NLD) or Asperger Syndrome (AS), we are different, but we try to conform to the mold. Yet no matter how hard we work, it's not good enough for the neurotypical (NT) world. The agencies that are supposed to serve the disabled can't assist us because we don't fit in with their usual population.

Career planning books have not been written with our difficulties in mind. The NLD/AS individual is a special case because often he/she is very intelligent, has high verbal abilities, and tends to have excellent writing skills. On the other hand, our challenges in the social, visual-spatial, organizational, and motor coordination areas cause us to stick out in the workplace.

The British newspaper, *The Observer*, in the articles "Adult victims of autism are left on jobs scrapheap" (Beaumont 2001) and "Signal failure" (Carlowe 2001), reports that nine out of ten Asperger adults are unable to hold a job and earn a living. Jerry Newport, who has founded several support groups for adults with ASD over the last ten years, thinks it's more accurate to say that 90 percent of the AS population is underemployed. "Of the couple of hundred AS people I have met, at least half have jobs, but very few are employed at the level you would expect if you knew their education," he said. Despite a university degree in mathematics, he has spent most of his life as a taxi driver and courier, but finally found work in accounting and tax consulting.

It is appalling that someone who is intelligent, educated, honest, and hard working is unemployed. To extend that figure to 90 percent of a given population shows something wrong with the system.

While there are career services for people with physical and mental disabilities, these agencies are not designed to help people with AS or NLD find and maintain employment. Few people have even heard of these conditions; most vocational rehabilitation workers and career counselors are clueless as to how to help us. A lack of information about the nature of our disability can be more of a problem than the disability itself.

Ours is a "hidden disability." Our differences are less obvious than those of someone with Down Syndrome or severe autism. We go through life pretending to be normal, trying to fit into a world that refuses to accept us. Most often, we are accused of being lazy or rude when in fact most of us work very hard to achieve – and yet all our effort and persistence is not good enough for the neurotypical (NT) world we live in. People don't understand how someone who seems so "normal" or "bright" has such problems with certain things. We need some way to educate the professionals, and to make ourselves better understood.

Our minds work differently. One mother describes her son as being excruciatingly slow, no matter what the task. In order to undertake and complete a task, he needs very clear, comprehensive, and linear instructions. His comprehension of body language and non-verbal social cues, which make up a lot of workplace communication, is almost nonexistent. Like many with the disorder, he has been unable to find a work environment in which he fits and can be successful.

That doesn't make us second class, though we feel as if we are second class. Despite the challenges we face, individuals with NLD/AS have many wonderful characteristics that can be useful in the right work environment. As a group, we tend to be articulate, thorough, kind, and persistent. Many of us are highly educated, have great verbal and writing skills, and are highly motivated, conscientious, honest, and hard working. But it can be very difficult to find the job that will make allowances and accommodations for our disabilities while making our abilities shine. Individuals with NLD/AS often suffer from:

- a pervasive sense of underachievement, of doing one's best but always falling short of others' expectations

- feeling that the world sees us as lazy, crazy, stupid, and/or irresponsible, when this is the farthest thing from the truth

- feeling "different" or like a "misfit" in many situations

- feeling overwhelmed with life
- an extreme lack of self-esteem.

How can we find a suitable work environment? How can we maximize the probability of workplace success and minimize the possibility of failure? We need to make ourselves better understood. Our difficulties need to be recognized and taken seriously. That's the only way we're going to reach some semblance of our true potential.

For example, while I work hard and have great determination, I've had more than 40 different jobs in 25 years. My problems over the years have led to job situations where I was repeatedly told that I just didn't fit in, or that I did not have the abilities to succeed at the career I was attempting.

There are supports out there for other individuals with disabilities. The physically disabled have many accommodations. Buses have wheelchair lifts. Public buildings must be wheelchair accessible. The blind person gets readers. The deaf have interpreters. Even individuals with Attention Deficit Disorder (ADD) have gained increased acceptance. But NLD/AS? No one knows who we are. Even the term "non-verbal learning disability" is confusing. We aren't non-verbal. We are in fact very verbal. We can learn fine. We can take tests and do well.

I tend to score high on civil service exams. Then comes the interview. Most often, I'm not the one hired. If I manage to get the job, problems arise, and I'm usually out by the end of the probation period. It's in applying that book knowledge to real world situations where my problems arise. My hopes are that this book will do three things:

- educate and enlighten vocational rehabilitation personnel and career counselors to the specific needs of NLD/AS individuals.
- help NLD/AS adults and teens who are entering the workforce
- help NLD/AS adults who are struggling in the workplace.

In order to accomplish these goals, in Part I, Career Voices, I have conducted numerous interviews with NLD and AS adults. Their stories offer examples of disability-related issues that arise at work and show how these intelligent adults have come to grips with them. While many have struggled in the work world, others have successful careers. Their stories encourage us, showing that, with the right match of career and work environment, we can indeed succeed.

Part II, Career Strategies, deals with employment issues – from career planning to finding a job to keeping that job – and how various NLD/AS characteristics impact this process. The first section deals with career planning, which must come first, before actual employment. I believe a good match is crucial to future vocational success. The transition from school to work is often a difficult time for ASers/NLDers, so I have included some tips.

The second section of Part II, Finding a Job, relates job-hunting strategies to the needs of the individual with AS or NLD. Since there are myriad books and websites with information on job hunting, this section is brief. I have attempted to make the job search as NLD/AS friendly as possible, and have devoted most of the space to interview strategies, often the most difficult part for NLDers and ASers.

The third section of Part II, Maintaining a Career, is the longest. I have attempted to discuss all the possible NLD/AS issues that impact work performance, positively as well as negatively, and to come up with ways to work around these. I have included chapters on disclosing the disability, a dilemma many struggle with; workplace bullying, which has been the downfall of many; and working with vocational rehabilitation personnel, as many NLDers/ASers will find themselves traveling that road. I conclude with my dream for a future where NLD and AS ways of thinking and doing are understood and accepted. This is followed by a list of career choices for NLDers/ASers.

Part III contains extensive lists of disability and career resources.

AS and NLD: descriptions, differences, and similarities

AS and NLD are neurologically based developmental disorders that affect the way in which the brain processes information. Based on a group of observable traits, both conditions are due to brain abnormalities, not emotional trauma. The AS/NLD brain is wired differently, though it's not necessarily faulty. People with NLD or AS generally have average to superior intelligence and above average verbal ability, yet have significant difficulty with job performance and social interactions. Because our society values social competence above knowledge or intelligence, such deficits often cause NLD/AS individuals significant, lifelong challenges in relationships, work, and recreational pursuits. Though the issues may change over time, the problems don't go away. In 1944 Hans Asperger wrote:

In the course of development, certain features predominate or recede, so that the problems presented change considerably. Nevertheless, the essential aspects of the problem remain unchanged. In early childhood there are the difficulties in learning simple practical skills and in social adaptation. These difficulties arise out of the same disturbance which at school age causes learning and conduct problems, in adolescence job and performance problems and in adulthood social and marital conflicts. (Asperger 1944, quoted in Bauer 1996)

Although neither condition prevents those with it from having a "normal" adult life, there's little information about the eventual outcome for most children with AS or NLD. Some NLD/AS adults have been able to achieve a level of personal and professional success in various jobs including teaching, writing, and even sales. For AS adults, childhood fascinations and special interests may form the basis for an adult career. Many great scientists and artists have turned AS into an asset, finding the seclusion and detachment they need to do their best work. Their single mindedness has allowed many bright individuals with AS or NLD to advance our knowledge in many scientific disciplines, making them a unique resource to society. There are speculations that Einstein and Newton had the condition (Muir 2003). With the right supports and accommodations, adults with AS/NLD can be successful, contributing citizens and employees. Many of these will never seek diagnosis. Since their differences do not cause insurmountable problems at work or in relationships, they simply accept their idiosyncrasies. Gillberg estimates 30 to 50 percent of all Aspergers go undiagnosed (Gillberg 2002), and the same is probably true of NLDers. Often, successful adults became aware of their condition only after having children with the disorder.

In many cases, however, adults with NLD or AS have several college degrees, yet are unable to find or keep work that matches their strengths and abilities. The reason for this is the disparity between a high verbal and a relatively lower performance IQ score of NLDers and ASers. While verbal IQ is most indicative of academic achievement, performance IQ points to the ability to achieve success at work. Thus, though they attain high levels of education and skill, they may fail to hold down a job and earn a living. A high percentage are either unemployed or underemployed. Just 12 percent of Asperger adults are in full-time employment, and only 3 percent live independently (Barnard et al. 2001). There is no current data on the employment of individuals with NLD, but almost half of those I know with the disorder are unemployed, and many others underemployed.

Their high intelligence, combined with their naivety, can cause NLDers/ASers to be perceived as oddballs. Subtle differences cause difficulty in social interactions and workplace relationships. Their socialization deficit makes it harder to interact with, respond to, and read other people's needs. For example, their inability to read non-verbal signals makes interpersonal communication a challenge. Their rigid style and peculiar perspective exacerbate the problems. Because the AS/NLD employee has trouble with eye contact, he can be perceived as inattentive, dishonest, cagey, or rude. Difficulty with modulating volume and tone of voice can make him appear angry. Problems with understanding body language, social cues, or facial expressions makes it hard to know exactly what is expected, causing frequent misunderstandings. Until he's verbally told, he may not be aware whether the boss is happy with his work or is disapproving. At that point, it is usually too late.

Though we appear intelligent due to our high verbal ability, we struggle with performance issues. While colleagues may be less intelligent, in a heavily performance based work environment they get the job done better and faster. Difficulty understanding idiomatic expressions or directions that are not explicit and step by step can cause problems at work. Our need for verbal mediation, or talking oneself through tasks, can be perceived as crazy.

Part of the problem is a lack of understanding. People are threatened because NLDers and ASers seem different. They face a societal fog of indifference and misperception. Intelligent and loyal, with a strong sense of justice and, often, a vast store of knowledge, NLDers and ASers can do great things if they're not stripped of their self-esteem by intolerant neurotypicals (NTs) who can't accept someone who is a bit erratic, a little different. They are often perceived as lazy, clumsy, socially inept, spacey, underachieving, incompetent, impetuous chatterboxes who lack emotional insight. When they try to explain their differences to colleagues and bosses, they're berated for making excuses.

There is a large amount of variability in the symptoms that occur in an individual with NLD or AS and the degree of severity of those symptoms. No two people display the same problems to the same degree or in the same way. With persistence and determination, many NLDers and ASers find that their difficulties seem less obvious.

Though there is no question that the two are different disorders, there are many similarities in social interaction and information processing.

Defining NLD

There is no entry for NLD in the psychiatric diagnostic and statistical manual, DSM-IV-TR (APA 1994). Researchers are still debating what exactly constitutes the disorder. Therefore, coming up with a definition is difficult and arbitrary. The diagnosis is still uncommon because the disorder is often misunderstood. It is not a disorder that causes people to be non-verbal. Rather, NLDers have a diminished ability for learning information that is presented non-verbally. NLD has been defined as a specific neuro-psychological profile. According to both Rourke (1995) and Thompson (1997), NLD is a syndrome with certain strengths and weaknesses tied to the underlying cause, which is alleged to be white matter damage in the right side of the brain. The strengths include strong verbal skills, attention to detail, and a good rote memory. Problem areas involve social interaction, motor clumsiness, organizational and executive abilities, and visual-spatial tasks.

Cognitive and verbal strengths

Individuals with NLD generally have exceptional verbal skills, do well in tasks requiring decoding and encoding (like spelling), have excellent auditory attention and memory, and learn primarily through verbal mediation. Most NLDers talk and read early. As adults, they are prolific talkers and tend to be quite articulate. Many learn foreign languages with ease and are excellent writers. On the other hand, they may have difficulty with higher level abstract or non-verbal reasoning, with inferences, and with making part-to-whole connections. That is, they may have problems recognizing relationships between an object and its component parts. The common analogy is not being able to see the forest for the trees. NLDers learn best by repeated practice of detail until they can apply the concepts.

Visual-spatial and perceptual skills

These are the major problem areas. The crux of NLD is a visual perceptual deficit, and many of the other difficulties revolve around this weakness. Many NLDers have difficulty processing what they see. Although their eyes work fine, their brain doesn't integrate the information they see. It takes them longer to recognize, remember, and work with visual material. Problem areas include faulty perception of space and objects within that space.

Most people are familiar with visual skills like *visual acuity* (the ability to clearly see, inspect, identify and understand objects) or *color vision* (the ability to differentiate colors). Most people are unfamiliar, however, with visual processing, or perceptual, abilities. Visual processing refers to how the brain interprets information taken in through the eyes. Individuals with perceptual disorders have trouble "making sense" of information taken in through the eyes. Some visual skills that depend on the interaction between our eyes and brain include the following:

1. *Tracking:* the ability to follow a moving object smoothly and accurately with both eyes, such as a ball in flight or moving vehicles in traffic.

2. *Convergence and eye teaming skills:* the ability of both eyes to aim, move and work as a coordinated team.

3. *Fixation:* the ability to quickly and accurately locate and inspect with both eyes a series of stationary objects, one after another, such as moving across a sheet of paper while reading.

4. *Focusing skills:* this is the ability of the eyes to maintain clear vision at varying distances, allowing the viewer to look quickly from far to near and vice versa without momentary blur, such as looking from the chalkboard to a book or from the dashboard to cars on the street.

5. *Stereopsis (depth perception):* the ability to judge relative distances of objects and to see and move accurately in three-dimensional space, such as when hitting a ball or parking a car.

6. *Peripheral vision:* the ability to monitor and interpret what is happening around you while you are attending to a specific central visual task; the ability to use visual information perceived from over a large area.

7. *Binocularity:* the ability to use both eyes together, smoothly and equally, simultaneously and accurately.

8. *Maintaining attention:* the ability to keep doing any particular skill or activity with ease and without interfering with the performance of other skills.

9. *Visual form discrimination:* the ability to see the difference between two similar objects and determine if two shapes, colors, sizes, positions, or distances are the same or different.

10. *Visual figure ground:* the ability to see or perceive an image within competing background, like finding the saltshaker on the dinner table, or picking one line of print from another while reading.

11. *Visual closure:* the ability to identify or recognize a symbol or object when only a part of the object is visible.

12. *Reversal frequency:* confusing letters or words (b, d; p, q; saw, was; etc.)

13. *Visual memory:* the ability to recall what you have seen.

14. *Object recognition (visual agnosia):* the ability to visually recognize familiar objects. Problems with this may be due to deficits in visual memory or inability to integrate visual stimuli into a recognizable whole.

15. *Visual motor integration:* the ability to use sight to guide movement, combining visual input with other sensory input. This refers to both gross motor and fine motor tasks, affecting hand and body movements, and includes the ability to transform images from a vertical to a horizontal plane (such as from the blackboard to the desk surface). People with this problem have a tough time orienting themselves in space, especially in relation to other people and objects. They are clumsy, bump into things, place things on the edges of tables or counters where they fall off, miss their seats when they sit down, etc. Difficulty with fine motor integration affects writing and organization and interferes with social, academic, and athletic arenas.

16. *Visualization:* the ability to form pictures in your "mind's eye" and store them for future recall.

17. *Spatial relations:* the ability to comprehend the position of objects relative to other objects or oneself.

Source: OEP Foundation 1995, http://www.oep.org/whatvt.htm

Many individuals with NLD have problems with some, or all, of these skills. Form discrimination, visual memory, visual motor integration, and visualization are among the skills most severely affected. These deficits don't have to do with the eyes, but with the way the brain interprets visual information. They cause problems with getting lost, finding an object in a cluttered area, remembering what was seen, recognizing and remembering faces, and problems with sports.

SPATIAL PERCEPTION

A related area to visual perception is spatial perception. Size, distance, volume, order, space, and time are important to spatial understanding. Examples are the space between people in a line, the arrangement of items on a desk, the location of one's seat in a room, the order of events in a schedule, or the layout of a publication. The spatially challenged person can't keep track of belongings or time, gets lost, and is often late. Creating and maintaining order in a desk or room, estimating how long a task will take, or organizing the content of an essay are common problems. Some people react by learning and imposing rigid, inflexible order on their world, while others reject order, living in disarray.

There are two types of spatial skills. *Visual-spatial performance* describes how we use sight to differentiate objects. People with visual-spatial problems have trouble with things like copying from the board, understanding dimension, reading maps, spacing letters and words, paragraphing, and math operations like subtracting.

Motor-spatial performance describes physical movement through space and time. People with motor-spatial problems are klutzy. They may have problems writing legibly, playing ball, staying in step in a dance or march, tying ropes, riding a bike, walking across a room without bumping into people or objects, shaking someone's hand, or reaching for and turning a doorknob.

Many daily activities require spatial skills. Some require a combination of visual-spatial and motor-spatial abilities. Time is spatial. Math requires visual-spatial understanding for tasks like place value or fractions and motor-spatial ability for ordering complex hierarchical tasks in virtual space. Reading comprehension necessitates following meaning through place and time in the story. Writing and drawing require knowing where to send the pencil (visual spatial) and making the pencil go where you want (motor spatial). Making change requires both visual-spatial and motor-spatial ability in handling the money. The person with spatial difficulties may have problems in social situations. He/she may invade others' personal space or be rigid and inflexible in their interactions with others.

Social skills

Social skills are another problem area. The visual-spatial difficulties noted above are often the basis of the NLDer's social troubles. Social blunders caused by the inability to discern and/or process perceptual cues in communication include trouble recognizing or remembering faces, as well as difficulty interpreting gestures, deciphering postural clues, and "reading" facial expressions. (Thompson 1996).

Problems understanding non-verbal communication can lead to difficulties, since 65 percent or more of interpersonal communication is non-verbal. Social problems related to work issues include misunderstandings (due to faulty interpretations of body language) and failure to recognize or acknowledge colleagues and customers.

Deficits in social judgment and social interaction (Thompson 1997, p.11) can cause further problems. Although individuals with NLD are eloquent and have good rote language skills, they may have problems with pragmatic speech, including tone of voice, inferences, facial expression, and gestures. For example, they may have problems entering conversations. Although they often have an excellent vocabulary, they may tend to ramble and have problems with the rules of conversation.

NLDers often have difficulty adjusting to transitions and novel situations (Thompson 1997, p.11). They need ample advance notification of changes that will occur in the work environment.

Motor skills

Motor skills are a problem. This includes visual-motor integration as well as both gross and fine motor issues. To varying degrees, individuals with NLD have problems with coordination and balance. They are clumsy and awkward. They lack the muscle coordination for many tasks. Their writing is sloppy; they tire easily with pencil and paper tasks. As youngsters, they often have difficulty learning to ride a bike, participating in sports, learning to eat with a knife and fork, tying shoes, or using scissors or glue. Most adults stay away from sports, arts and crafts, needlework, and other pastimes requiring visual-motor coordination. Due to fine motor difficulties, some NLDers are slower at manual tasks than other people.

Information processing issues

Many NLDers have problems with the synthesis of information and information synthesis speed (Thompson 1997, p.29). Because their brain takes longer to process non-verbal information, they require more time than the average person to complete tasks.

Executive functions, the mental processes that allow us to monitor behavior and make decisions, are another problem area for many NLDers. Rourke (1995) has identified deficits in executive functioning among the primary impairments in NLD. However, Roman (1998) feels that such deficits are more common in severe cases of NLD, but rare in more subtle cases.

Problems with executive function include difficulty with organization, planning, problem solving, prioritizing, focusing on a chore, completing tasks, obeying social rules and monitoring behavior. Executive function issues include organizing time, organizing materials and belongings, and organizing thoughts. In a nutshell, executive functioning is the ability to grasp a problem and come up with feasible solutions. The deficit can make it difficult for an NLDer to organize his work, plan and manage projects, initiate tasks, and follow multi-step instructions.

Defining AS

Although first described by Hans Asperger, an Austrian pediatrician, in 1944, Asperger Syndrome was only recently recognized by the medical community, and was not included, for example, in the *Diagnostic and Statistical Manual* until the fourth edition (APA 1994). Today it is still relatively unknown and not clearly understood, even among professionals. Therefore, many adults and children struggle through life, remaining undiagnosed. According to NIH statistics, one in 500 people in the USA has AS, a higher incidence of occurrence than Down Syndrome (www.N.H.gov or www.nih.gov). Tony Attwood (1998) suggests that it is one in 250. A population-based epidemiological study, carried out by Gillberg's group in Sweden, concluded that nearly 0.7 percent of the children studied had a clinical picture either diagnostic of or suggestive of AS to some degree (Gillberg 1989) and Australian statistics from the Autism Association of

NSW suggests it is as much as one in 100. Recently, the incidence of diagnosis has increased dramatically.

While researcher Uta Frith (1991) describes individuals with AS as "having a dash of autism", Klin and his colleagues (1995) demonstrate that the cognitive profiles of people with autism and Asperger Syndrome differ significantly. Individuals with autism display a relative strength in performance abilities with a relative weakness in verbal tasks, while individuals with Asperger Syndrome show the exact opposite pattern: verbal strength with a relative weakness in performance. Individuals with High Functioning Autism (HFA) have the early language problems typical of autism, while people with AS have normal early language development. While autistic persons are content to be loners and have little desire to interact, Aspies seek out social interaction, albeit with little success. They want to mix, but don't have the social skills to do so effectively. Stephen Bauer, Director of the Developmental Unit at the Genesee Hospital, Rochester, New York, writes: "It is not at all clear that Asperger's syndrome is just a milder form of autism or that the conditions are linked by anything more than their broad clinical similarities" (Bauer 1996).

By definition, Asperger Syndrome is not a deficit in intelligence. In fact, intelligence is often higher than average. It is a social disability, whose most obvious symptom is one's inability to engage in social interaction. Beyond this, Asperger individuals' inability to interpret other people's feelings, their steadfastness, social withdrawal, and over-sensitivity are characteristic of this syndrome.

While individuals with AS look and sound normal, they may be eccentric and behave in unpredictable ways. Their disregard for social protocol, together with their rigid rule following, and need for routine and organization may annoy others. AS can affect people from all walks of life and with varying degrees of intelligence, from moderate learning difficulties to intellectually gifted. They often have amazing minds, complex obsessions, and strange bodily movements. Difficulties in social understanding and social communication can make them seem odd, rude, gauche, or arrogant.

People with AS have abnormalities in the prefrontal lobe of the brain (*Archives of General Psychiatry* 2002). They show abnormalities in three main areas of development: social skills, communication, and odd behavioral characteristics (Bonnet and Gao 1996). They have deficits in fine and gross motor skills, visual motor integration, visual-spatial perception, non-verbal concept formation, and visual memory (Forrest 2001). Language skills are usually normal (Klin, Volkmar and Sparrow 2000). AS may also be characterized by a strong desire for perfection, a special interest or talent, a fondness for routine, poor coordination, high cognitive skills, low organizational skills, and uneven processing of sensory input – that is, being more or less sensitive than most. Probably the most serious AS deficits, from the point of view of employment, are in social and communication skills. Although intelligent and capable, they tend to be naive, and are often perceived as odd by their peers. As children, bullies often target them.

Social relations

Asperger Syndrome is, first and foremost, a social impairment. People with AS find it difficult to interact with others, and may *appear* uninterested in forming bonds. Although they use language to communicate, they have poor social and pragmatic language skills – the stuff most people take for granted, such as taking turns, listening, not repeating, looking at folks in the eyes, not being literal and realizing you can't always be the boss. Because of this, many prefer interacting with things rather than people. They have a limited ability to discern and understand the thoughts and feelings of others, and thus may not always recognize the power of emotions (Attwood 1998, p.112). Their range of facial expression and body language may be poor, and they may have difficulty reading the facial expressions and body language of others. Some social behaviors may be beyond them. AS adults might avoid eye contact, use an inappropriate tone of voice, misunderstand instructions, dress oddly, lack good personal hygiene, or talk about seemingly irrelevant things.

In addition to struggling with social interaction, people with AS view the world differently. They have trouble understanding society's unwritten codes, and must be explicitly taught the rules of social behavior that most people simply absorb through observation or osmosis. This can sometimes lead to trouble with the law. For example, a boy might be too aggressive with a girl he likes, not realizing that such behavior can lead to harassment charges. They tend to see the world in black and white and may have difficulty carrying over what they learn in one situation to another. Indeed, they may seem to lack common sense.

Aspies may have inappropriate responses to stress. For example, they may laugh when another person is crying. They often have problems following directions related to physical movements, and have sensory integration problems that prompt strong, unusual responses to touch, smell, sound, taste, and visual stimulation.

Motor issues

Poor motor skills, both fine and gross motor, are another characteristic of the condition. Many AS individuals are clumsy. Some have illegible handwriting.

Intellectual and verbal skills

According to the DSM definition (APA 1994) AS people must exhibit normal to superior language development and intelligence. Many are very bright, with superior memories, and excel in mathematical and logical thinking. It has been compared to having a video camera in your mind; you can remember everything you've seen and heard. This helps them compensate for some of the things that hinder them.

In spite of this, problems with communication do exist. They tend to be very literal and some want to talk only about their narrow interests. They often have unusual verbal prosody and have problems controlling or being aware of intonation, inflection, rate, and tone. They may have a stilted, formal manner of speaking, and sometimes exhibit "telegraphic speech" – abbreviated speech in which words not essential to the meaning of a sentence are omitted. Sometimes their unusually loud, high or monotonous voice can be annoying to others.

Odd behaviors

Repetitive motor mannerisms, obsessive interests, and rigidity characterize Asperger Syndrome. Frequently, AS people have a tendency to rock, fidget or pace. They may have a limited but intense range of interests, and often become fixated on one subject or object. They may also be very inflexible about specific routines or rituals. They can be overly sensitive to loud sounds, lights or odors.

Similarities and differences

The AS profile of neuropsychological assets and deficits (Forrest 2001) is very similar to the NLD profile described by Rourke (1995). Both have neuro-developmental abnormalities involving functions of the right cerebral hemisphere (Brumback, Harper and Weinberg 1996). In both conditions, there is no delay in cognitive development and speech. In fact, early verbal ability is one of the hallmarks of NLD: often NLDers are extremely verbal and early readers. Asperger Syndrome has been conceptualized as a "Non-Verbal Learning Disability" (Klin *et al.* 1995). A comparison of NLD and AS individuals revealed 20 out of 21 similarities, including a verbal over spatial discrepancy. (Klin *et al.* 1995). Both Brumback *et al.* (1996) and Vacca (2001) consider Asperger Syndrome to be an extreme form of Non-Verbal Learning Disability.

Both NLDers and ASers seek out social interaction, yet are not accepted by their peers. A related problem shared by both disorders is the inability to perceive or understand non-verbal cues, such as facial expressions, appropriate spatial distance or body language. For example, normal people (NTs) use eye contact appropriately and understand that you can tell how someone feels by looking at their face. Such cues are invisible to those with AS/NLD. They can't perceive subtle differences in facial features, tone of voice, and gestures that make up non-verbal communication.

For both NLDers and ASers, the largest problems are in the area of social relationships, whether at work or at home. They're often misunderstood. They're accused of rudeness, laziness, lack of caring, or a poor attitude. Exclusion and rejection become part of life. They can't make social connections. Wanting to make friends and fit in, but unable to, they may respond by withdrawing, acting out with emotional outbursts, or refusing to cooperate. Living with this social disability and constant rejection often leads to uncertainty, confusion, insecurity, and anxiety, which they may try to relieve by creating routines and rituals. If these things aren't addressed, a lowered self-esteem and psychological disorders such as anxiety and depression are frequent outcomes. In turn, depression can interfere with the person's motivation and ability to get work done. Seeing others having friends augments feelings of jealousy, adding to the downward spiral.

It is in the affective area that NLD and AS diverge. NLDers have normal emotions but are inept in expressing them and in recognizing them in others, to the extent that they are expressed non-verbally. Aspies, on the other hand, do not feel the same range of emotions. This is called "theory of mind" and refers to the ability to recognize that others have thoughts and feelings different from what we may go through. Though they may feel very deeply about many things, they may not cry or smile when it's deemed appropriate.

They often have a flat aspect, and have difficulty with initiating or experiencing normal social relationships.

AS individuals generally have greater social problems. Their frequently highly restricted interests create an additional obstacle to their social functioning. These restricted interests seem to be peculiar to Aspies; they're not mentioned in the literature about NLD. This is the main difference between the two disorders, as they are most frequently defined clinically (Forrest 2001). The ASer's odd behaviors, like rocking or flapping, can also contribute to their social problems. These are not present in NLD. In contrast, the NLDer's social ineptness is mainly due to their inability to read non-verbal communication, such as facial expressions and gestures.

Difficulties with visual-spatial issues, a major problem area for NLDers, aren't mentioned in AS literature. In fact, many ASers respond well to visuals and diagrams, and are visual learners. Many find work as engineers or architects. In contrast, NLDers don't respond to physical demonstrations and may not understand diagrams. They can't learn by watching, and need everything explained in words. Thus NLDers tend to become wordsmiths – teachers and writers – while ASers often excel in math and find work in computer fields or engineering.

There are similarities, but the two syndromes are different. AS and NLD each have unique characteristics. Each syndrome possesses terrific attributes as well as great challenges (Table I.1).

Table I.1 AS and NLD: similarities and differences		
Characteristic	NLD	AS
Cognitive Development		
No significant delay	Always	Always
Clinically significant impairment in social, occupational, or other important areas of functioning	Mostly	Always
VIQ> PIQ (above average verbal, impaired non-verbal skills)	Mostly	Mostly
Good rote memory; unusually accurate memory for details	Mostly	Mostly
Impaired executive function and organizational issues	Mostly	Sometimes
Problems with synthesis of information and speed	Mostly	Mostly
Slow processing speed	Mostly	Mostly
Non-verbal reasoning less developed than verbal	Mostly	Rarely
Learn by verbal scripts rather than visual diagrams	Mostly	Sometimes
Good in language arts (verbal, written, foreign languages)	Mostly	Sometimes
Good in math	Sometimes	Sometimes
Trouble seeing the big picture	Mostly	Mostly
Language		
Early or normal onset of language	Always	Always
Articulate	Always	Always
Early and avid readers	Always	Mostly
Good spellers	Mostly	Sometimes

Strong rote language skills like phonology and syntax	Mostly	Sometimes
Weak pragmatic or conversational language skills	Mostly	Mostly
Trouble differentiating between abstract and concrete	Always	Always
Literal in speech and understanding	Mostly	Mostly
Difficulty with figurative language (nuances, inferences, etc.)	Mostly	Mostly
Trouble understanding things they have heard or read	Mostly	Mostly
Unusual speech patterns (repetitive and/or irrelevant remarks; talking out of turn)	Mostly	Mostly
Social Interaction		
Impaired use of non-verbal communication, such as eye-to-eye gaze, facial statement, body postures, and gestures to regulate social interaction	Always	Always
Problems with peer relationships	Always	Always
Lack of social or emotional reciprocity (inability to respond emotionally to what someone says)	Mostly	Mostly
Viewed by others as odd; socially awkward and clumsy in relations with others	Mostly	Mostly
Compulsive, rigid	Always	Always
Naive and gullible	Sometimes	Mostly
Inappropriate body language or facial expression	Mostly	Mostly
Unaware of others' feelings	Mostly	Mostly
Tend to misread social situations	Sometimes	Mostly
Difficulty adjusting to transitions and other social situations	Sometimes	Sometimes

Lack of spontaneous seeking to share enjoyment, interests, or achievements with other people	Sometimes	Mostly
Behavior		
Intense, limited interests, abnormal in intensity or focus	Sometimes	Mostly
Repetitive motor mannerisms, like rocking or flapping	Never	Mostly
Inflexible adherence to specific, non-functional routines or rituals	Never	Mostly
Visual-Spatial Problems		
Problems with spatial skills – knowing where an object is in space in relation to other objects	Mostly	Sometimes
Problems with visual-motor integration – coordinating visual and motor tasks	Mostly	Rarely
Inability to find an object in a cluttered area	Mostly	Sometimes
Visualization – the inability to form mental pictures	Mostly	Rarely
Problems maintaining attention on visual tasks	Mostly	Never
Problems with visual memory	Mostly	Rarely
Motor Issues		
Gross motor		
Clumsiness	Mostly	Sometimes
Problems with sports	Mostly	Sometimes
Balance issues	Mostly	Sometimes
Fine motor		
Poor graphomotor skills	Mostly	Mostly
Poor arts & crafts	Mostly	Sometimes

Sources for NLD information: Sue Thompson; Byron Rourke.

Sources for AS information: *International Classification of Diseases*, 10th edn, World Health Organization, 1992; *Diagnostic and Statistical Manual*, Text Revision, American Psychiatric Association, 2000).

PART I
Career Voices

NLD Voices
AS Voices

NLD Voices

1 I Should Have Listened
Peter

When I was 17, I took interest and ability tests designed to help decide what I should be when I grew up. I scored off the charts on logical ability, very high on mathematical ability and language, and very low on visual thinking.

The recommendations were actuary, psychologist, or university professor. I should have listened, because I wound up getting a PhD in psychometrics, which is sort of in-between actuary and psychologist, and in my job I do some teaching. But I didn't listen.

Instead, I drifted from job to job. I worked many low-level office jobs during summers in college, and wound up writing and editing for a public relations firm as an associate. I was pretty good at most of it, although I had personality conflicts with some people, and didn't deal with these in a mature way at all. I am not sure how much of this was caused by NLD issues, how much by my innate contrariness, and how much by the obtuseness of the people I was dealing with.

While visiting my sister, I met a couple with a severely disturbed child. I played with her, and loved it. Since I'd always liked little kids, I decided to become a teacher of children with special needs. One of my own former teachers from the special ed school where I went as a child told me this was a bad idea. I'd gone to this special school because of my learning disabilities. At the time, NLD was unknown. However, my WISC (Wechsler Intelligent Scales for Children) scores match the NLD profile (the subtests range from 60 to 160). She knew me well, and, unlike a lot of well-meaning adults, was not one for saying things like "you can do whatever you want to do". She knew I couldn't. I should have listened, but I didn't.

The coursework for the MA was easy, but I had a lot of trouble with the student teaching. Dealing one-on-one with a child is one thing. Dealing with a bunch at once is something else again, and it is something I am particularly bad at.

Realizing this had been a bad idea, I drifted again. Then, in 1984, my parents and I visited Israel. I loved it, and moved there. One day, I was in my apartment when I heard a knock on the door. It was a friend of my former boss at the public relations firm, asking if I wanted a job as an editor and researcher at the Israel-Diaspora Institute. They were involved in improving democracy in Israel, and in getting Diaspora Jews (Jews who live outside of Israel) involved in Israel in more ways than just writing checks. I accepted the offer, and worked there until I decided to move back to the USA. Although I had a fairly easy time learning to speak Hebrew, I had a tough time learning to read, because of the different alphabet. In general, Israel is a good place for NLD-type people. Israelis tend to be very straightforward and verbal. They say exactly what they think, without relying on a lot of body language. Because there are people from many different cultures living there, they are more used to dealing with differences.

After my return to the USA, I got an editorial position at a company that wrote college texts. While I liked the actual editing, I saw that the publishing world was one where advancement depended on all sorts of social graces and skills which I lacked. So, while keeping that job, I looked around. Soon, I found a position at NYU working for some researchers who worked with special needs kids. I taught myself a bunch of statistics, and took some graduate courses in psychology and statistics. To get ahead in that job, I needed an advanced degree. I considered an MPH (master of public health) and a PhD, and decided on the latter. The background courses seemed more interesting to me, the prerequisites were less daunting, and the good MPH program in New York City is at Columbia, and I had heard bad things about going to graduate school there.

So, I went back to school to get my PhD in psychometrics. While I was getting my PhD, I taught undergraduate statistics, and didn't have a good experience. Though I can explain things well, I'm not a good motivator.

When almost finished with the PhD, I saw an ad for a job as a data analyst at the place I work now, applied, and got it. When the project I was working on was winding down, I got promoted to the job I have now, which is as an in-house statistical consultant at a non-profit research firm. We research AIDS, drug abuse, violence, and things like that.

When my colleagues have statistical or methodological questions about papers or grants they are writing, they ask me. For example, one woman is working on a grant which involves estimating the number of drug injectors in each of the 96 largest cities in the USA. She has lots of data, but none directly on point, and all the data has considerable errors. We are working together to find the best way to convert the data into some reasonable estimates.

I also work on my own ideas and papers. I am currently working on a paper discussing the use of statistical graphics to describe interaction; an interaction occurs when the effect of one variable on another variable is different at different levels of a third variable. For instance, the chance of a person having HIV is related to whether they inject drugs; but the relationship between drug injection and HIV is different for homosexuals and heterosexuals.

I organize a statistics support group that meets once a month at lunchtime. Sometimes I or another researcher presents a topic, sometimes we discuss things that have come up, and other times we devote the session to upcoming conferences. I arrange for outside experts to come and speak. Finally, I teach some short courses (mostly in the ten-hour range). Long term, I would like to expand my consulting and teaching so that I'm working in various places doing the sort of work I do now.

This is a very good fit for me. The people are very nice (non-profit work tends to attract such people, I think), the work has some social relevance (we are working on solving social and medical problems), and the general atmosphere suits me. No one cares what I wear; nor do they care what other people wear. There is a high tolerance for different ways of working, thinking, and acting, because the company attracts an eclectic group of people. The staff is very diverse, not just ethnically, but educationally. There are PhDs as well as high-school dropouts, and many in-between; those with advanced degrees have them in a variety of fields. There is also a great deal of variety in terms of what people do. For example, while I sit in the office and work on my computer some of my colleagues are out on the streets interviewing drug dealers.

I have found a spot that does not demand things I cannot supply. For instance, I have very poor spatial and motor skills. But my job demands almost none of these (although I do have trouble finding the fax machine and the color printer in the maze of cubicles).

However, there are some areas of difficulty. For instance, I don't read body language well at all, and I have told people this at work. Since I deal with a fairly small number of people, I have learned some of their quirks, and how they like to interact. I am not great at dealing with large group situations, and the statistics support group can be big. Fortunately, my work is highly intellectual and doesn't demand much emotional sense.

I am also not well organized. I have come up with several ways of coping with this. First, I have separate backpacks for work and weekends. That way, I can put work stuff in one place, and other stuff in one place. Second, I keep notes at work on one pad at a time, rather than lots of separate pieces of paper. Third, and perhaps most important, I have a Palm Pilot. This has really helped because it keeps everything in one spot, it can be backed up onto my computer, and I can set it to remind me of things I have to do.

My best advice to NLD people entering the work world is to try to find a spot where you fit well, rather than trying to force yourself into a spot where you don't fit. We are square pegs, and we need square holes. Depending on how well you know your own abilities, you might be able to benefit from standard job search books like *What Color is Your Parachute?* (Bolles 2003), take some standard ability tests, or find a career counselor. Once you have found a spot where you fit, or come close to fitting, try to find a person at the job who can help you with issues that you don't get.

2 The Lawyer

When Sandy was a kid, she decided she was going to be a lawyer. She couldn't stand blood and had no love for math or science, so she didn't want to be a doctor. She was never good in art, which was very visual and spatial. Teaching was out because she was shy and didn't like speaking in front of groups. None of these occupations appealed to her. But a lawyer, that's a different story. There were no lawyers in her family, and she didn't know any. But she loved Perry Mason movies, and she knew that was what she wanted to be.

In college, she majored in English literature. She loved books and reading, so that was a logical choice. And there were few math and science requirements in this major. But English lit proved to be harder than she had expected. There were papers to write, and coming up with original ideas to write about was a killer.

The study of literature goes beyond simple comprehension of what is read. The readers must learn to interpret, evaluate, and appreciate literature. In order to draw conclusions, they must understand not only what is said, but what is implied. At first, Sandy found this difficult, but little by little, she got better at it. Her understanding of literature grew, and she became a good writer in her own, dry way. She was best at the research angle, which required putting together others' ideas rather than coming up with her own.

Sandy's high scores on the LSAT (Law School Admission Test) and good GPA (Grade Point Average) ensured her acceptance to a good law school. Law was all about reading, understanding, and her favorite: verbal sparring, the art of arguing points back and forth. It was great! Everything was words, and words were everything. No math, no science. Who could ask for anything more?

Most people know law from television court dramas, where courtroom lawyers must make rapid decisions to defend their clients, but the reality is quite different from the stereotype. Much legal work takes place behind the scenes. Parties have a dispute they can't resolve and hire attorneys to do legal combat. The litigation process involves many steps that occur before, during and after an actual trial. The lawyers prepare the facts supporting their client's demands, and send papers to the other side. Often, issues are settled by agreement between the contestants, avoiding court. Many lawyers specialize in the research and writing that goes on behind the scenes of litigation. Real estate law, contract law, and tax law are examples of legal fields that rarely require courtroom dealings.

Sandy has worked in many different areas of law. Most of her work was in litigation research and transactional law, focusing on commercial contracts. These specialties require strong verbal and research skills, and there's little need for understanding social cues and nuances, since court isn't part of the picture. She told me: "I've only been in court a couple times early in my career, and barely spoke at those times." The goal of writing contracts is to be as comprehensive as possible. The lawyer must cover all bases by making sure all the pieces are present and fit well, with no ambiguities in the language. Sandy explained: "It's one big verbal puzzle, perfect for the NLDer's wordsmith strengths. This type of work requires lots of reading, writing, thinking, and editing. What's important is getting a good end product. There's no need to think on your feet, and people skills are not important." She adds: "Somehow I chose the legal specialties that work best for me, and I think would work for others with NLD."

In her first job Sandy worked long hours at a large law firm doing research and writing. She told me: "This was right up my alley. There was no dealing with clients, interviewing witnesses, or anything else that would have required social skills, reading people, or anything like that."

Sandy did very well at that job. She recalls one incident, however, which was a classic NLD moment: "A female partner at the firm asked me how my wedding plans were going. I took her literally and gave her a complete rundown of what was going on. I didn't realize that she was just asking to be polite. Later, during my annual performance review, she brought up this incident. She said she hadn't expected a 'diatribe.' This took me by surprise. I didn't know about NLD back then; with what I know now, it makes perfect sense. I've always taken people very literally, always thought in black and white terms, and apparently it's been obvious to others when it was not to me."

Because law is a matter of each lawyer trying to gray things up in his or her own way, such black and white thinking can be a problem. Life situations are almost always shades of gray, not black or white. A lawyer needs to be able to look beyond the facts, in order to consider possible gray areas, compromises, alternatives, and middle-ground positions. If a case says the law is X, someone who thinks in black and white terms has a hard time arguing against it, because that person has difficulty finding the nuances behind the literal meaning. Fortunately, Sandy was able to follow the lead of her partners in such situations. She comments: "They would give me a direction, and then my strong research skills would take over."

A related NLD issue Sandy encounters is the difficulty in seeing the big picture, which often is more than simply the sum of its parts. Ideas don't always flow logically, and it can be hard to know how and where they fit in the whole. This is another area where working hand in hand with her partners has been helpful. She explains: "Research has been perfect for me. When someone gives me a topic to research, I'm able to focus on the details and don't have to understand where they fit in the bigger scheme. That's my partners' job. My current boss is great at that. He sees the big picture, gives me the pieces to research, then he edits my work and puts it all together into a coherent whole. We're a great team, because our strengths complement each other."

Due to the methodical nature of legal research, organizational and executive function issues didn't arise. Sandy explains: "The work sort of organizes itself. And time isn't that much of an issue, if you do a good job and are thorough."

To keep her work organized, Sandy uses post-it notes. She breaks the tasks down into small, specific steps, and uses the stickies as labels. She gives an example: "When I need to write three letters, I'll write down all the consecutive steps for the job: write each letter, address it, write three envelopes, and so on." Because of this, each job takes her longer to accomplish than it would the average person. However, this method also ensures that the end product is thorough and accurate, and that's what counts. To keep up with deadlines, she has to start early and allow for the extra time.

Since her work is one on one or solitary, social skills aren't a problem. However, during a four-year stint as corporate counsel for a printing company, Sandy worked in a large office where she had to deal with many people, and found office politics stressful. She comments: "That whole office politics scene was beyond me. Often, I didn't understand what was going on. I just wanted to come to work and do my job well, but everyone else seemed to have an agenda."

While at that firm, she had an assistant whom she never understood. She recalls: "To this day, I don't know if she loved me or hated me. She acted like she loved me, but some of the things she did indicated otherwise. Sometimes, I thought she did these things not to hurt me but simply through sheer stupidity. But others would point out that she wasn't stupid, and that these things couldn't have been mistakes. For example, one day she purposely made me look bad in front of my boss. But she was always so nice to me, and I was good to her as her boss, so I couldn't imagine why she wouldn't like me. Close relationships with colleagues can be so confusing."

A large competitor bought out the printing firm and all positions were eliminated. Sandy got a "temp" job at a large food company, filling in for a maternity leave. It was a pleasant, friendly place to work. As a temp, she wasn't part of the social scene, and wasn't expected to attend functions or participate in business lunches. Sandy enjoyed the autonomy and freedom from office politics and social pressures. She told me: "People expected me to be there to do my job and then leave. It was all work and no play, which is how I like it. Work is structured, while play is not. I have trouble in unstructured situations where I'm never sure what is expected of me.

"For me, legal research works great. It's very methodical, systematic, one step at a time. It requires thorough, accurate work, but there's no need to work really quickly or to think on one's feet (a problem area for me). It's solitary, so there're no 'politics' to deal with."

Sandy feels that paralegal or legal research jobs – such as editing one of the legal publications – might make a good career choice for many NLDers. Today, Sandy works very part-time from home, so that she can raise her three children, one of whom has apraxia (a neurological motor planning condition), and one of whom has NLD.

3 The Long Road
Charlene A. Derby

Finding a satisfying career as an individual diagnosed with Non-Verbal Learning Disability is a long road. It is my hope, however, that those following me will find it much shorter and smoother than I did. Curious students who pick up this book may have several advantages. Among them are:

- a childhood diagnosis of NLD

- participation in occupational therapy

- participation in vision therapy

- social skills training

- experience in advocating for themselves during their school years.

All of these things help lessen the impact of NLD behaviors on a job and career. While you may enjoy my story, please be aware that you don't have to make my mistakes. And you can reach the success part. My prayer is that you'll reach success earlier than I did!

My initial career aspiration was to be a writer. I'd spend study hall time in high school writing poems and short stories. I found a book in the school library called *The Student Journalist and Creative Writing*. I started sending my materials to publishers. At the end of my senior year I'd had one poem published in a student anthology. My mother, herself a freelance gospel song writer, wasn't so enthusiastic about my goals. I remember her telling me: "I think you should become a teacher. That way you can support yourself." So, when it came time to select a major in college, I chose English and secondary education.

While working on my bachelor's degree, I worked as a volunteer with a youth organization. I was responsible, along with other college students, for putting together weekly club programs and special events. I loved it. My programming was very creative and used my organizational skills. I also worked various campus jobs such as library assistant and housekeeper to help with tuition expenses. These were jobs with a predictable set of tasks to complete. They also didn't require a lot of contact with others. I occasionally felt I had to scramble mentally to keep up with my peers. For example, my roommate's boyfriend would come over, stand in the doorway, and say "Where are you hiding, my little friend?" in a French accent. I had no idea he was parodying the *Pink Panther* movies. I just thought he was weird. In social situations, it seemed that everyone had more to say than I did, and were quicker to say it. I'd keep quiet while trying to make sense of the conversation flying around me. Once I had a friend tell me, "You don't say much, but when you do, it's really profound." For the most part, though, college was a positive experience. That's why my failure at student teaching, the last semester of my senior year, was such a shock.

I had experience working with young people. I had experience putting programs together. I loved my subject area. So, what went wrong? My master teacher said I didn't know how to control the class. She said I was unaware of what was going on. She asked if I never got angry. She never criticized my lesson plans, though. After consulting with the credentialing office at the college, we decided to terminate this student teaching experience and try again, at another school, in the fall. This time I was given more feedback and more specific direction on how to manage a classroom. This time I was successful, and I received a high school teaching credential. The irony is that I've never taught.

Immediately after finishing student teaching the second time, I moved to another, sunnier state to live with my cousins. To stay there, I took a job as a manufacturing technician for a company that made products for open heart surgery. The quality of my work was very good, and I was promoted to a more difficult and better paying area. After learning the job through the sink or swim method, I began to ask some questions. Why couldn't we have some products set out at various stages of assembly so that the trainees could see the steps? Couldn't one of the engineers draw some pictures of the assembly process? What about some slides or color photographs? I was told that these things weren't necessary. Those who could do the job would get it without extra help, and the rest would quit or be fired at the end of probation. It didn't sound like a good deal to me.

About six months after taking the medical products manufacturing job, the company began a training department. I was promoted to technical instructor, partly because I held a teaching credential. The first thing I did was write some procedures and put together some work samples. While I was considered a successful instructor, I started having trouble with my trainees. They thought I lacked empathy for their struggles. I was accused of being too much "by the book". I was told to let down my hair and have fun with them. "Have fun? We're talking about medical products here! Saving lives is serious business!" I was told to ask them how their weekends went. I didn't care about their weekends or their petty personal problems. I cared about getting the work done. Later, when production stabilized and there wasn't a need for so many trainees, I was transferred to the documentation department. I enjoyed the job, but wondered why I wasn't selected for a supervisory position. After all, I knew everything. But those jobs went to the trainers who had the best people skills. I don't think I knew what that meant at the time.

Seeking career advancement, I left medical manufacturing and took a job with a full-service restaurant chain. My job there was to write workbooks that could be used for on-the-job training. I did great for a while, and then I was promoted to manager of skills training development. I got along well with some of my employees, but others not so well. When I tried to correct a male subordinate, he told me I was power hungry. When an employee got a divorce, I was told I was cold and uncaring. I didn't understand what my boss meant when he told me, "Motivation means that people want to do a good job for *you*." I thought they should want to do a good job for the job's sake. After all, that's what I was doing!

Wanting to continue up the career ladder – and tired of being ragged on about lack of relationship skills – I took another job, this time with a fast-food company. Initially, I worked as a program developer writing workbook and classroom materials. Then I was promoted to manager of training program development. All went well for a while. I thought I had worked out whatever it was that was wrong at my old job.

The social skills specter raised its head again, though. I had one employee tell me that if she wanted to know what I thought of an idea, she'd check to see if my pupils had dilated. I could go out for drinks with the crowd on Friday after work and not contribute to the conversation. I just didn't know how to join in on a discussion about sports or manicures. It was all so boring and trivial. I was overly trusting in my work with other managers. I lacked the expressive language needed to participate effectively in meetings. When the group first began discussing a topic, I'd sit back and listen until I got a grasp on what was being said. Then, I'd formulate my recommendations, frequently bringing them up near the end of the meeting. Other participants felt criticized when I did this. They thought I felt superior and was waiting for them to make a mistake so that I could correct it. I also didn't understand corporate politics very well. My employees told me that one manager was slime, and I disagreed with them. A short while later, he did prove to be slime, to the detriment of me and my department. After about five years of management, I was asked to move back into a developer role. I was told that my employees didn't know where they stood with me, that they felt I was aloof and uncaring. I was devastated. I didn't understand how they could think that, but if there was complaining to do, I certainly had a few complaints about them, too!

I left the corporate environment after 16 years and when I was seven months pregnant. I decided to become self-employed so that I could work and be a mother at the same time. Over the past 12 years I've continued to write employee training materials, but in the privacy of my own home, one-on-one with my computer. It has been great. Most communication takes place via email or conference calls. I don't have to worry about body language or facial expressions. Now when I see a client, it also meets a social need, so being personable comes more easily. By nature, client and project meetings tend to be task oriented due to time constraints. This suits me just fine! It looks like my career is set for a while.

I can evaluate these experiences only in hindsight, which they say, is 20/20. My son's diagnosis of NLD six years ago brought some insights to other family members as well. As I look back, inability to read body language, infer meaning from conversations, or notice things about others was definitely a detriment when trying to supervise them. The first time someone asked me, "What are you trying to say?" I replied, "What do you mean, 'What am I trying to say?' I'm saying what I'm trying to say." As if "saying" it were an enunciation, articulation, or hearing problem.

My inability to appear warm and personable was another hindrance to effective management. I have what could be called a "flat affect" or lack of facial expression most of the time. Because of this, people feel wary, and don't know what to think of me. Unfortunately, many people don't try to get to know me. In contrast, I've had some successes. I managed to climb the corporate ladder (at least halfway up), generate some income, and establish a comfortable life style. I'd say this is due to the NLD strengths of organization, attention to detail, and information synthesis. My need to get my mind around a topic has made it easy for me to explain it to someone else on a training program. I don't skip steps or make intellectual leaps. And I can look at the way something's currently being presented and see the gaps in it. Wanting to fix bad presentations, though due to my need for closure, actually helps when conveying information to employees on the job.

I'd like to say, though, that I think I grew up during my forties. Possibly part of it was the responsibility of motherhood, or of being able to take a break from the corporate environment and evaluate it more objectively. I now understand what some of my bosses were trying to tell me when they said that leadership is different from management. I also understand that being personable doesn't mean that I have to become a giddy, silly woman whose trip to the hairdresser's is the highlight of her life. I've learned to express genuine interest in others and come across as sincere when asking about their lives and interests. I'd like to stress "learned" here. It's a strategy. It still doesn't come naturally.

My hope is that those students being diagnosed with NLD today will have an easier time of it. Many will learn from the experiences of the people in this book. On the other hand, because of early intervention programs, many won't have to go through the experiences described here. For that, I am thankful. Because of that, there is hope.

P.S. I've continued to get an occasional poem published. My most recent work is on Poetry.com. It hasn't gotten me any fame or fortune, but at least it's out there!

4 The Research Associate

Although Tina did well academically, she found college difficult. She majored in Communications and English with a minor in Psychology. "I didn't like the social atmosphere. I was interested in academics, while most of the other students were into partying and money! My problems with depression escalated in college. I think it's connected to the NLD, especially to being such a different child and not understanding what was wrong. I think I would've been better off at a smaller liberal arts school; I went to a huge university."

Law school was better, though the first year was a bit frustrating. "Because I'm an emotional person, and so much of law is based on reason or what passes for it, I found law school difficult. I loved legal philosophy. I made many good and lasting friendships while there. I became friends with one of my profs, and have done research for him off and on ever since. He and his wife are now two of my closest friends. When I passed the bar exam, though, I lost all interest in the practice of law. There's little relationship between discussing jurisprudence and filing forms to present to a judge."

The transition from school to the work world was difficult for Tina: "The job market was bad, so I worked as a temp. Fortunately, I'm able to type and use a computer, but being a secretary or receptionist was hard after law school. I worked at banks, publishing houses, insurance firms, law firms, and universities. My favorite jobs were at the universities. I don't like formality, especially having to dress up! I have a hard time working in the traditional office environment. Universities were always more casual, and the other employees were more like me – educated, smart people with little traditional career ambition, who sought a relaxed environment where they could work around professors, lectures, libraries, and multicultural people. I'm not image oriented, and I detest the corporate environment where making money is what's most important. I don't fit into the corporate world, so it was hard to find a place I felt comfortable in.

"While I liked meeting new people and seeing new offices, I would become attached, and had a hard time moving on to the next temp assignment. I had no health insurance, and I needed to feel part of something. I also encountered some very nasty, mean people, who hire temps because no one wants to work for them permanently! For example, one boss was known for being awful to temps and knew I was fresh out of law school. She told me there would be a staff party to watch Clinton's inauguration, but that I was to go get food for everyone and then sit outside and watch the phones."

The little spatial and coordination things others take for granted are difficult for Tina: "While temping, bosses would complain about my illegible handwriting, or that I couldn't fold a piece of paper neatly or seal an envelope properly. It was hard after finishing law school and passing two state bar exams to have people yell at me because of things like folding or handwriting."

Tina had always wanted to work for a public interest organization: "I thought it was a great place. However, the people there were not what I expected. My boss, the legal director, was very insecure, abusive, misogynistic. I had been warned that he resented young lawyers right out of school. He used my clumsiness as a way of belittling me, yelling and screaming at me because of my inability to fold letters and stuff envelopes. He would run into the hallway, hold the letter up for all to see, and yell, 'Unbelievable!' I was fired from that job when he claimed that I'd mailed his personal insurance information to a prisoner. I'm so gullible, and I was under such stress, that I believed him! Later I realized that I'd made copies and given them to him, but hadn't mailed anything. I think he might have done this just so he could have a reason to fire me. It was very demoralizing."

Tina's temping days ended when she found her present job as the research coordinator at a large university business school. She started as a temp, and was offered a permanent position. "I got in through the back door. It helped that I'm an alumna, as are my coworkers. They seem to hire their own; perhaps they know they're more likely to stay."

Her job is varied. "I help professors find data for different studies they're working on. I do web research as well as basic administrative work, whatever is needed. Sometimes I work with groups of visiting scholars; I enjoy that a lot. We take them to other cities, show them banks and other organizations. I enjoy getting to know them and learning about different cultures and ways of doing things."

Tina loves working in academia. She's fortunate to have found a friendly, supportive environment, with understanding people and interesting work. "I've been very lucky with colleagues at this job. I tell them up front about my problems with depression and NLD. Everyone, including bosses, has been accommodating and kind. If something comes up that's difficult for me, I simply ask for help. We help each other. They also make sure I keep my doctor's appointments; they're always checking up on me, as if they were family. Even those who've left our center and gone elsewhere still keep in touch."

One of Tina's biggest challenges is organization. "My coworkers tell me when my desk is getting messy, as this is something I'm unlikely to notice. I find it difficult to organize papers and things so they look orderly and neat, where to put things in relation to other things, how to put things inside a box so that they fit. I don't use file folders because to me, once something is in there, it's gone; things have to be in front of me, in plain view. I compensate for my lack of physical organizational skills with my excellent memory. It looks messy to others, but I know where everything is, because I remember where on the desk I put it. People are always surprised when they ask me for something and I pull it right out."

Tina is open about her disabilities. "My attitude is that I hide nothing and am open about everything. I'm openly NLD and openly bipolar. Before I knew about NLD, I said I was spatially and mechanically challenged. I see these as nothing to be ashamed of, and as something people should be educated about. If I try to hide them, I'm just making it harder for myself and for others. It would be very hard to hide my NLD; it's obvious from my poor handwriting, general clumsiness, lack of coordination, and disorganization. I can't drive; I walk into walls; I have to watch my feet when I walk down the stairs. I can't keep track of what's going on in a fast-paced movie or sports game. I can't picture something that's being described to me if I'm unable to see it. I can't maneuver myself in space or push one of those hand trucks around without bumping into things. If I tell them it's NLD, it gives them a label for what they know is there already. Being open allows me to ask for help when certain things come up. I always have to explain to people that things that are simple to them are hard for me. Many people have a hard time understanding this. But I have also spent my life in very liberal, tolerant environments. For example, where I work there are several atheists, many openly gay employees, people who are openly HIV positive, and people from a variety of cultures and ethnic backgrounds."

In addition to her day job, Tina moonlights as a mystery shopper. "The focus is on people, rather than the physical environment. They do ask if the stores are clean and tidy; anything looks tidy to me unless a tornado has just destroyed the place! It's mainly seeing if the employees in the stores and restaurants are helpful and courteous. I enjoy writing the reports, and some of the assignments require detailed observation."

5 The Professor

Today, Al has two master's degrees and is teaching at college level, but these achievements have come only through great effort and determination.

Al's mom realized from an early age that he had difficulties in social interaction, motor coordination, visual perception, and organization. Although he could read by age four, due to problems with cutting, pasting, drawing, and tying his shoes, he was diagnosed with a motor learning disability at age six. The structured environment of his Catholic school and the long hours he spent each night doing homework enabled him to be a good student in spite of his difficulties. His mom recognized his many strengths and was determined to help him succeed. She helped him organize his room and clothes, helped with homework, especially the art projects, and offered a great deal of emotional support. She instilled in Al the belief that he could do anything if he worked hard and put in the effort.

Al went to college in the Midwest. His first major was finance, but when he didn't do well in accounting, finance, and math, he knew this was a poor choice. Since he did well in psychology, sociology, communications, and English, he decided to major in communications, and concentrated on taking classes in which his writing skills and rote memory would be to his benefit. He did best in courses that had papers to write and take-home essay tests, where he could have the extra time that he needed, and use his verbal memory to good advantage. However, he encountered problems when asked a question in class. While he knew the information was in there, he simply couldn't get it out of his head. When he was called on out of the blue, his anxiety level would rise, and he would blurt out an answer that was obviously incorrect. Some of the answers were so ridiculous, they would draw giggles from his classmates. In spite of these problems, Al graduated with a 3.28 average.

After obtaining his BA, Al went on for the master's degree in communications. But he still had an intense interest in finance and investing, so he found work as a stockbroker. However, he couldn't make the necessary social connections, and wasn't willing to engage in the unethical behavior necessary to generate the commissions required. "It took me time to establish relationships with clients," he explained. "The brokerage house I worked for wanted immediate results in terms of commissions generated. I was honest with people about what I thought were good investments and what were bad investments. I didn't care if my brokerage house rated it a buy, or how much commission I would get. I wasn't willing to flip clients in and out of stocks, as other brokers were doing, to generate commissions for the short term. Although I was new to the profession, the branch manager would leave me in charge. On a few occasions, I ended up making mistakes when placing the stock orders. It got to the point where the regional manager was making threats on a weekly basis. I decided for my own personal well-being that this was not the place for me."

After his failed attempts as a stockbroker and mortgage originator, Al saw a career counselor and decided to go back to school to pursue a career in speech language pathology. Speech was a keen interest of his, and he liked working with people. He was aware of his excellent verbal abilities, but was unaware of other difficulties that would later cause problems in doing the job. His NLD was lurking in the background, ready to strike.

The intensive speech pathology curriculum included taking a full course load of four graduate classes, working as a graduate assistant by teaching a class in interpersonal communication, tutoring foreign students, and completing a practicum each semester. Al finished all the required coursework with a 3.65 grade point average and did well on the two on-campus practicums in which the number of clients was small. His problems didn't appear until the final two practicums, where speed and organization became major factors.

The hospital practicum was in an acute care setting. He never knew what patient he would be seeing the next day, and therefore couldn't prepare ahead, which is important to NLD individuals. He also had problems organizing and handwriting reports quickly and legibly. "In addition to my problems with organizing them, I just could not handwrite them in the ten-minute time period as required. My fine motor coordination has always been poor. I compensate by spending more time writing or typing something than the average person. I'm the type of individual who will stay up all night if necessary to get something done," he explained.

His hospital supervisors would test with rapid-fire questions. Al dreaded this process; his anxiety would skyrocket. "I would blurt out what I knew was the wrong answer because I couldn't think of the correct answer fast enough," he said. The head supervisor said she didn't know how to get the answers out of his head. Once, when Al couldn't think of the answer, she told him, "I'm not here to give you the answers!" He explained: "We sat in silence as my anxiety level increased, and she kept pressing me for an answer that never came until I left for home." Al's evaluations were based on his written patient reports and the questions that were asked of him after each patient. Although he asked to be observed and evaluated by the head supervisor, this was not done; he was told that it would increase his anxiety level.

At the school practicum, the large caseload combined with the fast pace worked against him. Although he helped the children improve their speech and language skills, he had difficulty with planning, organization, behavior management, and crafts. "When doing arts and crafts activities with the kids, I had a terrible time drawing, cutting, pasting, or putting something together. I remember my practicum supervisor screaming at me because she wanted me to draw something that seemed simple to her, but took me a lot longer than expected. Another time, the supervisor had me cutting out paper figures. Even though she had showed me how to do this with the scissors, I kept messing it up, and felt really embarrassed. When I was required to put together a bulletin board at this practicum, my mother put something together and sent it to me," he said.

His difficulties were related to perceptual, organizational, and motor issues. Problems in handling a caseload of 50 or 60 students included a lack of flexibility transitioning from one activity to the next, difficulty applying information in a fast-paced environment, and not moving at the required pace (organization/time management). He also had trouble interpreting non-verbal cues when diagnosing clients, and in socially connecting with teachers. The school supervisor said he had a dull personality, and that the teachers wanted to know what was wrong with him.

Al believes his supervisors were seeing his disability because they said things like "You're unable to see the big picture" and "You have difficulty communicating with others". In contrast, one of his on-campus practicum supervisors was able to help Al understand how to engage in a particular technique during therapy. Using a video of one of his classmates doing the procedure correctly, she explained the method step by step. This was immensely helpful. Later, she told Al that she suspected he had a learning disability, but didn't say anything at the time because he was passing. In work situations, supervisors are generally not willing to take the time to help us understand what needs to be done.

Although he passed the speech pathology licensing exam, he was not awarded the degree due to the two failed practicums. The things said by his supervisors, such as "You don't belong in this profession" and "If it wasn't for your hard work and effort, you should have packed your bags long ago' eroded his self-confidence and led to a major depression. Told that hard work was not the issue, and that while he always gave 100 percent effort he just couldn't do the job, Al felt he had no future. Speech pathology was a field he loved, and a career in which the demand was high. He desperately wanted to succeed and couldn't understand why, in spite of working so hard, he kept failing over and over again.

His mother came to the rescue once more. She felt that the learning disability he was diagnosed with at age six was affecting him, and found a neuropsychologist to have him tested. The testing led to the diagnosis of NLD. Al saw another neuropsychologist for treatment, who wrote a letter to the school containing the necessary accommodations he would need to be successful in completing his off-campus practicums. In spite of hiring a lawyer, however, the university refused to provide him with these accommodations, and the learning disability office was powerless to help.

Al believes getting the diagnosis was the best thing that could have happened to him. "I didn't know I had NLD, so I went through life thinking I had serious character flaws, such as being disorganized, incompetent, or just plain stupid. I attributed my problems to a lack of confidence or shyness. I didn't understand why I was having so many difficulties in terms of careers and social relationships. I failed to recognize all the things that I'd accomplished, such as obtaining a master's degree or becoming a stockbroker. I couldn't see the big picture and was engaging in a lot of self-pity. Constantly blaming myself for the problems I've had led to severe anxiety and depression. It hurt so much to work so hard, yet feel you're not where you should be. After being diagnosed with NLD at the age of 30, I understand why I am the person that I am, and finally have a reason for all the pitfalls that I have run into across the course of my life. I had some pretty severe obstacles in the areas of visual-spatial, organizational, and motor coordination that affected my success in the workplace. I learned that people at work want things done quickly – that time is money. Having a learning disability impacts my ability to perform at the same speed and level of effectiveness as a neurotypical individual who is performing the same job," he said.

With his mother's encouragement, Al picked himself up, went back to school, and obtained yet another master's degree – in reading specialization with an emphasis in adult literacy – that led to his current teaching position at the university. "If someone had told me at the age of 23 that I would be teaching at the college level someday, I would have said that you have to be out of your mind. I've found that teaching and tutoring at the college level fits in with my verbal strengths, and that I love helping students and making a difference in their lives," he said. Al has taught classes in freshman composition, basic reading and writing skills, reading improvement, and inferences.

Teaching at the college level is the first career in which Al has had success. For a 35-year-old individual with a significant learning disability, he believes this is a major achievement. Al believes NLDers need as much practice and training as possible in order to succeed in the work world. Because of the problems he has faced in the past, he has proceeded slowly and cautiously in order to gain as much experience as possible. NLDers need to be allowed to move on their own time schedule. With extra time and a great deal of patience, they can accomplish great things. During his SLP practicums, doing things at a reduced pace was not an option. With teaching, nobody sees the many hours he spends putting together the course, or preparing for what he's going to teach. Al spends a lot of time preparing by outlining the material, writing out lesson plans, and practicing what he's planning to cover. His organizational difficulties mean that he must spend more time doing things than the average person with the same abilities, whether it's preparing lesson plans or simply writing a letter. Because of his problems with motor planning, he realizes that he must spend extra time preparing to teach. Everything seems to take him longer. He wrestles with feelings of being overwhelmed and confused on a daily basis. For example, when the department asked him to find paragraphs and write questions in five different reading comprehension areas for a pilot test they were conducting, Al spent three entire weekends finding the paragraphs, writing the questions, and typing up the test. It was a difficult process, but worth it when his questions were considered very good, although he was working with a team of more experienced teachers.

Al believes the social difficulties of NLD are among the biggest challenges we face, because they affect us both in terms of careers and relationships. He still takes great care concerning his appearance to others. His desperate desire to succeed means that he often over-prepares. People at the college where he works are very accepting. He's not viewed as being different or socially inadequate because he seems to fit in with this environment, and it fits his strengths.

Intensive preparation and repetition has been the key to Al's success as a college professor. For example, when he found out that he was going to be evaluated, he did a lot of preparation work ahead of time, including summarizing the readings, writing out the discussion questions, writing out step by step what he planned to do for that day, and practicing. He even required the students to do a reading assignment to be handed in that day, so that they would be prepared to engage in classroom discussion.

In addition to intense preparation, Al has found that repetition helps. He has taught developmental reading for five semesters, and even though he has used a variety of textbooks and the academic subject that is paired with the course has always been different, the reading concepts are always the same.

Another thing that has helped has been Al's improvement in facial recognition. "The person who evaluated me said he was amazed at my ability to remember all the students' names and to relate with the students. He told me he had been in classrooms where the professor didn't know the students' names. I can remember teaching a course in interpersonal communication at Bowling Green State University, and having students put on their evaluations that I could not remember their names. I have to admit that I did have much difficulty remembering faces at that time, but my ability is improving. I incorporate a great deal of classroom discussion into my lessons, and I try to form a relationship with my students. Facial recognition has always been a weakness of mine, and I had over 80 students in my four classes combined, so it was not easy putting names with faces. However, through repetition and by developing strategies to get to know students, I've been able to overcome. With teaching, I'm finding that with practice and doing things in a slow and calculated fashion, I am becoming a better teacher. I honestly believe that with practice, the ability of NLD individuals can improve."

The former head of the developmental reading program, and a powerful individual in the department he works in, mentioned how Al was making a difference to the lives of his students through tutoring. She said the head of the learning assistance center spoke about the great job he was doing, and how she wishes she could clone him. "Imagine that, someone wants to clone an NLD individual!" was Al's comment.

That got Al thinking about what success is. He attributes his success to the fact that his strengths are being utilized, and believes that NLD individuals can succeed if given the opportunity and put in the right circumstances. The most important things in life are people, and having people who care about you and accept you for who you are is more important than any career. Al doesn't view success by what career a person has, how much money they have, or whether the individual is married or has children. Rather, he defines a successful individual as someone who has attempted to make a difference in the lives of others.

Al has worked hard his whole life and has had to face obstacles that the average person does not face. Even though his motivation and hard work have helped him accomplish many things, his mom's extra support has really made the difference. He believes that meaningful support is a key factor in whether or not the NLD adult is successful. That is why we need services like job counseling and vocational training. Hopefully someday the necessary support system will be in place so that all NLD individuals will have the opportunity to find a career in which they can succeed.

Al has been on the journey of trying to find something that fits with his strengths and does not emphasize his weaknesses. In his former careers as a stockbroker, mortgage originator, and speech pathologist, his weaknesses came to the surface and his deficits were displayed. Teaching adults at the college level appears to show Al's strengths. He enjoys working with people and seeing them achieve their goals. This is what he liked about speech pathology. He sees that experience as an overall success because of all the things he was able to do despite the challenges he faced. Despite the problems he had with supervisors, Al loved working with the patients, and seeing them progress. He felt he was doing something meaningful. When he was a stockbroker, Al's main interest was in helping people, while his company was interested in generating commissions. Al believes that nothing is more fulfilling than making a difference in the lives of others.

In addition to teaching, Al works part time in his mother's rental business and his father's medical office. He finds the fast pace of the medical office stressful; his anxiety skyrockets when he's trying to do many tasks at once. He's also a board member of the Nonverbal Learning Disabilities Association, and is a liaison to the NLD adult community. He has organized the New York City NLDA support group.

Al wants to be a leader in helping NLD individuals become successful. He has this message to NLD adults: "Never give up hope, despite the struggles. I believe that NLD individuals are some of the most intelligent, honest, determined, persistent, motivated, caring, and hard-working people I've ever met, and they can be successful in following their dreams. Many of us are highly educated with great verbal and writing skills. Although we're just as competent as anyone in the NT world, we have to face additional challenges that make it very tough to compete with others who have similar educational backgrounds. These challenges interfere with our ability to perform different types of jobs, yet I believe we have a great deal to offer employers, if our difficulties are recognized and taken seriously. Motivation, effort, hard work, and the ability to compensate for weaknesses are our keys to success. Once we're shown how to compensate for our difficulties, we can do a great job because we're willing to go the extra mile."

6 For the Love of Books

My first career choice was early childhood education. I'd babysat some, and enjoyed it. I liked children, and found very young children pliable, accepting, and non-judgmental.

I did well in the academic courses leading to the early childhood education degree, but failed the teaching practicum. Too late, I realized I'd made a bad choice. Good teachers have eyes in the back of their heads. I barely have eyes in the front! I'm oblivious, too unaware of what's going on. Good observation skills are essential when working with young children. So is the ability to switch quickly between activities and be able to pay attention to many things at one time. But I didn't have any career counseling then, and wasn't aware of all that.

Since I didn't know what else I wanted to do, I dropped out of college and did menial jobs for three years. These included selling cut flowers from a flower shop street stand, packaging potato chips, and a variety of office functions. None lasted more than three months. The potato chip packaging stint only lasted a few hours before they sent me home. I spent more time during that period being unemployed than employed.

One disastrous office job was at a firm where I had several bosses. They all gave me assignments, and I never knew which were to be done first. I had no guidance in prioritizing and was always behind.

At another temp job, I worked as a customer service rep on the phone. The management wanted us to do phone soliciting when the phones were quiet, but most of the employees resisted because it was not in the job description. We were seated at desks in a big open room. There was a lot of banter and playing; paper airplanes flew across the room. While this was going on and we waited for phones to ring, I would most often have my nose in a book. Whenever the supervisor walked in, the others would stop their games – but I would be caught reading. I didn't last too long at that job, although I was more conscientious than the rest.

At first, I thought my difficulties were due to incompetence. I was aware of my motor coordination problems, and managed to avoid work that required good coordination and speed. That is why I avoided factory and restaurant work from my youngest days. However, I was less conscious of my visual/spatial/organizational and social difficulties and the impact they had on my work experiences. NLDers often don't notice things. So when the boss walked in, everyone quickly noticed, but I continued to read.

In the business world, "time is money". A job well done isn't valued unless it is also done fast. It was difficult to produce enough output and keep up with the demands of an office job. This is due to my slow mental processing speed – because I must verbalize everything and am unable to think in pictures – as well as my slow motor skills, which require more time to file, make copies, staple, collate, and perform general clerical tasks.

Tasks that require both visual-spatial skills and motor coordination take me longer than they do someone who's average. If you add organization to the mix, it gets even slower. Although I know the material and am familiar with the information, applying that knowledge in a fast-paced environment is my downfall. When it comes to my fine motor coordination, I often feel like I have two left hands.

By this time, because of my love of reading and the suggestions of a couple of well-meaning friends, I decided I wanted to be a librarian. One of my better jobs was as a part-time library clerk in a university medical library, shelving books and checking out materials at the circulation desk. It was a minimum wage job, but at least they didn't fire me. Since I had spent much time in libraries, I felt comfortable. The quiet environment had few distractions, making it easy to concentrate on one thing at a time. Perhaps best of all, accuracy was more important than speed, and there was no time pressure. I also enjoyed working with people. So I decided to go back to college and become a librarian.

But there were no library degrees at the bachelor's level. I majored in geography, then went on to graduate school in library science. After graduation, I spent four months looking before finding a librarian position at a prison.

There were problems almost from the start. The prison guards were as bad as adolescents, poking fun at me and getting me in trouble. They perceived my obliviousness, and viewed it as a security risk. I had to call on the union and Affirmative Action several times in order to keep my job. Twice they tried to get rid of me. I fought my ground as a woman working in a male facility and won. In retaliation, they made life more difficult for me. My shift was changed to evenings, making any type of social life all but impossible.

I was unhappy. I lived in a small town, I was in my late twenties, and there weren't many adults my age. The churches were small. After five years I got tired of the struggle, and decided it was time to move on. There was an opportunity to go to Yugoslavia to work for a church-sponsored seminary. I quit and became a missionary librarian, following God's call. Since I was a volunteer (you raise your own support by speaking at churches – which I thought would be hard but I found surprisingly easy), I had no real boss. I enjoyed helping the students and managing the seminary library. I was able to obtain grants and funding, and I cataloged the collection.

It was also here that I began to write. People back home in the USA praised the newsletters I sent home. Encouraged, I began to write for magazines. My first article was published in *Christian Single* in 1992.

Of course I was living on a shoestring: no health insurance, no retirement, no savings, just basic food, housing, and shelter. It was a great time, but even here, I noticed that other American missionaries didn't view me well. I felt shunned. I had good relationships with the seminary students, but felt that most of the Americans didn't accept me. One particular gal, a summer intern, wrote in her journal: "There is something wrong with her…she talks slow, she moves slow, she does everything slow… I wonder if she's retarded." Of course I was not supposed to read this (or perhaps I was; it was left open on the desk for me to glance at). This was a rude awakening. I realized this is how I came across to some people. Though I knew I was "weird and different," I hadn't yet been diagnosed with any learning disabilities.

I stayed in Europe for four years. I worked in Yugoslavia, Poland, and Slovakia. The job in Slovakia was terrible. John, a former colleague from Yugoslavia who had started up his own network of schools, was a definite Type A choleric with huge expectations. When I couldn't keep up with his inordinate demands, he thought I was lazy, defiant, and uncooperative.

Deciding I would be a career missionary, the next step was to go to a Bible school affiliated with my mission board. But going back to dorm life with much younger girls proved to be a disaster. Bible school was a new and very definitive culture, requiring a very narrow, specific "fit". I was unable to adapt to their narrow, discriminating standards and undefined expectations. The fact that I didn't fit in became very obvious. I wasn't accepted by other students, and the rejection stung. I found myself lashing out against the very strict attitudes and rules, and unable to conform to the school culture.

So I gave up missionary life and attempted to get back into the library world. But I'd been gone over five years, and much had changed. I had to start at the bottom and it was not easy to get a job. I obtained a library director position in a small town. At the initial interview, the board seemed supportive and positive. But after I took the job, it became obvious that I was unable to ascertain what the board and staff wanted. No one told me what needed to be done, or how, and I was unable to read the signals of their growing displeasure. They wanted a clone of the former director, which I was not. When the library board told me I was not working out, I was mystified. I had no knowledge of anything going wrong. Yet the entire staff of five part-time library clerks had turned against me. I realize now that, due to my inability to perceive and understand non-verbal communication, I was unaware of how bad the situation had become. I was unable to handle the political and social demands expected from a head librarian in a small community. I lasted less than three months, and became severely depressed as a result.

After this experience I began considering alternate careers, and went for career counseling. When I explained that I might have a slight disability, they suggested I contact my state's vocational rehabilitation office. Upon hearing my tale of woe, the caseworker ordered a psychological evaluation and, eventually, after a year of prodding on my part, a neuropsychological evaluation. The tests showed a 34 point discrepancy between VIQ (Verbal IQ) and PIQ (Performance IQ), indicative of NLD or "right brain dysfunction." At this time I was 42 years old.

My next library position was at a small, private secretarial school. The pay wasn't great, but I loved working with the students. It was a small family atmosphere. By communicating with the teachers, I was able to predict student needs. Knowing the curriculum allowed me to prepare materials in advance. I found I enjoyed teaching library skills. When students came to the library, I assisted them with research. I was proactive and created library guides. If I couldn't find something right away, I would research the answer and get back to the student later. The academic dean, my boss, was not with me in the library. I was "queen of the castle" and could plan and organize my own work.

All good things come to an end, and the school closed for financial reasons. But now I had a good reference, and soon got another job, this one in a busy urban public library. Here the situation was quite different. The clientele was not defined. Anyone could come in – from street people to the mayor. It was a high pressure, intense work environment. Most of the day was spent at the reference desk, answering an endless stream of questions that came like piercing arrows. There was little time to formulate an answer. You had to think on your feet, and make instant decisions about where to look or where to send the patron for information.

In addition, we were a team of five librarians. We worked together at the reference desk, and my weaknesses became immediately obvious to my colleagues. If I was absorbed in a search on the computer, I didn't notice the person standing at the desk, silently demanding my attention. If the customer said something or cleared his throat I would look up – but that was too late. Most of the time, my colleague would say, impatiently, "Yvona, you have a customer."

In the hectic, bustling environment, I couldn't remember all of the people I'd helped. I was polite, saying "Hi, how can I help you?" to everyone. But I was unaware that I'd helped a customer earlier, and so didn't ask what more they needed. I didn't recognize key employees from other departments, and got lost in the large building.

I was unable to apply my knowledge in the very fast paced setting of a busy urban public library. Neither could I compensate, as I had done at the secretarial school, by putting in extra hours of effort, in this environment. My supervisors recognized that I was working as hard as I could, but it was not good enough. My responses were too slow, and I was unable to make the many instant decisions fast enough.

I lost that job in July of 1999 and, knowing about NLD, it was obvious that all my performance problems were NLD related. The fact that I was oblivious to customers standing five feet in front of me had to do with my limited field of vision and the customers' polite reluctance to bring their presence to my attention. The fact that I didn't remember a patron I had assisted a couple hours earlier was related to my poor visual memory. My inability to think on my feet was due to my slow mental processing speed. Organization, another NLD weakness, was also an issue. When my troubles began, I approached Vocational Rehabilitation Services and requested a job coach. But he was clueless as to my needs and blamed my problems on a lack of self-confidence. After losing the library job, I spent almost two years working with the state's Vocational Rehabilitation's Services Employment Connection, to no avail. They sent out my résumé, but I could have done this on my own.

My experience with state vocational rehabilitation services revealed their inability to help NLD or AS individuals. These agencies are used to dealing with people with reading and writing difficulties. In contrast, we are very intelligent, have high verbal abilities, and excellent writing skills. However, our challenges in the social, visual-spatial, organizational, and motor coordination areas make production or service-oriented jobs, such as janitors, waiters, dishwashers, or cashiers, difficult. These jobs require speed, accuracy, multitasking, and people skills, which are often areas of weakness for the NLD or AS person. We need jobs that capitalize on our strengths: our high verbal and written abilities, kindness, perseverance, and dependability. We need work that emphasizes our ability to work independently rather than forcing us to conform to a team, and self-motivation rather than external pressure.

Finally, I decided enough is enough and moved back home. Today, I live with my mom and work from home as a freelance writer. Over the past ten years, I have had many articles published on health and career issues in a dozen small magazines.

7 Try, Try Again
Kim Stocum

My career experience could best be summed up in the words of a few former employers: "You're just not picking this up fast enough."

As a college freshman, my financial aid package required a work study job. I found a job as a "gopher" for the college library, but soon discovered that, even though I'd been on campus a few weeks, I didn't know where offices, buildings, and rooms were located. My supervisor couldn't tolerate the fact that I didn't know where to take important items from the library, or my continual need for explicit directions, so I was left without a job for the rest of the semester. Now I realize this lack of a sense of space or direction is a significant part of my NLD, but this was before my disability was recognized or acknowledged.

At the end of that crazy freshman year, the discrepancy between my efforts, apparent intelligence, and academic performance caught the attention of an unusually perceptive instructor, who suggested that this perplexing situation could be due to an unrecognized learning disability. This concept came as no surprise; my academic and neurological history supported this idea.

The testing experience was, in one word, peculiar. The intricacies of my cognitive and perceptual functioning were examined in ways I could never have imagined. The result: I was diagnosed with a "right hemisphere LD" based upon the total discrepancy between my high verbal abilities and my poor performance on tests involving visual memory, visual perception, spatial ability, and numbers. The psychologist commented on my memory problems, stating that auditory was better than visual. As material became more complex, however, there was poor recall all the way around.

Suddenly the quirks of my academic experiences – both in college and long before – made sense in an astonishing way. On the advice of the perceptive college instructor, I got in touch with my state's office of vocational rehabilitation. Although all I had to go on was the report describing my disability, I was determined eligible for services.

After receiving my associates' degree, I decided to get some real work experience before going off to finish my education. I had a passion for medicine and wanted an introduction to the field of health care, so I figured I'd get some exposure to the rigors of this field at a local nursing home. There was a two-week training program that took place after you were hired. I didn't even survive that. After just two days of bombardment with a lot of new information, I knew I was in trouble.

The job of nursing assistant is quite physically demanding. Patients must be lifted, carried, transported, bathed, and fed. These activities demand a great deal of motor coordination, speed, and efficiency, which I didn't have. These issues also arose from my NLD, but my disability was still an enigma.

My supervisor there was one of the first to say, "You're just not picking this up fast enough." I was shocked. This was the first time I had any serious inkling that my slow information processing was an issue anywhere other than in school. That summer, I got to know the company I now work for while trying to find my proper niche in the world of work.

My mother worked at a local grocery store. Although my ability with numbers was far from sufficient to try cashiering, they had many openings for service clerks or "baggers". Because the hours were flexible enough to accommodate my schedule as a part-time college student, it seemed like a good choice for a part-time job. Soon, however, they started telling me I wasn't meeting their items-per-minute quotas. But at least they didn't fire me for it.

I realized that, due to my perceptual and motor problems as well as for psychological reasons, the job was not a good fit. I knew I wasn't reaching my potential, but I hung on because I liked the people I worked with and the flexible schedule.

A manager suggested that I try the cashier test just to see what would happen. Two major problems surfaced: the test was timed, and it required proficiency with both visual memory and number manipulation. I failed miserably.

A couple years later, frustrated with the service clerk position, I took the test again. Luckily for my sanity, I managed to pass. After a few months as a cashier I realized that, no matter how hard I worked, they had a problem with my inability to meet the quotas which were also in place for cashiers.

It had been over two years since I'd been formally diagnosed with a learning disability (which I later recognized as NLD from its description in the literature), but I was still in deep denial. I was still trying to get through college, working towards a BA in sociology. In order to get a job in the human services field, I would need a driver's license. Although I'd had drivers ed in high school, I was unable to get enough practice behind the wheel to master the necessary motor sequences for the safe operation of a car. So now I signed up for lessons at the local driving school. After several months, the instructor felt I was ready for the road test. This abysmal experience resulted in utter failure, after which the instructor proclaimed there was nothing more that could be done to increase my chances of passing the test. I was too disgusted and too busy with school to pursue it further.

A few years later, I tried to tackle the driving issue again. This time, I worked with the occupational therapy department of a local hospital. I didn't realize that this involved an extensive and peculiar analysis of my neurological, perceptual, and cognitive functioning. They worried about far too many things, including a purely cosmetic eye muscle imbalance, my visual perception, and problems with visual–motor coordination. It was, to say the least, nightmarish.

In addition, I had a serious problem with the way this therapist responded to me. His endless prying questions made me feel that he was trying to keep me from ever learning to drive. So I approached my vocational rehabilitation counselor about obtaining a different evaluation with another therapist.

The second occupational therapist was, thankfully, nothing like the first. After running the same bunch of tests, she reached the opposite conclusion: I could learn to drive. But the axe fell when I stepped into a car for the first time in five years. The guy who was doing my road evaluation had very little patience, and did not allow me to take control of the wheel at any time. I knew as soon as I stepped away that my chances of getting a license with him as my teacher were virtually nil.

After seething for a few weeks, I approached my counselor about finding a different way to get this accomplished. On her advice, I returned to the driving school where I'd taken lessons previously. Imagine my relief when one of the instructors said he'd be willing to take me on. Once he showed up to start lessons, I laughed. It was, in fact, the same guy who'd tried to help me the first time! Now, however, he was armed with information about my specific areas of difficulty, and I'd had some ugly experiences.

I was relieved to learn that it would be just the two of us, and discovered that he was patient almost to a fault. This helped me relax, increased my sense of confidence, and allowed me to concentrate on compensating for my motor and perceptual impairments. He talked me through the driving process, which was a big help because NLDers learn by way of words and need to talk through their actions. After a few months of intensive lessons, he decided I had enough skill and confidence to attempt the road test. I was on tenterhooks as we waited on the corner for the results. My instructor offered reassurance, but I was not certain. Imagine our glee when we discovered that I had passed the test!

After surviving this experience, and also managing to secure a college degree, came the tricky game of trying to find a job in which I wouldn't fall into the usual problems. That turned into another giant project involving several people and a lot of discussion of the ins and outs of my NLD. After a number of months, we all realized what I had been trying to tell them all along: the field of human services was not, in fact, a good fit. One of these people finally saw that what I was still seeking, after getting that degree that I didn't really know how I'd use, was a niche in the field I'd dreamed of ever since I could remember: medicine.

Over the years, teachers and counselors had managed to brainwash me into believing that there was no place for me in the health care system because of the motor, perceptual, and processing speed issues coming from my disability. Now the light finally went on in one of the counselor's heads. What was making them so sure there was no place in that vast field for someone like me, who wanted it so badly? She had previous experience in medicine, and didn't quite buy their argument.

This counselor had a friend who was the director of a local medical clinic, and she felt I would benefit from discussing this peculiar situation with one of the physicians at the clinic. She suggested using my talent for writing to explain my predicament in a letter to this doctor. The results were astonishing. Both the clinic director friend and her physician colleague were amazed by my story of struggling with the paradox of high intelligence, a learning disability, and a passion for the art and science of medicine. I was floored when the counselor relayed their reaction: "This girl is intelligent enough to go to medical school." Somewhere in the back of my mind I always knew that, but by the time this was going on, I had lost any sense of my true intelligence beneath all the worries over my NLD.

Later on I had an extensive discussion with this physician about the whole crazy situation. It was bewildering to think that perhaps I wasn't delusional after all, and that maybe there *was* some way to make this medicine thing happen. It wouldn't be easy, and it wouldn't be quick, but at least I wasn't going to have to throw my dream away because of the problems I'd had with academia.

Encouraged, I went back to college once more. After some definite success with biology, I hit chemistry, which I hadn't seen since high school a decade earlier. Although I was beating the class averages on exams, the labs were impossible to get through. This was like being back in high school, and I knew then that I was in for some deep trouble trying to make my idea come to fruition. I had difficulty handling multiple tasks, sequencing tasks, organizing data, and manipulating lab equipment. I also needed concrete, detailed "talk through" instructions. Professors were starting to notice these problems, and I was going crazy trying to figure out ways to squelch them.

It all came to a screeching halt when a chemistry instructor said in lab, "This looks like a sequencing problem, and I have no idea how to help you, since I'm not a learning specialist." I wanted to fade into oblivion, to run and never look back, to scream. Here it was again. The same old batch of problems that had trailed me all the way through my education were surfacing again.

It was the tutor who'd tried to help me survive chemistry who came up with a new idea: health information technology, also known as medical records. This is the area in which I'm currently pursuing a degree. The college professors, academic counselors, and the vocational rehabilitation caseworkers all concur that this indeed is a good career choice. Dealing strictly with medical information obviates the need for good motor skills or math ability, and it is accuracy, rather than speed, that is of utmost importance in this field. Although it's not quite what I had in mind when I started my educational journey, it may be the best compromise between a passion for medicine and the issues arising from NLD.

8 The Corporate Backpacker
Lisa Marti

Lisa Marti, an avid backpacker and Masters swimmer, has not only learned to live with Non-Verbal Learning Disability, but to thrive within it. She discusses how her ability and handicap affected her career within an urban environment. This is her story.

As an avid backpacker I would like to tell you about a career I had for seven years in which I had to navigate a very different kind of world, the urban wilderness. I was traversing the cities of California with an internal frame backpack filled with materials I needed to succeed in the corporate world.

One of my most meaningful accomplishments was a four and half day solo backpacking trip in the Maroon Bells Wilderness near Aspen, Colorado. I hiked up four 12,000-foot mountain passes with 50 pounds on my back, and often spent 12-hour stretches entirely alone. I've always seen a significant survivalist parallel between this adventure and a job I had for seven years marketing credit cards on college campuses. Successfully navigating both the natural and urban world with an NLD brain that doesn't have a fine-tuned navigation center, yet never remaining lost permanently, is a challenge. I believe it was my success in finding my way around LA that gave me the confidence to venture by myself into the Colorado wilderness for several days.

In this sales job, I was an independent contractor for two marketing companies, and sometimes signed up 100 people a day for credit cards. I had planned on doing this after graduating college until I found a real job, but it turned out to be very lucrative; I was one of the best representatives in the country, consistently reaching bonus levels. When the president from the second marketing company called to recruit me, I negotiated to get one of the best pay rates per application nationwide. This is a sharp contrast to my prior employment experiences.

For the first six months my territory was close to my home in Colorado, venturing up to 60 miles at most. Then one day the phone rang. It was the operations manager. She said with enthusiasm, "Would you like to go to California for six weeks?" I didn't know what to think. My husband, who was still in school, was all excited and said, "You definitely should go. That's a really cool opportunity!"

I was 25, recently graduated from college, and adventurous. Since I worked the same schools over and over, they got saturated. My work was solely commission. The new frontier was financially promising. I called a travel agent and packed my bags, stuffed my internal frame pack with office supplies, applications and clipboards instead of freeze-dried meals, clothes, water bottles and a camping stove. I filled cardboard boxes with promotional free gifts, figured out how to pack my portable copy machine, and flew to San Francisco.

These trips involved a monetary challenge that required significant resourcefulness. The company gave me an extremely tight budget to live on during my journey: $35 a day for hotels and $15 a day for food – a ridiculous figure for the cities of California, even in 1988. I was stubbornly adamant about not spending a penny of my commission money on travel expenses. I wasn't seeking luxury; my only standards were a clean and safe hotel room.

I had a very hard time finding something within the budget in upscale Berkeley. I settled for a motel that I felt pretty insecure about for around $35 a night. I noticed the parking lot was empty. Suspicious? I settled into a room sporting furniture on a slant and hair in the sink. I was concerned so I called the police, asking if they thought this was an OK place. They said, "It's not that great." I said, "Where am I supposed to stay? In the homeless shelter on a business trip?" I got off the phone, sat on the bed and cried.

Then I got an idea! Maybe I could rent a room from a student at a pro-rata rate for two weeks. I went to a local grocery store and picked up a student paper. The advertisement read: "Law Professor seeking roommate for house in the Berkeley Hills". I met the professor and we agreed for me to stay for $17 a night. I blew off what I'd paid for the motel the first night. It wasn't worth negotiating with the motel owners that I had to talk to through a tiny peephole in a plastic window. I moved my luggage and self to the

Berkeley Hills, which were near a great park with hiking trails. I had a break from restaurants, had a laundry machine and the company of the professor.

I traveled all over California on these trips, covering 20 schools in the state. I had to work at a different school in a different city each week. Each destination involved finding my way to several locations, including the campus, parking lot, the parking office, where to unload, where to set up and the student activities office to check in. Because I'm a masters swimmer and desired to keep fit while traveling, I wanted to find a masters program everywhere I went. At the end of the day I had to find a restaurant for dinner and once again find my way back to my hotel. By the time I got all my directions down the week was over and I was on my way to the next destination.

With NLD I find it difficult to use maps, and I spent a large percentage of my time lost. In the morning I would ask the front desk staff at my hotel for directions to my schools and pools verbally, and I would write these down. But it's easy to make mistakes, even with directions. I stopped at many a gas station for directions. Most clerks will say "Let me draw you a map." And I would tell them "I don't understand maps, I need it written or I need to write take a left on this and a right on that." And those damn neurotypicals insisted "This will be an easy map, you will have no problem." Neurotypical is the word we use for people who fall within the neurological norm. How can a stranger assume what abilities I have or do not have?

There was no annual fee on the cards, which included a major credit card and two or more other cards, generally gas and department store cards. When the students came up, I made it a requirement for them to fill out a package deal, even if they just wanted one card. This is part of how I made this job work for me, while it didn't work out for many people. I was unrelenting, not letting anyone apply unless they filled out the entire package, assuming those deterred by this would return.

I arrive at San José State University, unload, haul mounds of materials to my booth, and begin to set up. I take the boxes and bags off my luggage cart. Free water bottles fall everywhere as the garbage bag they are stored in rips. I pull out my extra long extension cord and find a place to plug it in and set up my portable copy machine. I say hello to my longtime vendor friends and proceed to stand on a chair and hang my poster on the bulletin board attached high above my booth. I then place all my applications, office supplies, and free gifts on my table so I can work efficiently and my customers can see what the most appealing options are in credit cards and free gifts (bait).

Students stop by, glancing at my sign, and I spout out my sales pitch. I rattle off a list of instructions to everyone who decides to apply. As students finish and leave, others sit down and begin the process.

A friendly engineering student from Egypt arrives. He wants a radio headset, which I am offering for applying. He can't believe he can get that free just for filling out the forms and begins the process. A few minutes later seven other Egyptian engineering students arrive, then a Vietnamese business major. Soon I realize I need to get my adrenaline going so my body can move fast, my brain can think fast and I can speak fast. I need to be on the ball, so I take a swig from the large cup of coffee on my table.

All four credit card companies we're working with want a copy of the student's ID and sometimes their driver's license for me to get paid and for them to get a card. I have to bend down to my copy machine, which is on the floor, without missing any activity at my table or any potential new customers in the vicinity. I also need to place the IDs effectively on the flatbed of my copy machine so I can get as many IDs and drivers' licenses as possible on there at once. I didn't want to let any of my ten customers leave without filling out all four of their forms perfectly. Some make mistakes that seem inconsequential but matter – like crossing out important numbers such as the social security number or date of birth. I am determined to keep them there until they get all the forms right. Otherwise, they wouldn't get their card and I wouldn't get paid. Some get frustrated, and the large bag of peanut M&Ms that they are working so hard for starts to look less appealing.

Chaos begins. Tien is upset because one of the headphones of his "valuable" new radio headset is not working. Mohammed has filled out all of his applications by only signing his first name for the signature. I'm trying to figure out how to kindly get him to fill out all the forms over again while I go through boxes of headsets to find Tien one that meets his standards, so he can get to his economics class across campus. Then 18-year-old Alyssa approaches meekly. She's a freshman who doesn't know anything about how credit cards work, and I am explaining the world of credit.

It's 6pm. Things are petering out on campus. I pack up my booth, call the company on their 800 number, and report my "numbers" for the day.

NLD on the job

One of the reasons I stayed at this job for so long is because I didn't think I could do anything else I could make a decent living at. I was concerned I wouldn't survive an office job where my work could be criticized. This job was like having my own business. I do think NLD made finding my way around much harder. It also made the organizational skills involved in travel harder. One way I beat those difficulties was by leaving my hotel very early in the morning to give myself lots of time to get to a campus. If I didn't have trouble getting there and got there early, I started early. I worked many very long days. I spent a lot of time lost, but I was the only one who knew or suffered the consequences.

NLD got in the way when I had to try and fit a large suitcase, a portable copy machine, and an internal frame backpack and boxes and bags of free gifts in a Metro Geo. I handled this by developing patience with the challenge this posed for me and spending more time at it. Fortunately there was no boss in the passenger seat of my rental car rushing me to tap into my problem-solving ability faster than my poor NLD brain could go.

Because the work was so repetitious, I didn't have to use executive function skills all the time. Executive functions involve making decisions, solving problems, planning and initiating tasks, prioritizing, sequencing, establishing goals, regulating motor and emotional output, inhibiting impulses, monitoring results of actions, and self-correcting. This is my area of most significant impairment.

Multi-tasking is often hard for NLDers, and other NLD adults commented that they could not do the multi-tasking involved in this job. But repetitive tasks don't require as much use of the frontal lobe or executive functions. This work was so repetitious that I could do it in my sleep. This explains why I was able to multi-task here, but not in other situations.

Another common problem for NLDers became a strength in this situation. Many NLDers tend to focus on details and are unable to see the big picture. This work involved paying attention to many details, and I was able to succeed since I wasn't distracted by having to process and learn a lot of new information. Jobs that involve the constant learning of new info are very difficult for me. There were always new situations and challenges, but these were similar in nature and pattern.

Perseveration is often another problem NLDers face. In this situation, it translated into persistence. My tenacity helped me to ensure that all the students filled out their forms correctly and that I didn't miss any potential customers.

I worked very well independently. My sense of humor came in handy. My excellent verbal and communication skills, a common NLD trait, were important at work on campus and on the road. I have a good sense of humor and was able to negotiate in an assertive and persuasive manner. Resourcefulness, ambition, determination, and my sense of strategy were among my biggest keys to success.

Although social skills are often impaired in NLD, this is not always the case. I have excellent people skills, which is critical for sales, and was able to tap into these even when under pressure. I am playful and can relate to a wide variety of people. I was tactful, diplomatic, honest, kind and friendly. It's rare and refreshing to see the level of honesty and kindness that's often present in NLD. However, diplomacy and tact require a greater ability to read between the lines and understand non-verbal communication. NLDers also tend to be literal and straightforward. That is why these skills are difficult for many individuals with NLD.

While writing this story I noticed similarities between this job and another successful job I held as operations manager at the Volunteer Connection, a non-profit agency. This was the hardest, most challenging job I've ever had, and would be difficult for many people. I ran this agency, whose mission is to match prospective volunteers with volunteer positions at over 300 non-profit agencies. It is clear why my NLD did not seem such a detriment in these two very different jobs. At the Volunteer Connection, I was the one running the show. My boss, the executive director, was appreciative and patient; this is critical for someone with NLD. He was rarely there. I either worked alone or supervised up to seven in-house volunteers. No one was hovering over me. This was also true in the credit card job. In that case my boss was all the way across the country. In both situations, my work involved considerable self-motivation as opposed to external pressure, and I worked very well independently. There was nobody rushing me and pushing his or her way of doing things.

Like many NLDers, I don't process information quickly. When I worked at the Volunteer Connection I spent a lot of non clocked time learning things for the job and planning how I was going to approach projects.

In a sense, I was in a supervisory role in both positions. I have a lot of skill in delegating and coordinating. My verbal, communication and social skills are very good. At the Volunteer Connection this was helpful in dealing with the public, other non-profit agencies, our in-house volunteers, prospective volunteers, co-workers and my boss. These same skills paid off in dealing with customers, campus officials, and anyone else I had to deal with while traveling at the credit card job. I was able to use my creativity and resourcefulness at my own pace without external pressures. I would imagine it is not uncommon for an NLDer to thrive when given a chance to work on her own. Attention to detail, another NLD strength, helped me to succeed in both jobs.

In contrast, I have had problems keeping jobs in the past. In college, I pounded the pavement for low paying cashiering and waitressing jobs, because I felt these were things most people were capable of. But I was fired from my first job as a supermarket cashier, and from every other cashiering and food waitressing job that I tried. Surprisingly, I was successful at cocktail waitressing. There, your tips depend more on your personality. If you bring the wrong beer, they usually drink it anyway. But if you bring the wrong, burnt, or late dinner, it's a different issue. Food waitressing involves a great deal of memory, organization, and multi-tasking.

My NLD touches all aspects of everyday life, impairing me academically, vocationally, and in general living skills. Due to this disability, my abilities are quite uneven. Over my lifetime it has felt like my strengths reach toward the sky and my weaknesses fall below the earth. Often it seems that my weaknesses climb all the way up to my strengths, knock them on the ground, and beat them up saying, "We won't let you taste the good in life."

Many adults with NLD, including myself, are on a journey to figure out how to lean into their strengths and compensate for their weaknesses. NLD is a disorder of uneven abilities. Our job as NLDers is to find a way to balance that out. All NLDers have a personal profile of strengths that are clearly there if they take the time to look for them and find a work environment that helps promote them. I want to help improve the lives of people with NLD of all ages. I would like to turn a handicap into a gift and devote my time and energy to advocating for those with NLD.

9 Teaching
Debbie Green

I am an adult with NLD who has been teaching for seven years. It's been a tough journey, but teaching feels right and I've grown more successful as I've learned how to compensate for problem areas. Experience is truly the best teacher.

After graduating from college, I had a hard time finding a job. I didn't interview well and my body language gave off a sense of fragility and over-zealousness that killed my chances at actually getting hired. Finally, after a year of subbing, I was hired over a phone interview to teach elementary school music.

Flying across the country, I met my new principal. I was confident that I would work at this school for the rest of my life. After all, I was loyal, committed, open to feedback, caring, creative, and hard working. I didn't know this principal judged people immediately, basing all kindness or pettiness on her initial impression. If she liked you, you could do no wrong. If she didn't like you, you could do no right. Unfortunately, my body language and insecurity alienated her immediately.

For the rest of the year, she harassed me, put me down, and finally fired me. Part of this was due to my inability to fit in socially. I spoke about my homesickness, not realizing this made me seem whiny and complaining. When the principal acted unjustly, I reported this to people, not realizing they listened sympathetically, then went to her with the information. Not noticing that everyone stayed until late in the afternoon, I left when the bell rang, doing my work at home. Not noticing the colorful decorations in the other teachers' rooms, I left the same posters up all year, oblivious to the impression I was creating of an inappropriate environment for children. I was branded as lazy and not caring. Not knowing how to promote myself, I allowed the other teachers to think that I had all this free time and a cushy job. If I had been more experienced or more socially savvy, I would've asked them about their work and incorporated their classroom themes into my lessons.

In any case, the principal fired me with scathing words, leaving me devastated and unsure about my teaching ability. I genuinely liked teaching and had worked hard. Her perception of me seemed so far from the truth I didn't comprehend what had happened. All I could do was pick up the pieces and keep going.

However, my next job was no better. In fact it was worse. In elementary school, classroom management was not a big issue. I only saw the kids once a week and music was exciting enough to hold their attention. Teaching ninth grade was a horse of a different color. I was unsure of myself, and it showed. When I asked the kids to do something, they would ignore me. When I talked to parents, I said the wrong thing, infuriating them. Because I appeared weak, parents, teachers, and administrators saw me as weak, incompetent, and a liar. People actively picked on me because they knew I wouldn't fight back or if I did that I wouldn't be believed. Soon the older teachers were complaining that I was monopolizing conversations. The kids openly disrespected me. The administrators refused to support me. At the end of year, I gladly left, moving to middle school in the hopes of finding a more supportive environment.

At first, this seemed to be the case. The kids were younger and more willing to listen, and I had a few great teammates who supported me and helped me with lesson plans and with discipline. Things weren't perfect. Sometimes my honesty would get me in trouble. While I was never deliberately cruel, if a kid asked me something, I would tell him/her the truth. And sometimes the truth was not politically correct. Often I would believe excuses. I laugh at the memory of how many kids had hospitalized parents/grandparents every time a major project was due. It took me almost the whole year to catch on. I was terrible about hall passes too. If a kid said he/she needed to go to the bathroom, I always let him/her go, not knowing this was field trip time.

Things went well for three years. Then a new principal came who had to have everything a certain way. He wanted us to prove that we were teaching, submitting copies of every lesson plan, stating all our objectives, and following the same program as every other teacher in the same subject/grade. This was too much for my organizational skills. Unfortunately, my helpful friends had moved on to other things and the group of teachers that replaced them were cliquish, highly conventional, and sycophants. They made all the rules and if I didn't follow, I wasn't a team player.

My creativity was seen as chaos. My suggestions were seen as disagreement. I missed subtle cues, and this was interpreted as not caring enough to go with the flow. By the end of the year, the principal became openly abusive. It got so bad I would only meet with him if a union member was present. I found out later he had done this to several other teachers. It was simply the way he operated.

It was time to move on. I applied to a new school opening near my home, and was fortunate enough to be accepted. The new school has been wonderful. I teach all sixth graders. By now, I am experienced enough with this age group that classroom management is excellent. I refuse to listen to excuses, maintain consistent discipline, and have high expectations. I decide on class rules and enforce them consistently like crazy during the first month of school. I spend the first month walking around the class with contracts. A whisper to a friend – bang – a contract. Out of seat without permission – bang – a contract. Missing homework – bang – a call to a parent. This establishes the basis for respect, and once that foundation is in place, you can teach.

I am now experienced enough to know what works and what doesn't work. If my expectations are unrealistic, I am confident enough to say, "Hey guys – this isn't working. Let's try it this way." I am also able to be more flexible. If the kids make a suggestion, I listen and if it works, I go with it.

I've gotten better at self-promoting. Like any job, teaching success has to do with politics. Joining certain visible committees, becoming team leader, joining literacy groups, and sponsoring Battle of the Books makes a difference. People want employees who not only do the job, but then some. You have to make yourself invaluable.

I run an after school music club, and asked the principal if they could perform at the faculty lunch. He agreed and they were a big hit. Later, the principal thanked me, commenting on their excellence. I also asked the principal if my kids could put together a school newspaper, and made sure to give him a color copy of the finished product. This too went over well and was presented at the faculty meeting as an example of literacy in the classroom.

I've gotten better at listening and sharing and being vulnerable with my fellow teachers. The teachers I work with are warm and supportive. They love activity and hands-on stuff and are excited to learn about new ideas. At staff meetings, I feel I can sit next to any person and be comfortable. My body language is much more confident; I am much more confident. This shows, and people treat me accordingly. I feel like I am a teacher, instead of someone playing the part of a teacher.

There are still problem areas. Organization is a disaster. Teaching has many forms – progress reports, psychological evaluations, department forms, school forms, missing homework assignment forms, etc. There's planning and grading and entering. Sometimes when work is turned in after the due date, it gets buried under piles of stuff or is stuffed into a corner of my backpack, and I don't find it for weeks.

When planning, I have trouble stating my objectives and doing complex lesson plans. It's all there, but I find what I'm doing as I'm doing it and adjust accordingly. I was always the kind of kid who wrote the outline after the paper, and my teaching is the same way.

Grades are another problem area. Thanks to computer programs, I don't have to deal with math. I just type numbers into the computer and let it figure it out. My problem is filling in bubble sheets for report cards. Every time grades are due, I spend hours laboriously filling in bubbles, and then check and double-check to find my mistakes. It's easy to skip a bubble or fill in the wrong bubble, and this reflects inaccurately on the report card. I suppose I could ask for help, but I like to do as much as I can by myself, even if it means extra time at home.

Over the years, I've been fortunate to find people and activities that have boosted my self-confidence and improved my body language. A dear friend of mine often affirms me and makes positive observations about my abilities. Working out at a gym has given me a new sense of surety and mastery about my body. Approaching challenging situations and succeeding at them has boosted my self-esteem. All of this translates into more self-confidence, which leads to greater success.

I feel respected and supported at my new school. Exercising and working on my body image allows me to project myself more self-confidently. Experience has given me the ability to be an effective teacher. And practicing active listening has allowed me to get along better with my colleagues.

Teaching is a challenging job, especially for those of us with social and organizational issues, but it is worthwhile and interesting. For those with the inclination, I'd say go for it. After all, every failure is just another step on the road to success.

AS Voices

10 The Prodigal Son

Steve works as a production clerk at Cedar Industries, a sheltered workshop that employs people with disabilities as well as those recovering from substance abuse. For the last seven years, he has maintained a database of the 80 employees at Cedar's warehouse. When I asked what he did, he explained: "My job is to keep track of their hours, and the specific tasks each person does on the assembly jobs. Everyone has a card. Each job has a code. I keep a log of the jobs and codes, and make appropriate changes when job tasks change. The work includes data entry as well as running reports and printing labels and time cards."

Because of his computer skills, he's also the office computer trouble-shooter. Cedar Industries offers computer training, and Steve is in charge of the facility's computer lab, where he has taught classes in word processing and Windows. Steve explains: "Teaching the classes, you need to be very patient. Some of the clients don't grasp the information very fast. Many of them are on medications which tone you down, so they seem drugged. You have to explain things more than once."

Steve's interests have always included computers and competitive chess. In high school, he won three state chess titles. At the State University of New York at Buffalo, he began as a computer science major, and was on the Pan American chess team. He worked hard to maintain a 3.0 average. The computer science courses proved to be very difficult for him, so his Dad, a successful businessman, convinced him to pursue more of a business curriculum. He graduated with a degree in management information systems. "I've always been close to Dad. He influenced me to switch majors and go into the School of Business," he told me.

Although involved in chess club and a few campus ministries, college at times was a lonely experience. "I didn't drink and wasn't into the party scene," Steve told me. "In class, with the exception of some English courses, there was no conversation among classmates. You try to understand what you're learning and figure out what this has to do with the real world. You're left walking the halls alone, then just going home."

When I asked what he did after college, Steve replied that he worked for a computer consultant. They installed an accounting computer system for a local business. He also did property research, and taught employees how to use the new computers that were installed. After the installation was finished, however, the company laid him off.

Still, it was a good experience. Soon, an opportunity to work at a bank doing individual and fiduciary taxes presented itself. Steve had worked at this bank part time years ago, and had a good reputation there. The new job doing taxes took him in a new direction – taxes – but didn't use his computer skills. Though he knew next to nothing about taxes, he was optimistic about the training and accepted the offer. "My Dad was very proud of me. It was a very prestigious job," he said. "I was in the world – the business world, on the track, and successful."

But success came at a high price. Although he worked there for three years, taxes were not the right fit for him. When I asked why, he explained: "I didn't have confidence that I could do the job the way it should be done." Even though his family was proud of him, he felt alienated from them. They didn't share his religious experience, and were hostile towards his newly found Christian faith. He dated a girl with similar beliefs a few times, and got close to her family, but when she broke off the relationship he lost her and her family as well. That was his first dating relationship. It ended in sorrow and was crushing. "She said talking with me was like walking on thin ice," he recalls. "I never got upset with anything she said. I don't know why she said that."

During this time, his boss at the bank was promoted, and the working conditions changed. Steve explained: "We were no longer being supplied with accurate tax information. An owner takeover took place while I was there which led to a computer conversion. The new owners didn't take into account the tax department's needs. This made it almost impossible to do the work. After my boss got promoted, I was being groomed to run the entire tax department, with limited tax knowledge, doing illegal things. This was very stressful."

Steve was an emotional wreck. Once, after a church service, he was pressured by several people to go up to the altar, and then everything seemed to hit him at once. "I freaked out…a friend had to come rescue me and take me home – I even had to pay him!" he told me. That was his first breakdown. Following the advice of his good friend and spiritual mentor, he resigned the position at the bank and enrolled in a Bible school. But in his Dad's eyes, he was now the prodigal son. Steve felt he had let his Dad down.

"I'm not a quitter," he said. "The job at the bank was the first thing I'd ever quit in my life. Whatever I start, I finish. College was tough, but I stuck it out and persevered."

Bible school, however, was very different from college. He began with real enthusiasm and excitement, but as time went on, it proved to be a very difficult time emotionally. "I didn't have the support system I needed," he said. "My close friend and mentor, who's like a second dad to me – a spiritual dad – influenced me to go there. He had gone there. I wanted to make him proud," he sighs. "But things didn't work out as I'd hoped. I liked what I studied and could handle the academics. But Bible school was a whole new culture… It was culture shock. There were no outlets. You were expected to eat, sleep, and drink Bible. Many people love this and can handle this; I can't. Ninety percent of the people that went there had family and church support. But because the school was a different denomination from my home church, they did nothing to support me. No send-off, no prayers, no financial help – nothing."

Steve's crying episodes, which had begun while working at the bank, intensified. "It was too much. I had problems and requested counseling, but was denied. They said, 'The regular courses we have here for the freshmen will be enough'."

Steve continued: "After two months at Bible school, one day I started crying in the middle of a chapel service and had to go to the restroom. Later that night I had trouble breathing. Each breath was a struggle, they had to call an ambulance." It was another breakdown, requiring a night in the hospital. "That was the worst night of my life… I got out the next day, packed up my things and drove home for good." The prodigal son was coming home.

Steve slowly recovered, took a few classes at a community college and did some temp work for a couple years, but couldn't find a permanent job or even an internship through the college. He also was looking for a girlfriend, but got many rejections from the women at his church.

In order to remedy his work situation, Steve worked with the state Vocational Rehabilitation Office through a vocational program offered by Transitional Living Services. "They would help me look in the classifieds and send résumés to different places," he told me. "It was kind of bizarre that, for three years, they kept asking me what type of job I was looking for!" He had a few interviews, but with meager results. Finally they said his time was up.

"They didn't have any connections," Steve continued. "It's their job to help people like me, but they can't do it. They had a program that would pay my wages for the first three months on a new job, but even promoting that, we couldn't find anything."

VR sent him for a vocational assessment. "They sent me to BOCES," he told me. "The tests weren't vocational at all. They were second and third grade reading writing and math tests...for three days. What did this have to do with the real world? They didn't test any computer aptitude at all... When I told the tester I felt misled, it was interpreted as a lack of cooperation, and I was quickly removed from the Vocational Rehab program." He felt betrayed. "I met with those counselors every week... Yet not one of them has called me to see how I'm doing. One day they're on your team, helping you, rooting for you. The next day they won't talk to you; they just say they can't help you any more, you've exhausted the funding and you're on your own. They can help a disabled person get a janitorial type job, but they don't have a clue how to help someone who has a college degree, yet has a gap or disability like Asperger's or NLD. The business community wants the young guns, people fresh out of college, and with no problems or weak areas. Something needs to be done to close the gap between the charitable organizations that help people find work and the business community."

Steve's experiences with vocational rehabilitation services are very characteristic, and similar to those of other individuals with Asperger or NLD. State DVR (Department of Vocational Rehabilitation) agencies are used to dealing with mentally retarded individuals who can be placed in low level jobs like dishwashers or janitors. They also are able to help those with physical limitations, who can be employed with the use of accommodations like wheelchair ramps. But they are clueless as to how to assist individuals with neurological dysfunctions, such as NLD or AS, who are intelligent and have college degrees but have difficulty with fast-paced, production-oriented, and socially demanding work environments. This society is very tough on anyone who deviates from the very fake social veneer required to succeed.

Steve's father tried to find a business they could do together. They looked into buying a specific fast food franchise where Steve would have worked in the franchise's computer area. The food chain wanted Steve to be familiar with the restaurant end of the business first, so he went to work as the assistant manager at a busy restaurant. I asked what this experience was like. "I worked my butt off. There were no breaks. Managers weren't allowed to take breaks," he said. "The pace was frantic. You had to move very fast to get the orders out. Each order was timed. Everything had to be very, very clean. The owner was very strict. One woman collapsed on the job. I experienced more episodes of crying during work. One particular day, by 2pm it was exceptionally busy. I'd started the shift at 6am. I collapsed and had a very difficult time breathing. Fortunately one of the customers was a nurse. I went to the hospital." That was his last day working there.

As a result of all these negative experiences, Steve was hospitalized for depression. Later, a friend helped him to get involved in an outpatient program, IPRT, which helps people make life changes through classes in self-esteem and goal setting. For the first six months, he worked part time while attending the courses. He found the ad for his current job at Cedar Industries on IPRT's bulleting board. He applied and got the job.

At work, Steve tries to be friendly and helpful to everyone. On his breaks, though, he goes to the computer lab to escape from people. "I need time to regroup, time to myself. Time when I can rejuvenate, then go back to the grind."

"People at my current job are very friendly," he says. "It's not a cutthroat environment." In contrast, he explains, "At the bank and other places I've worked, people would talk behind your back and even curse at you in front of other employees. That happened a few times in three different places I've worked."

Steve has difficulty in social groups. He has a hard time mixing in. "I've always had more difficulty in social situations than other people have. I wasn't diagnosed AS till I was in my early thirties. Though I have a good number of friends, I'm 36 and have hardly dated. Often, I'm not sure what is appropriate and inappropriate to say," he told me. "I tend to be too cautious... In the past this has caused me to lose out on some social opportunities, but I'm changing."

Communication can be tough. "Sometimes people at work talk fast. It's difficult for me to process everything they're saying if they're very fast talkers," he comments. "A couple hours later, I may think of what I should have said. Chess is the exception. I can find moves and strategies in the game very quickly and play quickly. I've given simultaneous exhibitions where I've played 30 players at once, going from one board to the next. Work, though, is different. I can't be in a very fast paced environment with fast talkers."

"I like to have time to think things through," he adds. "At the fast food restaurant they would always say 'Don't think, just react'. This is hard."

Though many Aspies need a structured, scheduled environment, Steve has learned to be flexible. Compulsive thinking, however, is an issue. "It's very hard to get a problem out of my mind until it's solved. Sometimes, you need to be able to put a problem on the backburner and get to it some other time. This is challenging. Everything inside me is saying 'Get that thing solved!'"

Doing a number of things at once is a challenge as well. "I'm best at doing one job or task at a time rather than doing many things or having several things going on at once. When I started my current job at Cedar, it was very difficult, because I had to keep track of many things at once." He elaborates: "Many people change jobs at once. Joe is going to do the filters. Sandy will seal the bags. And so on. You need to write it all on their cards, change their cards, enter the information into the computer… It was overwhelming at first. If it wasn't a sheltered workshop with counselors in place, I may not have been able to do it." But, with the right environment and supports in place, he was able to do even this. He comments: "You learn from experience. I've learned what environments to avoid, and what settings are good for me." Most people with Asperger work best in a quiet, structured setting.

Steve also took up ballet. "Everything I'd done before was mental: chess, astronomy, computers, college," he explains. "I lift weights, but ballet has given me more of an artistic, romantic, creative, and physical outlet. It has helped me to feel free. Dance has helped me become less of an introvert. So have other hobbies. If I'm in a group where there is a focus – chess, dancing, Bible study – it's easier for me to talk to people. It's much easier than going to a party. There's more structure."

Looking to the future, Steve says, "I like my job, but I feel I'm underemployed. I don't make much more than minimum wage. There are no benefits like health insurance, and the job was only intended to be a one year temporary position so I get no more raises. I was denied SSD/SSI. I hope to get back to a regular job. I hope to get into an environment where I know I won't be fired for the first mistake that I make. You have to hope you get a good boss, someone who can work with you, who can understand your abilities and your limitations. I have a lot to offer a company: I'm a very hard worker, dedicated to what I do, very detail oriented. I'm dependable. People can trust me. I give my whole heart to everything I do, and I believe my Dad knows this."

11 The Eccentric

Lars always knew he was a bit eccentric, though others often attributed his unconventional behavior to his Danish culture. Ironically, he had much more trouble fitting in in Denmark, since Danish society expects a greater degree of conformity than is true in the USA. "For example, I was pressured to go away on a week-long field trip," he said.

Young Lars didn't like school. He had trouble understanding others' perspectives, and abhorred group assignments. After coming to the USA at the age of 14, Lars found that he was much better able to be himself and to be left alone with that. In high school, he became a better student, but continued to cause headaches for administrators and teachers. His handwriting remained poor, despite efforts to improve it. One of his high school teachers commented that Lars was a good student so long as he typed his assignments.

Planning to become an attorney, he began college with a political science major. Soon, however, he realized this was not a good choice. "It was too adversarial and action oriented," he told me. Finding that psychology helped him to understand himself better, as well as comprehend others and how they think, he took as many psychology courses as possible. "Psychology raised some intriguing questions. When I took my first psychology class, the text referred to a question that only a psychologist can ask: 'Why does an infant love its mother?' I was hooked. I went through several fields with psychology, such as social psychology and cognitive psychology (looking at how people think). Ultimately I settled on industrial/organizational psychology since this would provide me with an opportunity to apply psychology to work settings. For example, I was fascinated with the idea that psychologists could study pilots flying and make suggestions for changes in design and training that would reduce the likelihood of accidents."

In order to gain a perspective on business, Lars next pursued an MBA. This exposed him to marketing, which fitted in with his interests in individual behavior and motivation. During this time, he decided on a university career. "I quickly realized that professors are paid for thinking, researching, and talking about things they're passionate about. Their enthusiasm for their topic is applauded, while social indiscretions are often overlooked. As an academic, I have come into an environment where eccentric people, at least within reason, are tolerated and sometimes even admired. As Tony Attwood puts it, 'Universities are a sheltered workshop for the socially challenged'."

Lars continued his academic pursuits, obtaining a PhD in marketing and launching his career as a college professor, teaching consumer behavior, international business, and marketing. It was during his PhD studies, at age 31, that he sought help for perceptual and attentional issues, and was diagnosed with Asperger Syndrome. "At the time, I thought I might have attention deficit disorder (ADD) since I had difficulty concentrating under some circumstances and would have to play my phone messages over and over to get down the phone numbers I was being asked to call back. When the psychiatrist showed me the description of AS, it all made sense," he recalls. "The fact that I am a bit on the clumsy side, do not like confronting people, am often perceived as staring, have difficulty recognizing faces, and have problems with non-verbal communication were not news to me. Many AS symptoms are ones that 'normal', or neurotypical, people experience to some extent now and then. Most people know the frustration of being misunderstood, experiencing frustration in traffic, getting lost, and having difficulty recognizing faces. And we are not the only ones to be naive. Therefore, it's not surprising that many of us have had our symptoms dismissed as normal or things that can be conquered." With AS, these traits occur more frequently and with greater intensity.

Obtaining a college position poses unique difficulties for the person with AS. The networking needed to make contacts is arduous for someone with limited social competence. Lars has found a way around this mountain, however. "At professional conventions, I'm much better off getting an early night's sleep, in order to recover from the numerous impressions and interactions of the day. I no longer force myself to go to cocktail parties and receptions despite the value of networking. These are not a good use of my time, and I generally don't make the best impression. One technique I use to network at these conventions is to have planned, thought out questions, and discuss them with people during the breaks. Another thing I do to develop professional relationships, in lieu of some of the more conventional forms of networking, is to send articles and information to colleagues when I see something that might interest them. That way, I can maintain positive contact in a non-stressful way."

Interviews can be daunting too. "The interviews that are held in hotel rooms at national conventions aren't well suited to my needs. There are many people, all over the room, and it's difficult to maintain eye contact. Often, their first impression of me is that I'm reserved and standoffish. This changes once people get to know me."

But there are other ways to get jobs in academia. Lars has obtained teaching positions solely through email contacts and telephone interviews. "Most academic jobs are filled through ads, rather than the old boys' network, because of affirmative action constraints. Now that I've taught for a while, my reputation has traveled, and others have heard about me through conferences and my websites. It's also helpful that I have some strong letters of recommendation from colleagues at places where I have taught."

It took Lars a while to get into the groove with teaching. "My first experiences weren't successful," he explained. "It has taken me longer to become an effective teacher, but it's something I enjoy and has been stimulating for me. My unique perspective helps, because the subjects I teach examine the things we take for granted. Intense preparation has been a key to my success. I put more effort into teaching than other professors I know, and I spend more time preparing the lessons than most people would. But I perform well, and my teaching has improved. At first, some students took advantage of me, because I erred on the side of being too nice and too accommodating. I have cracked down harder in recent years. Reading student evaluations has helped me to pick up on what works and what doesn't. Over the years, I have also learned a great deal about what motivates business students. Many are extremely results oriented and tend to judge a course in terms of how it might help them get and succeed in their first job. I now structure my classes in such a way that students can see many applications at the outset, and thus become more receptive to the course."

Many people with AS have problems with organization. Lars has developed some strategies to limit this as a problem. "My home, which other people do not see, is usually a mess, but my information is very well organized on my hard drive, as are my course materials. In part due to my poor short-term memory, I am a compulsive note taker, which helps me keep organized. I have numerous binders in which I file information, so many colleagues come to me to locate documents they themselves can't find. One way I have found to keep student papers in order is to have a manila envelope with each student's name on it. As soon as I have graded a paper, I replace it there, and don't need to worry about returning it. I email-merge out grade reports to students so that they can see that all their assignment scores are properly recorded."

Like many with AS, Lars finds changes in schedule or procedure frustrating. "I work hard to hide that frustration, and am working on becoming more assertive. Another challenging issue is explaining to others when something I'm asked to do feels uncomfortable. I don't like making requests, especially if they involve bending the rules. When my contacts with people require a negotiation of sorts, I try to avoid phone calls. I much prefer email, because I don't need to respond immediately. I'm also very uneasy driving – more so than most people can comprehend. By now, I have allowed myself a fairly firm no passengers policy.

"In the classroom, I have problems with eye contact, my monotone voice, and learning students' names. At the beginning of each quarter, I photograph the students and use cue cards. Today, students see me as a committed teacher."

Indeed, comments from his evaluations show that his students view him as dedicated, caring, and approachable. While some think his lectures are dry, others appreciate his sense of humor. Many also like the projects, the choices offered, and the notes provided via the internet.

Lars uses his website (www.larsperner.com) to interact with students and reach out to people. Students have a positive reaction to the information he provides here, which includes class notes as well as supplemental material, and helps promote class interaction. The fact that one of his websites is listed first on Google under the topic of consumer behavior also helps his credibility.

He's very open about his disability and mentions AS in his résumé as well as in the syllabus he hands out to each incoming class. He asks for others' understanding, and explains that his odd mannerisms don't indicate a lack of interest or regard. "With it out in the open, I don't have to worry about what other people are perceiving. Since academia is made up of eccentrics, I hope to create a positive rapport with students and colleagues."

His advice to others entering the workforce: "I've come to realize that what works for others doesn't always work for me, and I have learned not to take others' advice for granted. As Aspies, we need to look at things differently. It's important to understand yourself. Realize that advice given to others may not work for you, be receptive to taking a different path, and search for novel strategies."

12 The Transcriptionist

Unable to find work in the town where he grew up, Tony left home at 23 and moved to a distant city. He found an employment agency, told the person he could type, and was immediately offered a typist position with an insurance company. That was in the late 1960s. Since then, he continued to work as a transcriptionist, typing in response to taped letters, memos, or reports from a taperecorder or dictaphone. He was with his last employer, an insurance brokerage, for 22 years.

Transcription was an ideal job for him. "I was required to sit and type what I heard on tape and nothing else! It was great. I was naturally good at spelling and grammar, was detail oriented, and had the ability to work at one thing for a long time," he explained. All three of the companies he worked for were impressed. It was a good fit because Tony didn't need to use the phones, do any kind of customer service, or otherwise communicate with people.

Tony kept to himself, absorbed in his hobbies and concentrating on doing a good job at work. Because of his excellent work ethic, quiet demeanor, and tendency to avoid socializing and just do the job, he was called an ideal employee by one supervisor. He was reliable, had an excellent attendance record, and didn't like to be idle. He could remain in the background, typing and concentrating on doing his work well. "I was good at my particular job. While others in my department constantly complained that the work was boring and that they would like more variety, I felt just the opposite. I was lost in my work, contentedly typing letters all day. I could filter out most background noise, though loud radios were annoying. Voices in the background sounded like a foreign language swirling around me. As long as they weren't talking to me, I was able to concentrate on my work. They put up with my eccentricities, like inability to do well with small talk, often sloppy dress, loner tendencies, and other things that made me stand out from the norm," he told me.

Then times changed. People he had been doing transcription for began getting their own computers and doing their own writing. At the suggestion of a colleague, and because he was always griping about people's poor dictating skills, Tony began sending a weekly email newsletter to all employees about better dictation skills, grammar, punctuation, and spelling. A few people said they liked these.

Work slowed down in the word processing department. Tony's boss began to pressure him to learn new things and develop new skills not directly related to his job. The management wanted people to familiarize themselves with the tasks done in other departments by watching, interviewing, and documenting.

Tony has a hard time learning new tasks. The anxiety of trying to understand something new may cause him to zone out. "Supervisors often talk very fast, rushing through the explanation and leaving out steps they think are obvious, or that I should already know. I try to explain that they need to slow down, because I need to take notes so I can refer to the instructions later. I prefer a brief explanation, then a written sheet telling me each step I am to perform – leaving nothing out. However, this seems to be beyond their experience," he explained.

Tony resisted change. "I couldn't think of a thing I would be willing to do other than the same old thing I'd been doing all these years," he said. "I kept getting talking-tos from Human Resources about this. We were supposed to document what new software or other new skills we were learning. I didn't do any of this. I simply didn't know where to start. I'm not technologically inclined. It didn't interest me at all, and seemed far too difficult for me."

The company provided free classes, but the titles didn't mean anything to Tony. He didn't know what they were for. "I balk at classroom-type situations, because my early school experience was traumatic, and I do not learn well in a group with other people sitting close by and teachers watching me and asking me questions. Perhaps if I'd had a more understanding human resources person who could have explained a bit more about the software, and was more direct and explicit, I might have consented to take a class or two. I didn't pick up on their subtle suggestions, and didn't see the threat to my job. She was trying to subtly warn me that if I didn't get with the program and learn some new things to show my worth to the company, I'd be in danger of downsizing. I simply wasn't able to read between the lines; I need people to tell me things directly. Since I didn't have any real friends in the department, I wasn't in the know about what was going on, and didn't care what people were gossiping about."

In addition, Tony didn't get along well with his boss. "I didn't understand my supervisor, nor he me. I couldn't talk to him. He had a nasty temper and liked to yell. There was little work then, and we were always being told to look busy. Since many of my colleagues would leave early, I began coming in late. He got upset and yelled at me. I didn't think I had done anything that deserved this, so I complained about his temper to Human Resources," he told me.

The supervisor moved to another department, but Tony soon clashed with the woman who replaced him. "She asked me to merge some letters with envelopes, and I didn't know how. This surprised her. Apparently, I was supposed to know this task and had put off learning it," he said. Not long after that, his company merged with another large insurance brokerage, and Tony was downsized. "I'm sure my unwillingness to go with the flow and learn new things contributed to the decision to downsize me when work volume slowed down," he comments.

Since the layoff, Tony has been working with his state's department of vocational services. They administered a three-day battery of tests, designed to place people in various job categories. Because he did well on tasks involving spelling, grammar, and punctuation, Tony was placed in the clerical category. He didn't do as well on tests involving verbal memory or math skills. He's not happy with the results. "The testing should have been more thorough. They didn't tell us our scores, and didn't discuss the results with us," he complained.

Although his vocational services counselor is a nice person and a good teacher, Tony doesn't feel he understands him, or the issues arising from his AS. "Even after several months of trying to explain my problems with social situations and my inability to do certain kinds of work to him, he just doesn't get it. They think it's up to me to cure myself of my social inadequacies, to 'just try harder', and that giving my problem a name like Asperger Syndrome is a copout. I emailed him bits of information about AS, but he never mentioned the information or websites I sent him. I feel totally ignored by him regarding this. He can't accept my AS, yet he readily accepts the fact that I wear hearing aids to help with my hearing impairment," Tony explained.

Tony would like the vocational counselor to talk more about job placement techniques and what is being done to market the clients. "I don't understand why my counselors do not communicate with me regarding what they're trying to do to market my skills with employers. I would like to see and hear about some of their successes – people they've found jobs for," he said.

Temp agency personnel are even worse. At one time, Tony was registered with 17 different agencies in his search for a job. "I don't think the agency people asked enough questions about what I wanted to do. They have not had enough experience with job seekers who differ from the norm, and could not understand people who are very high in some abilities but very low in others. One young woman couldn't deal with my not being able to multi-task. Two were verbally abusive and rude, and blamed me for not being able to do the jobs they sent me out on," he said.

Job interviews are a major problem for him. A current trend is to have two or more people interview a job seeker, something Tony finds very difficult. "I can't pay attention to the questions and eye contact of more than one person. I have read and heard a lot about what to do and say on an interview, but once I'm there, my mind tends to go blank and I forget what I should do and say. I've messed up with multi-person interviews twice now, saying the wrong things to them. I don't do well with interviews to begin with, but when I've been required to listen and respond to two or more people, it's been a disaster," he said.

Today, it is difficult to find work where one does the same thing all day. Simple data entry, transcription, envelope stuffing, labeling, and mail opening and sorting are some examples. Tony has difficulty multi-tasking, a key element in many office jobs. "One 'temp job from hell' required me to answer the phone, and I would push the wrong buttons, say the wrong things, and then I'd forget what I was working on," he explained. Tony was let go from this temp job due to his problems with multi-tasking and answering phones. Currently, he's working as a temp with mail-opening machines. He likes what he does, but needs a permanent position with greater security and medical benefits. Because of his need for sameness and routine, Tony detests temping. "I get used to a particular job, get more or less comfortable with it, and then it ends and I'm out looking for another one. It takes me a long time to get used to a new job," he said.

Small talk, office politics, and socializing are other issues that Tony, like many Aspies, has difficulty with. He rarely goes to casual office parties, and didn't like it when they brought a birthday cake for him. "Once an employee complained because I constantly forgot to say 'Good morning' to her. I try to remember to say 'Good morning' and 'Fine, thank you' or similar remarks in the office, but I have never quite fit in with the others. When someone says 'How's it going, Tony?' or 'What's going on?' I tend to mumble 'Fine, thanks'. Feeling obligated to reply to small talk or general comments where an actual question isn't asked of me drives me nuts. I can't keep the conversation going while working. Often, I can't tell when someone's about to speak, and have sometimes spoken before they're done talking. If someone comes up to talk with me, I have to turn my machine off and stop what I am doing to listen to and attempt to respond to him, or I forget what I'm doing and make mistakes. I can't concentrate when others are physically close – for example, if someone comes in the room and reaches up to a shelf over my head, or if someone is watching. I wish people would just do their work and not talk so much because it is distracting. As long as people are talking in the background, their overall sounds wash over me. I can block them out and concentrate on my work," he said. "Because I am not very social, I imagine that people think I'm not capable of much, but that isn't true. They think I'm a bit odd; they're turned off by my awkward gestures, odd responses, inability to make eye contact and difficulty with small talk. But while people in my office are yakking about cars, sports, and other people, I am sitting there blocking them out and doing my work. For repetitive-type jobs with tasks that have to be done over and over all day that would drive many people nuts, I am their man. I wish they would realize this, overlook my quietness, and give me a chance."

13 Great Expectations

A hyperlexic child fascinated with books, Lana hung out at the public library. That was her refuge. A library volunteer since age 12, she was more familiar with the collection than some of the staff.

In school, she was known to correct the teacher's spelling in front of the whole class. Annoyed that her authority was being undermined, the language arts teacher handed Lana a red pen, saying, "Now you do all the grading." That is how Lana became a teacher's assistant, grading student papers in grammar and literature courses. In addition, she was a staff writer for the school newspaper, and participated in numerous poetry recitals.

In contrast to her strong language abilities, Lana was socially naive. Although she excelled academically, she was known to fail PE, music, craft and trade classes. Hyperactive and impulsive, she came across as odd, klutzy, sarcastic, and arrogant. Despite a strong desire to fit in, she stuck out from her peers.

The pieces didn't begin to fit together until years later, when, with her husband, she saw the movie *Rain Man*. "He started pointing out vague, subtle, yet multiple and consistent similarities and parallels between the main character's habits and mine. There were so many that he started calling me 'Rain Woman'. However, neither of us took it seriously, since I didn't fit the classic autism profile: I never rocked, learned to talk and read very early, succeeded academically in mainstream school without any special supports and despite a language barrier, and held steady jobs all my life."

The school system in the Soviet Union, where Lana grew up, allowed transferring to vocational schools and junior colleges straight after middle school. Therefore, she had to make an initial career choice by the end of eighth grade. Aware of her limitations, she quickly eliminated jobs requiring good balance and motor skills, like waitressing, assembling, or construction.

She also ruled out nursing, hairstyling, or medicine, which require touching and handling people or animals. Driving, delegating, or supervising were out as well. So were jobs requiring lots of public speaking or prolonged people contact, such as teaching, due mainly to her unshakeable habit of talking to herself, which looks odd to others.

At her parents' insistence, she enrolled in an engineering junior college. "It was a bad choice from the start," she said, "because engineering requires strong spatial perception, good craftsmanship and math skills, and mechanical and drawing ability, all of which are my weak areas. I'm not a technical person at all; my strength is in word-oriented subjects."

In spite of this, her instructors were impressed by Lana's academic prowess, strong memory, attention to details, and excellent clerical skills. She continued to work as a teaching assistant for various instructors. At her PE instructor's suggestion, she donated her clerical skills to a local athletic society in order to earn extra credits and pass PE. She graduated at the top of her class.

In the USSR, you were assigned your first job upon graduation, so Lana didn't have to worry about employment. She landed at a technical department of a large machine-building company and worked there for eight years, until the collapse of the Soviet Union forced the closing of her department, which was financed from Moscow. "Although I was always the odd one, I was accepted because of my strong work ethic, high productivity, and eagerness to please. I charmed the other staff by making sure every colleague got their own birthday poem each year. I was an authority on literature, poetry, writing and crossword puzzles, interests shared and appreciated by many of my co-workers," she comments.

After being laid off due to downsizing, Lana found her next job in just three weeks, by using family contacts. It too was a clerical job at an industrial factory. She was fortunate to have a nice supervisor and co-workers, and stayed there until her family received permission to move to the USA.

Coming to the USA gave Lana another chance to pursue her interests, though now she had a family to support. She earned a vocational certificate in office skills, followed by an associate degree in accounting with honors from a community college, and then a BA in business administration, magna cum laude, all while juggling full-time work, full-time school, and family responsibilities.

"At first, I thought I may not be as good with words in my non-native language, so I decided to work with numbers which are the same in all languages," she explains. "That's why I chose accounting. This presumption turned out to be wrong, since math is my weak spot, while my hyperlexic traits and excellent memory helped me to become adept in English, my third language, to the point where I aced grammar and spelling tests dreaded by native speakers. The business degree had broader applications and less of a math requirement. I got my foot in the door towards my first full-time job here through the same pattern as before: by being spotted in college as a capable student worker."

While studying at a local community college with a very diverse student population, Lana became part of the English as a Second Language (ESL) student community. She became involved in building bridges of mutual understanding between students and faculty, and developed a database project, "Adapt-a-Friend", designed to match ESL students with native speakers based on common interests, parts of which were later used to design a mentoring program. Her efforts were noticed, and she was offered a part-time campus job.

For the next two years, Lana assisted the counseling and ESL depart-ments as an interpreter, helping with student orientation and advising new students with limited language and cultural comprehension. Soon, she got a second part-time job in the financial aid office. For two years she worked in both jobs. She was glad to be able to make a contribution to the college, made many suggestions to improve and streamline the efficiency of office procedures, and initiated various projects to benefit the college and its students. Within ten months in the financial aid office, she was promoted to a substitute for a senior financial aid assistant, and temporarily took full charge of that position while a co-worker was on leave. She also frequently assisted other departments as an interpreter for applicants, students, and visitors with poor English skills. At the request of the ESL department, she participated in several staff development events for faculty, giving presenta-tions on serving ESL students. She was invited to a strategic planning meeting to help develop the college's plan for improving services to ethnic communities.

At the financial aid office, Lana suggested a change in office filing proce-dures which ensured timely processing of student financial aid awards and loan applications, eliminating certain types of errors and delays. By using simple logical thinking and problem-solving skills, she was able to pinpoint and resolve a delay of financial aid disbursement affecting over a hundred students. She also suggested and developed a step-by-step guide, "Steps and

Timelines to Apply for Financial Aid", which was used as a handout and an insert for copies of Free Application for Student Financial Aid (FAFSA) distributed by the financial aid office.

When she became aware that many college scholarships limit applicant eligibility by imposing citizenship or ethnic requirements, Lana created a database of local ethnic, cultural, and professional organizations that could be approached to establish scholarships to benefit their members, thus generating more scholarship funds.

She was the department's walking dictionary, and was often the first to answer questions about proper spelling of a word they were about to use. "That was particularly funny," she explained, "since I was the only non-native English speaker there, and had only lived in an English-speaking environment for a few years. Once, when such a thing happened for the umpteenth time, the colleague, who had a professional background in learning disabilities, asked, 'Lana, how do you do this?' Trying to answer on a professional level, I replied, 'I guess it's my learning style… you know, some people have dyslexia, so I must be just the opposite… how would you call this…maybe, hyperlexia?'

"I coined the word on the spot, almost mechanically, as the opposite of dyslexia. At the time I had not heard the term, and had no idea it existed. A few days later, while surfing the net, I recalled our conversation and, curious, typed 'hyperlexia' into the Google search engine. In a moment, I was in for the surprise of my life, for the first time ever reading a perfect, precise and comprehensive description of myself. Such a term did exist, and was exactly what I've been living with.

"That's how I found out about the autism spectrum. Further research led to communicating with other spectral persons and professionals. I came to believe that I could be affected with Asperger Syndrome and hyperlexia as one of its primary manifestations. Qualified professionals later confirmed this assumption."

The financial aid office where Lana started as a student worker was well structured. All of the employees followed their job descriptions, were familiar with their designated duties, and were led by a work-oriented, straightforward, fair, reasonable and consistent supervisor who was very appreciative of hard work and commitment. There were office friendships, but no signs of favoritism or cliques. Most of the department employees were mature, tolerant of individual differences, and not very competitive. "We enjoyed common office activities and events like potlucks and birthday or holiday celebrations, but didn't socialize much outside of work. I got along with them well; at least I tried my best to do so and never heard otherwise. I'm certain they noticed my quirks, especially my habit of talking to myself, but it didn't affect our relationships. I was appreciated for hard work, commitment, constant willingness to help (no job too large or too small) and suggestions for improvements. The only thing that my boss wasn't thrilled with was my habit of staying in the office and working beyond my work schedule, although I never asked for overtime pay."

This office environment was the perfect place to put Aspie traits to productive work, turning them into applicable, valued assets that benefited the department and the students. Lana could capitalize on her strengths while keeping her shortcomings out of the daily spotlight. "I have to do a lot of planning to get around my limitations and make them less noticeable, while presenting AS traits like rote memory, attention to detail and linear thinking not as a disability, but as highly applicable skills and valuable assets. For example, the students were impressed by my ability to remember the correct spelling of their names after seeing them in writing only once. Linear, efficiency-oriented thinking, together with my in-depth understanding of office procedures, helped me to quickly locate misplaced student files. My strong work ethic, bilingual skills, and multicultural competence were also highly valued here."

Lana feels that the office setting is a good work environment for Aspies. "Working with books or documents is very comfortable and gratifying for someone who's fascinated by the written word. A quiet library or archival setting feels calming, soothing, safe and relaxing to the individual who's sensitive to noise, light and commotion. Jobs which include a lot of word processing, proofreading and editing allow hyperlexics to blossom, since their strong grammar skills and large vocabularies are appreciated. Medical office paperwork is ideal for a hyperlexic to demonstrate proficiency with big words and terminology. The clerical/public office service field is the best place to capitalize on such traits as high attention to details, strong language/grammar skills, and the inclination to classify, categorize and organize information. Office jobs allow you to downplay physical clumsiness and poor motor or spatial skills. Interpreting and explaining policies and regulations, and providing information to the public, effectively accommodate the Aspies' tendency to lecturing tone. Repetitive (echolalic) speech patterns make them very comfortable repeating the same information to different visitors for the thousandth time without any irritation. Schedule and structure help keep daily activities organized. And last but not least, public sector jobs which usually offer good benefits, pension, union protections and, in case of any problems, right for due process, provide an extra degree of security and financial stability for naturally anxious Aspies."

This academic office environment was of tremendous benefit to Lana as well. She made a huge social leap, became more socially aware, and improved her communication skills and visual perceptions. She gives an example: "Because I had trouble remembering faces, I began to mentally match students' faces with images of written name labels from their file folders, which I remembered in much greater detail. That little trick helped immensely, and soon co-workers started commenting on how well I remember and recognize so many students (campus enrollment was about 17,000 students)."

Lana remained with the department, on part-time temporary status, until her graduation from the college. She received an associate degree with honors in a double major, winning several scholarships and a grant that allowed her to pursue further education.

When a permanent position became available in the department, her supervisors and office friends encouraged her to apply. Lana went through the selection process, and was named one of two finalists. However, she was rejected at the college president level in favor of the other finalist. This caused uproar in the office; the entire full-time financial aid office staff went to the vice president, requesting to reverse the decision. Though their request was not granted, this was a true vote of confidence.

A few months later, with strong support and glowing recommendations of her supervisors and co-workers, she was hired for an identical entry-level position on another college campus within the same district. And that's when the nightmare began. She arrived at her new campus full of anticipation and expectation. The office she joined consisted of several departments that served economically and socially underprivileged students.

"I expected this place to be accepting and understanding," said Lana, "because several employees have degrees and experience in counseling and disabilities. Unlike my previous office, however, this one was highly political. Most of the staff knew each other long before joining the office, and socialized outside of work. Interpersonal relationships were often given first consideration during hiring, promotions, and assignment of tasks and projects. Favoritism was rampant. Socially, this group resembled a school gang rather than a work team. Those who didn't have established informal personal ties with the department seniors and wouldn't play office political games didn't last long. Those who did could expect rapid advancement and got away with anything.

"I quickly noticed I was unwelcome there. They were giving me the cold shoulder. Two months passed before I was given a tour of the campus and offices. It seemed that they held this position for another person, had given me the job only due to diplomatic relations with my former bosses, and were pressuring me to quit."

Lana expected to be familiarized and trained in her new duties. Instead, she found that the duties of her position were split between several temporary student workers; one of them kept using Lana's personal assigned voicemail and refused to surrender its password to her. Her boss gave more authority in office duties to the work-study students than to Lana, who was a full-time classified employee. The students were assigned work she was supposed to be doing. She explains: "During the following year, I was frequently and randomly interrupted by the student workers and asked to get up and leave my desk, so they could do my job at my work station. Often, I didn't even have a place to sit down for hours. I felt that I was being pushed around the office. When I complained to my boss that I had nothing to do, he told me to 'relax, sit and listen to music'. My training and work were openly sabotaged, my pleas to superiors ignored. The people assigned to train me were busy performing their duties and kept forgetting, although they routinely remembered to train other new employees." Lana genuinely wanted to serve the college and its disadvantaged students, but soon realized that the drastic cutbacks in her authority, assigning her work to others, and refusal to provide adequate training signified a lack of intent to keep her in this department from the beginning.

When the cold shoulder treatment proved ineffective, problems escalated. "The boss regularly subjected me to sudden verbal assaults and put-downs in front of others, obviously enjoying my frustration. This was very stressful. During one staff meeting, she suddenly began shouting at me in front of several people, calling me stubborn and hostile. I froze in shock. She went on, 'Lana, you don't even want to look into people's eyes. Look in the eyes, now!' I couldn't even leave because she and one of her cronies were blocking the only exit."

This treatment was not only affecting Lana, but interfered with work duties and was counterproductive to serving the needs of the students. Here, office politics came ahead of work priorities. "I couldn't comprehend that an administrator would deliberately derail and sabotage the work within her own department in order to create a hostile environment for her employee, thus causing liability for the district. Or that intelligent, educated adults would attempt to deliberately smear a competent, experienced, dedicated co-worker who always tried to do her best to help them and make them look good."

Lana had been trying to transfer out of the department, but her efforts were blocked. Suddenly, however, her top boss gave her a promotion. "I wanted so badly to believe her change of heart… I was incredibly naive," said Lana. Her boss realized that after almost five years of an excellent record on two campuses, a sudden decline would not be believable. She promoted Lana only to create the impression that she wouldn't perform as well in a different position.

This promotion, though at a higher salary, had fewer responsibilities. "Sabotage of my training and duties increased. As soon as I assumed the new position, its duties were cut down," said Lana. "Later, they even began phasing another employee into my position, transferring my duties to her while I was still there. I fully realized the trap set for me by that promotion when, after a few months in my new position, my boss and her friends began making sudden, petty, ridiculous, unsubstantiated, and inconsistent complaints against me. My requests for investigation and proof of my alleged misconduct were denied. Even when I could prove that the allegation was unsubstantiated, I received no apology. In fact, someone told me openly that they would 'record only negative information about me'. My boss started prompting other employees to speak up against me during staff meetings. When one person refused, she was soon denied a permanent position and had to leave the department. This was a deliberate, calculated, systematic campaign of professional and personal humiliation, with the goal to provoke me into quitting or snapping in order to give grounds for disciplinary action and dismissal."

But Lana was not a quitter. She desperately tried to keep providing quality services to the students, which was becoming increasingly difficult as her health and ability to function rapidly deteriorated. Despite her commitment, good will, hard work, loyalty, and multiple praises from students and staff, her top boss told her that "every person in this office complains about your behaviors, but I'm not going to give you any details". When Lana requested clarification, she was immediately accused of having an attitude, being defensive and stubborn, and not wanting to be a team member.

Lana has learned a tough lesson. "My only fault here is that I'm not part of the social clan and cannot navigate office politics, largely due to the way Asperger Syndrome affects my social and communication skills. People in this office have very close social ties. Those who walk into this environment from the outside can't expect to be valued on their performance, competence, commitment, and goodwill. Being a productive, skilled and dedicated worker isn't appreciated here. Being part of the boss's clique is all that matters."

Trying to keep serving students, not to respond to nonstop provocations, and constantly having to look over her shoulder was becoming too much to bear. Lana contacted the union, which served only to further outrage her boss and trigger immediate retaliation. Three years of steady harassment, including disempowerment, exclusion, isolation, public humiliation, unsubstantiated accusations, and deliberate provocations, took their toll on Lana's physical and emotional health. She began to suffer from loss of concentration, memory problems, inability to focus, anxiety attacks, sleeping and eating disorders, and other physical symptoms. Her request as an ADA (Americans with Disabilities Act) accommodation to be transferred to a different department has been stalled for almost a year. The combination of Asperger's and workplace-induced post-traumatic stress has forced her career to a screeching halt. She's currently on medical leave.

14 Survival in the Workplace

Stephen Shore

After receiving my bachelor's in music education and accounting and information systems, I set forth to work in a medium-sized certified public accountants firm. Boy was that a mistake! I was let go after three months. I spent hour after hour preparing financial statements by hand for the auditing of mutual funds; so much so that I got tendonitis of the wrist. As the low man on the totem pole, I would spend much time verifying the work others had done. Even though I had just graduated as an honors student with a bachelor's degree in the field, I often felt my co-workers were talking in another language when they explained procedures and where different documents were located. It seemed as if I had been dropped into a foreign culture. I felt like I needed to be shown step by step in a discrete manner to get a grasp of what was expected of me. No one was willing to do that for me.

I was closely supervised and expected to fit in with the other accountants and business employees. The business uniform is the suit and tie, which drove me nuts. I can't stand to wear a tie. The only way I could survive was to ride my bicycle from where I lived (about seven miles) to work and enjoy the out-of-doors for an hour and a half each day. It took 45 minutes to get to work this way as opposed to the two hours by public transportation. Made sense to me.

Riding my bicycle to work and changing into my suit in the basement of the office was too weird for them. The personnel officer told me that I had better take public transportation and arrive at the office in my suit. Thinking back to that time I realize that I could not have chosen a place that was more conservative and conformist had I tried. Probably all financial institutions are like this. After a while I spent most of my time in their library reading business reference books as the supply of work seemed to dry up. On occasion, I would seek out work from other co-workers, or drop into one of the senior managers' office for a chat.

An assignment with a fellow accountant at the firm didn't work out well at all. I could never really understand what he wanted, and he seemed irritated at the things I did. The bank where we worked was overheated. In response to that I would often open the window and take off my shoes when I was sitting at the desk out of view of other people. He didn't like that at all. While auditing a ledger I mentioned to him that it was difficult to read some of the numbers.

One day the personnel officer called me into his office and told me he was letting me go. He said that I just didn't seem to fit in and suggested that there may have been a disability that I had failed to disclose to him when I interviewed for the job. That disability may very well have been there. To me, however, it was something of the past and it never occurred to me that accommodation may have been needed. I just thought I was stupid because I didn't "get it". Getting fired was very humiliating and embarrassing to me. With a fuzzy, heavy feeling in my head I gathered my belongings and left.

My next job was at a large bank as a portfolio accountant. I made trades for, received interest and dividends for, and created regular financial reports for $750,000,000 of pension fund money. I had now learned better how to blend into the business world. They tolerated my riding my bicycle to work. However, I was miserable being involved in the business culture. I thought I'd left the bullies behind in junior high school, but I was wrong. They were here too. Save for friends from India and Ethiopia, I kept to myself. I simply was not interested in spending the day yakking about team sports and how much a certain couch cost. I stayed at this large bank for the next year and a quarter but was unhappy there. I love the study of business, accounting and taxation but I cannot stand working with the people who choose these areas for their careers.

I left this job after 15 months to teach business at the vocational and college level. I find the study of business, taxes, the stock market, etc. fascinating. I also enjoy teaching business subjects, though not as much as teaching music. However, I just can't tolerate working with the personality types who are attracted to this field.

A better fit

I realized that teaching was for me. There was no close supervision with someone watching my every move. My supervisors and students were closer to accepting me as myself than in any previous position. They actually respected the fact that I rode my bicycle to work. My next job was at a finishing school for secretaries. A warning, like the one issued by the robot on the TV show *Lost in Space*, should have gone off in my head – too strict a dress code. I was let go from that place after two years.

The best fit

When I got my job as professor of music and computers in January 1994, I knew I had found my niche. I could do what I loved and expend much less energy trying to blend in. As long as students are happy, learning what they are supposed to, the administration is happy too.

There are some people there who respect what I do for the school and serve as mentors. They inform me of potential political blunders I may be about to make and are ready to help bail me out if I get into trouble. It is often difficult for me to read the political wind of things, and I'm terribly susceptible to bully-types that cross my path.

Those of us in the fine and performing arts are expected to be somewhat quirky, which suits me fine: I love not having to wear a tie. Some people at work may sense that I'm a bit different, but most of the school community has no true sense of what I'm really about.

By this point in my career adventure, some things became clear to me. In order to survive as a full-time employee of an organization, I must follow these tenets:

1. I must know myself well enough to know where in the workplace I fit in. I seriously misjudged that as I entered the business world. The conformity, along with the suit and tie thing, just doesn't work for me.

2. Close supervision of my day-to-day activities doesn't work for me. I do much better if I'm given a task and a period of time to figure out what must be done, usually in a way that it hasn't been done before.

3. Find a mentor or mentors I can trust. They can save your employment life.

4. Having an interest in a particular field doesn't mean that it is good for me to work in.

5. There is more to life than work. [Really?] Yup! I'm still learning that.

My work at the college, however, was circumvented by a politically oriented challenge that I was unable to meet. As a new full-time faculty member at this school, I had the full backing and support of my dean in teaching my classes along with course and curriculum development. Upon her direction and with the approval of the chair of my department, I set out to restructure the music area degree offerings and add new courses to the curriculum. Where it was only possible to declare a general major of music, my idea was to create different options within that degree. My sense that students would more readily identify with a specific program rather than a general music degree came to fruition as the number of declared music majors doubled soon after the change was implemented.

After following the bureaucratic maze of policies and procedures along with much collaboration with other faculty and staff, the restructured program was approved by an all college vote. Within this victory for my department and the others involved were sown the seeds of destruction for my continuing as a professor at this school.

Subtle social situations rear their ugly heads

There was one long-term and powerful faculty member who felt put out by my failure to consult with him in the restructuring plans. This person taught a single music class, had been in the college for almost two decades, and was very influential in determining academic policies within the institution. Since I was new to the college, it never occurred to me to consult with the chair of another, seemingly unrelated, department as I went about my plans to reconfigure the music program. While I did confer with other members of the music department as I went about these modifications, I should have expanded my inquiry towards additional people who were working within the music department. Perhaps my over-reliance on the documented organizational chart rather than the informal organization led to my overlooking this person.

My failure to detect this situation, combined with the challenges of my inability to read subtle social situations (office politics), resulted in this person's initial displeasure with my working at the college. Unaware of the gravity of the situation in this person's mind I never took steps to make amends for my transgressions towards him. From that point on he was always ready to oppose further plans for developing the music department.

For my first three years at this school I enjoyed a well-established support system that encompassed colleagues as well as administration ranging from the dean all the way up to and including the president of the college. Despite the attempts of the faculty member I had offended, along with his cadre of those who supported his wish to have me let go from the position of music professor, the administration saw that I was continuing to make a substantial contribution to the college and kept me on. Some of these contributions included the doubling of declared music majors and the donation of almost $40, 000 of musical equipment to the school via grant proposals.

Unfortunately, over these three years, the support base I had established with the administration and other faculty eroded away as they left the college for various reasons. Lacking this support, the offended faculty member was able to get the school to conduct a nationwide search for the music position I had now held for three years. Two national searches were mounted. With the first, I was one of the top three candidates for the position. Another person was chosen, but declined the position. The second time, I received the greatest number of votes from the search committee. Despite the search committee's recommendation of my candidacy for the position I had already held for three years, along with the agreement from the dean of the department, the music position was suddenly terminated.

Emotional aftermath

This greater than one-year process of losing this job has been very painful to me. For a time I had thought, like others at this college, that I had a good shot at a chance for having a job for life that I could enjoy. This position seemed to be a dream. I could do what I loved, and still have time to pursue my other interests like autism and bicycles. Losing the job, in spite of following all the procedures I thought necessary to retain the position, was a blow to my belief that by adhering to the rules I could attain my goal to keep this position.

As this long drawn-out process continued, I realized that losing the job was indeed to become a reality. I needed to do something to sublimate the energy created by the angst of the looming possibility of becoming unemployed. This made me very angry towards the perpetrators responsible for my job loss. As this seemed so terribly unfair to me, with much trepidation, I filed legal action with governmental agencies and with the union. It seemed, since the school had so blatantly gone against the teacher's contract, I should be able to win my position back. Since confrontation is very difficult for me, I was very reluctant to request assistance from the teacher's union. I suspect this is because confrontation involves strong, unpredictable emotional behaviors and reactions. Being a person who likes things to be scripted out before they happen, the unknowns of conflict can be very frightening.

The result was an additional year, and no more, of employment. Even though I was still working and the actual prospect of joblessness was yet to occur, I experienced a big change in attitude towards the college. Until now, aside from my wife and family, I gave this position first priority insofar as devoting my time and energy. Because I received such positive feedback from the president of the school and other superiors, I felt what I did there was good and needed by the school. After realizing that the school – or rather, a few key people – didn't view me on that basis, I chose to redirect my energies elsewhere. It no longer seemed necessary to be friendly with most of the people there, and there was certainly no need to perform any job functions beyond those that were described in the teacher's contract. It was these additional things beyond the bare teaching and advising of students that gave me a lot of satisfaction in doing an excellent job.

This caused my emotional withdrawal from the school which had been a source of great pleasure. The position became a mere shell of its former self. I did as I saw many other teachers do: arrive, teach, help the students, and leave. Changing my work philosophy to this minimalist approach was difficult, since it's my nature to continually work towards making the school a better place for the students. Seeing that there was no future here made anything that related to continued development of the school irrelevant.

Whereas this position had been a source of enthusiasm and energy for me, it became an emotional drain. Suddenly I realized a possible reason why others at this institution seemed to put in minimal effort. Perhaps they too had been burned by office politics and felt unappreciated.

Onward and beyond

I'm now happily enrolled in a doctoral program in special education with a concentration on helping people on the autism spectrum reach their fullest potential. When not working with people on the autism spectrum and studying, I teach computers and statistics at various colleges.

Acknowledgement

Excerpted with permission from Shore, S. (2003). *Beyond the Wall: Personal Experiences with Autism and Asperger Syndrome*, 2nd edn. Shawnee Mission, KS: Autism Asperger Publishing Company, pp.111–118. AAPC's website: www.asperger.net.

Stephen Shore, diagnosed with "Atypical Development with strong autistic tendencies" and nonverbal until age four, is now completing his doctoral degree in special education at Boston University, with a focus on helping people on the autism spectrum develop their capacities to the fullest extent possible. Stephen presents internationally on adult issues pertinent to relationships, employment, and disclosure as discussed in his book *Beyond the Wall: Personal Experiences with Autism and Asperger Syndrome*. He also serves on the board of the Autism Society of America, and is board president of the Asperger's Association of New England.

15 The Salesman
Jeff

I have always felt that I was different. A shy, introverted youngster, I didn't know how to express feelings appropriately. As a child, I was serious minded and fearful, often expressing anger and frustration. I dreaded any changes that affected my life, such as starting school or attending church at a different location. Show and Tell, where students stand in front of the class and talk about their interests or activities, was one of my greatest fears. I knew I was expected to participate, but my anxiety was incapacitating. On one occasion, I forced myself to stand in front of the class and talk about a new toy cowboy pistol that had been given to me. It was a total disaster. Everyone laughed. I was so embarrassed, I never made another attempt. It took many years to get over this incident, and I didn't learn that I had public-speaking abilities until high school. Speech class was a tremendous confidence builder. I learned many skills, such as how to place proper accentuation upon my words. By the end of the year, I was entering speech competitions. I believe that what I learned in that class provided the basis for my future in sales.

After completing high school, I enrolled at a two-year college. Lacking long-term goals and a sense of educational direction, I lost interest, dropped out, and found work at a local Italian restaurant. Another employee showed me how to operate the dishwasher and prepare the food for the salad bar. I understood the instructions for using the dishwasher, but the numerous tasks associated with the salad bar totally confused me. I felt intimidated by the manager, and was too embarrassed to ask for help. Because of my inability to stay organized and keep up with the hectic work requirements, I became frustrated and quit this job before they could fire me.

Later that year, my father helped me get a job at a paint store. I started out stocking shelves, unloading freight trucks, and making deliveries. I quickly adapted to this work environment, where numbers and colors categorized products, and stock locations were clearly defined. As my confidence grew, I was allowed to assist retail customers and contractors. At this stage of my life I was detail oriented, but not very good at diplomacy. I could match paint colors precisely, but was also prone to being argumentative with customers over policy or opinion. I preferred to spend my time in the back room working on color matches for architectural projects.

A few years later, I was entrusted with opportunities to make outside sales calls. On one occasion, I was asked to inspect a project where a primer was being applied to some large industrial equipment. When I discovered that the primer being used was not precisely the best product for that particular application, I felt compelled to inform the customer that we had sold him an incorrect primer, and that we would replace it with the ideal product. This spontaneous decision of mine was costly and not well received by my manager, so I wasn't asked to make any more sales calls for that company. However, I did continue to work for them as a sales clerk. My thought process was very black and white, and gray areas were confusing to me.

I have continued in the paint industry, working for several different companies in various functions, including sales, for 25 years. During this time, I was unaware of my Asperger Syndrome traits. It was not until January of 2003 that a counselor pointed out that I seemed insensitive to the feelings of others. I became very inquisitive about this, since I knew that I wasn't being intentionally rude or not empathetic. A few days later, as I continued to dwell on this thought, it dawned on me that lack of empathy is often associated with autism. I spent most of that night researching autistic spectrum disorders on the internet. When I read about Asperger Syndrome, the puzzle pieces of my life began to fit together. The knowledge of my sister's profound autism, my son's high functioning autism, and my own self-awareness led me to believe that I was also on the spectrum. A psychiatric assessment later confirmed my beliefs. I was diagnosed with AS, an incurable neurological disorder that affects the way I think, feel, act, and talk. My symptoms include high levels of anxiety that require medication, depression, egocentricity, difficulty interpreting humor and figurative language, a limited range of interests that can become obsessive, self-isolating, difficulty recognizing faces, pedantic speech, analytical thinking, problems with depth perception, coordination difficulties, and visual and auditory sensory issues.

After working as a sales clerk, my next step was store management, wherein I supervised as many as 12 employees. The responsibilities of

managing a store necessitated learning many new skills. Delegating authority and duties was essential for my survival in management. At first I tried to
take on too many responsibilities, thinking that if I wanted the job done
right, I needed to do it myself. When it became evident that this was counterproductive and extremely stressful, I decided that I must trust other competent people with some of the burdens. Over a lengthy period of time I put
together a crew of employees who I felt were capable. I was only fully comfortable with crewmembers who were loyal and in harmony with my philosophy of how things should be done. I needed to feel that my co-workers
were an extension of myself and not too independent. I could accept some
independent thinking if it proved to be profitable.

Although successful as a manager, I wasn't content. Being under the
leadership of district managers, marketing directors, financial directors and
numerous vice presidents was not something that my Aspie mind was very
tolerant of. Executives who use a lot of subtleties in their speech sometimes
intimidate me. Subtlety leads to confusion, and I'm in danger of being
manipulated. If I have time to become better acquainted with these people, I
can generally work out ways to deal with them, while protecting my vulnerable areas at the same time. But this takes time and a great deal of thought.

When that company decided to expand its outside salesforce, I applied.
When I learned that I had been chosen to manage one of the new sales terri-
tories, I was excited about the opportunity, but I was also unsure whether I
could successfully deal with the social situations. In general, I don't form
close personal relationships with fellow employees, supervisors, or customers. I am not one who hangs out with the guys at the tavern after the workday
is done, and I don't socialize with them on weekends. There are some excep-
tions to this, such as company Christmas dinners, which I feel obligated to
attend. I may also share a joke once in a while if I learn one that amuses me.

Business lunches and just normal socialization are major challenges. I
cannot rely totally upon scripts under these circumstances, so I resort to listening while my customers do most of the talking. With customers who are
less talkative, I can sometimes turn the discussion towards my interests, such
as computers or one of my recent research fascinations. Purchasing agents
and other contact people often want to enter into social talk that is of little
interest to me. I do my best to give attention to their conversations, but find
that my mind often wanders and I lose focus. It can be difficult to contribute
to these conversations, and I'm often fearful of appearing stupid because I
can think of little to comment on. Sometimes I fail to recognize their humor,

and they look at me with a quizzical expression and say "that was supposed to be a joke".

Customer complaints sometimes feel like a personal attack against my opinions or beliefs, which can be agonizing. I have learned to mentally remind myself that the customer is always right, even though that seems contradictory to me. To cope, I've created two separate rooms inside my mind, one where I deal with the customer, and another where I place my feelings and opinions, then temporarily close the door. The main problem with this is that although the feelings and opinions are repressed, I still need to deal with them.

My first sales territory was composed of many small to medium sized contractors and sales figures fluctuated according to the weather and seasons. I would frequently feel depressed during the winter months when sales figures would plummet. I also felt somewhat out of place and creatively hindered.

A few years ago, I made a change in employment to a paint manufacturer whose primary focus was on industrial customers, and for whom I still work. I like this job because it offers a virtually unlimited territory with considerable potential for growth. Several factors have contributed to my success with this employer.

I have learned from past mistakes, and today I'm more professional and functional. I have unique qualities that are of value to my current employer. Since my special interests revolve around research, I have found great pleasure in identifying niche markets that are often overlooked by larger paint companies, and then establishing our company as the best choice for quality products and service. The internet is an excellent tool for finding opportunities, and it's one of my favorite places to explore. I also enjoy working along-side our chemists in developing environmentally friendly products, including some bio-based products. One of our chemists has many Aspie characteristics, and we seem to have a mutual enthusiasm about new discoveries.

While calling on customers, I'm in contact with various levels of personnel: purchasing agents, quality control managers, plant superintendents, supervisors and workers. Purchasing agents are generally the ones who require the most socialization. It's important to remember personal information that they relate to me. Any references to family, vacations, activities, interests, etc. can be noted and then reviewed prior to future meetings. This provides subject material for conversations and business lunches. I have found that if I can get someone started talking about the things they enjoy, it can help eliminate lengthy and awkward pauses in the conversation.

I have the most success working with quality control managers. Their interest revolves around product performance, efficiency and safety. Technical talk is like a primary language for the average QC manager, and working with him/her can be an exciting adventure for me.

Plant superintendents and supervisors are very busy people with enormous responsibilities. They're usually not interested in chitchat, but they do want the assurance that they are receiving regularly scheduled visits. It's always a good idea to ask them if they have any specific concerns, and if they do, to give prompt attention to their instructions or requests. If I help them by monitoring product usage and performance, and by offering other useful services, I can help relieve some of the pressures of their job, and maintain a professional relationship with them.

Keeping a good rapport with the workers who directly use my company's products is absolutely necessary. These individuals will provide a considerable amount of useful information, and they truly seem to appreciate the fact that I focus attention upon what they are doing. I need to be cautious about offering advice and doing so in a constructive manner, as I can easily damage my relationship with them if I'm overly critical. An honest compliment works wonders for building someone's self-esteem, and I must constantly remind myself to offer praise to these hard workers.

Many of the factories and mills I visit are very noisy. Even if earplugs are not required, I still carry them with me so that I can quickly install them when I need to. Failing to do so can result in a feeling of painful vibration inside of my head. I have discovered that earplugs reduce sensory overload, which can lead to confusion and anxiety. I also need to stand very close to people who are speaking to me so that I can distinguish their words from the other sounds that are all around me. I don't like to ask people to repeat themselves, but sometimes I need to.

One other subject that I believe is important to mention is driving. My primary sales area is spread out along a 600-mile stretch of highway, and it's not unusual for me to travel 300 to 400 miles in one day. This is actually a good thing. I try to plan my travel times so that I can avoid traffic congestion as much as possible. I enjoy the solitude and love the beautiful green scenery, with snowcapped mountains, fertile valleys, and lush forests. The long distances between some of my customers allow me time to think about my previous stop and to plan for the next one. I use my travel time to think about projects and to mentally analyze details that require much thought. In my previous job, I made frequent stops to visit customers and potential customers within a relatively small territory, which was very stressful. While traveling, I must remember to eat meals at the correct time intervals, or my stress and anxiety will increase. Sunglasses are essential even during the winter months because I never know when there will be a break in the clouds, or sunlight reflecting off the road. Road and engine noise can also be disturbing to me. Smooth jazz or other relaxing forms of music can help filter out the noise and soothe my soul. Music can also reduce the sounds of rain and windshield wipers, and ease the distractions associated with driving in congested areas. If sensory overload becomes too intense, I will find a quiet place to park where I can relax for a few minutes.

It is important for me to know my strengths and weaknesses. I have already mentioned some of these specifically, but I have not yet directed attention to my Aspieness in general. My life goes up and down and round and round, kind of like a roller-coaster ride. While I live with constant anxiety and tension, when I'm at the bottom of an emotional cycle these feelings may increase until I feel stressed and overwhelmed. Then depression will set in. Medication and other strategies do not always correct these moods, and I must accept them as a part of my life. From a business standpoint, it is imperative that I remain as functional as possible. During these times I focus on maintaining only. I do not attempt to call on potential customers or begin working on complex new projects. To do so could result in disastrous consequences. I always know that these periods of emotional turmoil will subside, and that times of productivity and creativity will ensue. If I organize my priorities and time wisely, I can reduce the negative effects of my down moods, and increase the possibilities for positive results when I am on an emotional upswing. This is a tremendous challenge, and I continue to work on self-management. I believe that self-awareness along with cognizance of how other people are reacting to me are the best indicators of when I may need to slow down and go into a maintenance mode.

Stimming is another component of my Aspieness. Much of my self-stimulatory behavior is internal and is not directly obvious. At any given time, I may appear to be quiet on the outside, but inside my mind I am often repeating numbers, words, sentences, songs, etc. This can be distracting and sometimes leads to frustration because my thought process is slowed down. When I am in the office I will gently rock myself back and forth, or spin side to side while sitting in my swivel chair. While standing and talking with someone, I may rock myself from side to side. I do not think that I draw any significant attention to myself with my stimming. I always spend some time in the early morning and evening rocking myself vigorously in my chair at home. This is a personal joy that I always look forward to. It helps me to get through the workday because I know that my chair will be there when I get home.

If someone were to ask me what my greatest challenge currently is, I would probably say facial recognition. If I make contact with someone in a busy manufacturing environment, it is likely that I will forget what they look like before I leave the facility. At one plant I visit weekly, they've recently laid off about 350 employees, including several of my main contacts. These positions have been filled or consolidated, and I'm unfamiliar with the faces, personalities and expectations of these individuals. Adapting to these changes in an environment where people are constantly on the move and difficult to find is really putting me to the test. Focusing on both a conversation and a person's face is nearly impossible, especially if it's a new contact. I wish that I could take a digital picture of everyone I meet, but since this would not be kosher, I do my best to mentally record their face during breaks in the conversation. Name recall is equally challenging, and requires the same diligent effort.

In conclusion, I feel that my current job satisfies my desire for analyzing opportunities, using creativity in pursuing them, and giving attention to detail so that I can maintain my customer base. My employer benefits from my persistence, and my ability to look at situations and opportunities from unique perspectives, rather than being restrained by paradigmatic thinking. If I could go back and start over again, it would have been helpful to have a college education that would have included studies in marketing and psychology. I have been able to learn these skills and essential knowledge by trial and error, but it has required a lot of time. I think that some of the higher functioning people with AS could have success in sales, especially if they are marketing products or services within their area of special interest. Current business trends are focusing on service and efficiency rather than socializing. Aspies could take advantage of these changing times by building customer relationships based upon expertise instead of the former focus that centered on social interactions and gratuities.

16 The Graduate

At 46, David states, "The height of my life was college graduation." He spent the next ten years looking for work. "I almost gave up," he said. "Despite having a BA in English lit, I was poorly suited to hold down college grad jobs. Unfortunately, Aspies make great students, but lousy employees. Too bad there's no job just for studying (is there?)."

In college, David first became a computer/math major, but found advanced math too difficult. "I couldn't hack calculus and computer science, but I loved literature, so I changed my major to English lit. This was fun! Although a slow reader, I loved reading and discussing books." What does one do with a major in English literature? David held many jobs, with little success. "The worst attempt was trying to be a public school teacher. I worked as a substitute teacher, but couldn't control the kids. They simply defied me, refusing to do the work. There were many complaints, and I was thrown out by more than one district. I returned to college to pick up the required education courses, and got a teaching license. It only lasted three or four years before being disqualified for medical reasons. After explaining my strangeness and limitations to the Board of Ed medical division, they canned me. I was declared an unfit teacher."

David always knew he wasn't normal, and was called brain damaged as a child. He was smart, but often unable to show it. This led to a poor self-image and a lot of self-doubt. He never fit in. With his disability dragging him down, and continual problems finding and maintaining employment, he sought help, and was diagnosed with AS four years after college graduation. The diagnosis explained his difficulties with social situations. "I don't interview well, and can't handle tense situations. Driving causes too much tension, so I rely on public transportation," he comments.

Today, David works for a unique non-profit agency, Special Tees Custom Screen Printers. "We put custom designs on shirts, hats, shorts, towels and any other textile thing. I spend the days cleaning tools and screens or working on the production line, throwing shirts onto the press. My shop is a wonderful institution because it only hires people with mental disabilities. You must provide letters from your psychotherapist saying you're work ready: Then you can begin the application process, but don't expect to work for us anytime soon. We have an application list about as big as our staff, about 25 applicants.

"The downside is that it's not very creative work. Nothing more note-worthy than how many shirts you can print in a day, or fold and pack in a day, or how many tools and screens you can clean and reclaim in a day. Real boring, very repetitive, drudge work.

"Don't ask about pay. Most of us are on social security disability payments, which put strict limits on how much you can earn in a week. But if you have nothing else to look for, it's a living. The worst part of it is I'm not very proud of anything I do there or anyplace else.The last time I took real pride in myself was when I graduated college!"

David's boss and the founder of Special Tees, Tom Siniscalchi, describes David as large and heavy, with a profound limp. "He has a nice face which he keeps hidden behind a beard, and his hair is generally unkempt. He travels to work in his work clothes which, although machine washed clean, are full of dried ink. He wears big suspenders to keep his pants up, and because he has an unusually shaped body. He has impeccable eating habits, although he can't keep food out of his beard and often leaves a mess behind him.

"Though he's very intelligent, he's also very forgetful and becomes confused easily. He looks and acts a little odd, so people shy away from him. He bites his hand or scratches himself. He's clumsy and sloppy. When cleaning ink from a screen, he'll get ink all over himself as well as all over the walls. He has a short attention span, difficulty concentrating, and is extremely disorganized – after two hours, his desk would be a mess and he would misplace his written assignments. Because he's bored quickly and frustrated easily, he often takes on more than he's asked, which sometimes gets him into trouble.

"After seven years at Special Tees, David still feels that the print shop work is somewhat beneath him. He doesn't hesitate to belittle other employ-ees, pointing out that he has a college degree. His grandiose, condescending attitude alienates other employees at times. He's annoying, doesn't think before he acts. On September 11, he wore a T-shirt with the logo 'I'm an American Atheist'."

Tom explains that Special Tees is a special place: "We are proving that people with mental and emotional disabilities can be a productive part of society. These people are eager to work, and here their work is appreciated. They're part of a team, working together towards a finished product they can be proud of, loading shirts on the presses, straightening them, printing the design, taking them off the press, placing them on the dryer, catching them off the dryer, folding and shipping them. We also depend on them to take orders and design artwork. The only allowances we make for David and other employees are that we understand each individual's difficulties while attempting to push them to the highest level that we feel they can reach. This is done with the understanding that there's no pass or fail here. These people welcome the thought of someone helping them find their potential as opposed to casting them onto the scrapheap."

Tom speaks favorably about David: "He's one of the founders of the company, and has been with us more than seven years. Although he still doesn't excel at any part of the printing process – which he thinks is boring – he's a great guy, with a very generous heart. He's very articulate, speaks on behalf of the company, and has excellent computer skills. We're a million-dollar business now. He's great at advocating for Special Tees, and has helped immensely with computer work and promotional advertising. He's an excellent, eloquent speaker, and has represented us and spoken about the company and how we help people at civic functions."

One example of David's promotional abilities is how he was able to get Special Tees an interview with *Impressions*, a national trade magazine serving the imprinted products industry. David explains: "We subscribe to them, and I noticed that they do articles on screen printing shops which fill special niches, such as shops that serve college students or religious groups. I then called the editor and told her about us. They sent someone to interview us, loved us, and wrote about us. As a result, we were featured in the December 2002 issue."

Another example of the contacts David makes for Special Tees is with a non-profit agency which runs services for autistic kids, including a summer camp. David spread the word about Special Tees, the camp bought shirts, and David worked with the kids over the summer. "Others I worked with were aspiring psychologists," he notes. "I worked as a counselor in the summer camp program, did various activities with them. My favorite was story hour. We went up to a reading rock, sat in a circle, and I read stories to them. Because autistic children don't look at you and don't respond, it was difficult to tell if they were listening. I think they liked seeing what an autistic adult is like. It was a good experience, because I wasn't responsible for behavior management. Other counselors did that."

David appreciates greatness. He has a dream, and is trying to find his niche. He would like to publish a book someday. He has poor menial skills but is very intelligent, and gets frustrated because he feels he should be able to do more, but can't. In a way, his intelligence is a handicap. Because the gap between his verbal abilities and performance is so great, he's often unable to fulfill others' expectations.

17 In Pursuit of Approval

Reynaldo knew he was different. He behaved and thought differently from his family. Although he had a large vocabulary, he had trouble expressing his feelings or understanding how others felt. When agitated, he would rock back and forth or do other strange bodily movements to calm down. He seemed just a bit odd.

His experiences with doctors were positive from an early age; he didn't even mind getting shots. The instruments at the doctor's office were fascinating. The staff members were friendly. His parents got him doctor kits, and he enjoyed playing with them. This early interest grew, and when he became an adult, he chose the field of medicine.

In his twenties, Reynaldo was able to get work, but found it harder to hold on to the position. I questioned him about this. "When I was young, I could get jobs easily," he told me. "I did a variety of things, depending on what was available. My first job was as a dishwasher. I had other restaurant jobs as well. Later, I gravitated towards medical technology."

Most jobs in the medical field require certification. Reynaldo had no problems taking the certification tests, receiving high scores. Because he had an interest in the subject, he studied on his own, then took the tests. He scored in the 100 percentile on the medical assistant certification exam, and received a score of 92 percent on the phlebotomy certification test.

Reynaldo also did well on interviews. He told me, "At the job interview, prospective employers were very impressed with my skills, my subject knowledge, and with the articulate manner in which I spoke." Once employed, however, Reynaldo had many problems maintaining a job. Nevertheless, he kept trying. He had various jobs as a nursing assistant, medical assistant, and phlebotomist, but none lasted more than six months. Most of the time he was fired. He quit one restaurant job where he was being exploited. He comments about that one: "I was mistreated, made to work overtime without pay. I did this in order to please my superiors. I was looking for acceptance." Reynaldo's need for acceptance and desire to please became his downfall.

Once he was hired at a nursing home as a medical assistant. It was a brand new facility, and they had him doing maintenance. Although this wasn't in his job description, he went along. Other employees were in the break room while he was doing the work. Yet when he complained about it, he was told he had a poor attitude and was let go.

This lack of professionalism and a desire for approval caused Reynaldo problems at many of the hospitals, medical offices and medical laboratories in which he worked. He had problems getting along with colleagues, and would sometimes become too personal with patients. His odd sense of humor wasn't always appreciated. Wanting to please, he would cross boundaries by exceeding the duties of the job, sometimes performing nursing procedures he wasn't qualified for. He gives an example: "A phlebotomist collects blood samples and body fluids from patients for laboratory testing. Once I was working in the hospital emergency room. There was no one available to catheterize a patient when I heard the doctor order it. Because he was standing next to me, I thought he wanted me to do the procedure, so I took over. They said I had done a good job – but this is a nurse's job, not the job of a phlebotomist." He sighed. "Although they thanked me, they also reported me."

Another time, Reynaldo gave an injection, which is also a nursing procedure. A phlebotomist is limited to drawing blood, and is not permitted to give a shot. At the time, although he was working as a phlebotomist, he was certified as a medical assistant – and thus could give injections.

He had many such experiences of failed communication, not realizing what was expected of him and going beyond the scope of his job in an effort to please. Though his intentions were good, because of his social ineptness, he was not well liked, and was often misunderstood by colleagues and supervisors. The hospitals used these and similar instances to terminate him.

Reynaldo even had the opportunity to teach phlebotomy. He liked teaching because he could plan for the lectures in advance. He told me: "As long as I was prepared and knew what to say it was nice. However, many students used devious schemes and tactics. They tried to get me to bypass my grading system by offering me gifts. Some even threatened to get me fired if I didn't give them a good score. One student to whom I had given a 94 (of

100) got upset, said I was being racial, and charged me with discrimination. Ninety-four was still a good score!" Because of incidents like these, Reynaldo is no longer teaching.

Such situations led not only to lost work, but also to legal trouble. Reynaldo explained: "I tried to use my medical knowledge to treat people, but I was not a doctor or even a nurse. Some patients turned me in. I was tried and convicted of practicing medicine without a license. To escape jail, I accepted probation."

Reynaldo had gone back to college before his legal troubles began. Due to problems with technical rule violations of his probation, he was diagnosed with major depression and missed many classes. Though he was exonerated each time, the time lost affected his academic studies. Today, he's on financial aid suspension and can't afford to pay for school. Fortunately, his mother has offered to help with the tuition, allowing him to finish his studies.

It was during this time that Reynaldo was diagnosed with Asperger Syndrome (AS). His probation officer, who was studying to become a social worker, recognized the Asperger's profile. Reynaldo went for tests, and the diagnosis was confirmed. "Things began to make sense," he told me. "It's too bad it took legal trouble for me to learn this." Reynaldo always knew he was different, but now, in his mid-thirties, he was beginning to understand why.

"Now that I'm older, it's more difficult to get a job," he said. "They want the young kids, fresh out of school, or someone with a good employment track record." Today, Reynaldo works as a volunteer for the County Criminal Justice Commission Community Court, interviewing defendants and trying to get to the bottom of the issues. He also serves as a job search specialist, helping clients find jobs. He has been with the Florida Vocational Rehabilitation Department for the last three years. Though he has a job specialist working with him, they haven't been able to find him suitable work.

Because many AS individuals need to be in a supported employment setting, vocational rehabilitation workers need to be familiar with the condition. Reynaldo says: "Your employer needs to know your capabilities, as well as your limitations. He can't expect as much from you as from others. This is because a person with Asperger's has odd behaviors. These include strange movements, like rocking back and forth, and talking about things that are of no interest, or exceed the interest spectrum of those he talks to. The individual with AS may seem rude or snappy toward co-workers because of his lack of emotional reciprocity. He may also challenge the authority of another worker, whom he may think is 'bossing him around', when he is instructed by someone not in apparent authority."

Therefore, it's imperative that the employer can explain the AS sufferer's oddities to others in the workplace. A job coach can also help with this. It's very important that the boss refrain from scolding or yelling at the AS employee, and that all procedures are clearly explained. The person with AS needs to know the reasons behind the rules. Reynaldo illustrates this: "You can't just say 'If you speed, you'll get a ticket, it will cost you'. It's important for the AS individual to understand why speeding is bad – that it will endanger others on the road and could cause accidents. You must explain similar things in a job situation." He gave another example: "The para-transit service I use forbids their drivers from using I-95. It's a very busy highway and there are many accidents there. But if scare tactics are used, that would make a driver with AS want to do it more."

Reynaldo has this advice: "Stay away from production oriented jobs. Try to find work that's more independent, where you're not under close supervision." Professional jobs are better in this respect than production jobs. "Social workers, insurance adjusters, and auditors are examples of more independent work environments," Reynaldo explained. "Consider any job where you have your own office or can create your own work environment, rather than working in close proximity to other employees who can observe – and often annoy – you. This is a good work setting."

Today, Reynaldo is involved in advocacy for people with Asperger Syndrome. In January 2000, he formed a non-profit organization, The Advocacy Center For Adults with Asperger's Syndrome, Autism and Related Disabilities, Inc. In addition, he attends and helps to facilitate a monthly support group at Florida Atlantic University Center for Autism and Related Disorders (FAU/CARD), a satellite of the University of Miami Center for Autism and Related Disorders (UM/CARD).

18 The Entrepreneur

Scott describes school as "a 13-year nightmare". Although his parents sent him to prestigious private prep schools, he was a poor student. "I only did well in subjects that interested me, like music, and ignored the rest. The prep schools were training camps for bullies, career liars, social climbers, and back stabbers. Although intelligent, I was a slow learner. I was different, and was harassed, made fun of, picked on, and beaten up ever since sixth grade."

He grew up in large cities, and relished the excitement. "I loved to walk around and take in the smells, sights, sounds, tastes, and feeling of the city. Sometimes, however, the excessive sensory stimulation would cause me to zone out and retreat into my own little world. More than once, a good Samaritan pulled me away from death by taxi."

To deal with the abuse, Scott resorted to drugs. "The half decade between 13 and 18 is one foggy haze. I also discovered classical music and girls. Between the sex, drugs, and music, life became bearable, though I barely graduated."

He also discovered yoga when a teenager. His father had lots of yoga books, so Scott began reading them and doing the exercises. Yoga is non-competitive and teaches you how to take control of your body and your emotions, focusing on one piece at a time. You learn how to block out the overwhelming stimuli and how to break a big thing (your whole body) into small components, working on each part individually.

Yoga helped Scott to deal with the sensory overload. "It helped me get rid of a lot of the nervous facial tics, foot tapping, finger drumming. I learned to look people straight in the eye. It also taught me to filter out much of the anger and rage. I became more physically and mentally patient and more disciplined. Once you get control of these things, you become more confident when you're around normal people."

Scott began taking piano at age ten, and found an excellent instructor when he was 15. "She said she would take me, but I had to commit to two or more hours a day of practice. This was not a problem for me. Although my lessons were an hour, she often kept me for two, drilling me and raking me over the coals. I take criticism well as long as I have respect for the critic. She got me interested in music theory, which I found fascinating. Music theory is a huge body of knowledge, which takes years to master. I enjoy working on complex studies that offer a challenge."

His early twenties were spent working in his father's business, studying music, and hanging out with a group of middle-aged musicians and composers. "I studied with professional musicians for several years. Being around musicians and artistic people was good. They tend to be much more accepting of differences than people in the mainstream." His experiences with this group built Scott's level of confidence.

"Then I did a year in college. While on vacation, I visited a friend at an Ivy League school and showed my portfolio to a composer there. When a Pulitzer Prize winner calls the admissions department and tells them to admit you, it's a done deal. I was accepted into the graduate music program on the spot.

"This was an important lesson for me, though learned by accident. I discovered that if you're smart and talented, you can usually get in through the back door. The mavericks at the top tend to appreciate other self-styled eccentrics. If you show ability, perseverance, and willingness to work like a fiend, they'll help you out."

Graduate school proved overwhelming, however, and Scott experienced his first major bout of depression. He dropped out and joined the army. "Basic training, like middle and high school, was full of neanderthal brutes who ridiculed anyone who was different. Once I got into actual training, however, things improved. I began running. Running helps you control and master your body. A good five-mile run can burn a lot of anxiety, too. There were lots of smart social misfits in this group. I spent over a year studying an Oriental language and other interesting subjects."

Along with several scholarships and fellowships, the four years in the military helped pay for four and a half years of grad school in music composition. "This was a good time. With a fellowship, teaching assistantship, and the GI Bill, I had enough money. I was pretty well conditioned by the army, so I was disciplined and competitive. I had an office in the department, and was often there from 7am till midnight.

"I developed techniques for dealing with difficult courses. For example, I have a hard time reading and remembering certain kinds of dull text. I tend to zone out and get lost in less than a page, and can't remember anything I've read. To deal with this, I outline everything in a word processor. I take one paragraph at a time, and transcribe the essence. I also make time lines, diagrams, tables and pictures."

During his final two years of grad school, Scott found a flexible job in the engineering department of a large semiconductor manufacturer. While there, he discovered he was good with data, computers, and large systems. "Once more, I found something I could immerse myself in and learn about. I loved the challenge. I worked with engineers whose social skills were no better than mine. They liked me, and encouraged me to become an engineer. I felt very much at home in this environment."

In his last semester of PhD course work in music, Scott quit school and moved back to his family's home to help his dad with a business opportunity. He looked for work, but then found out what people would pay someone with an MA in music, and changed direction.

A local entrepreneur heard of Scott's computer skills, and came by to talk. "He asked if I could fix his network. I figured out the problems with his system, and he referred me to other businessmen." Soon, word got around about his computer work. "I had no formal training in computers or networking, but have an intuitive understanding of those systems. It's just there, just like music is. I 'get' data. I understand a lot about finance and accounting (it's all just data), so I'm able to talk the talk with financial people."

Scott has developed his IT consulting business over the past ten years. He designs systems that will work on an organization-wide basis. "I get all of my clients by referral, usually after they've been burned by sales people, bad advice or lack of planning. I tend to work directly for financial types, who like the bottom line, or MIS directors. I stay away from the basic computer tech stuff because it's not profitable, is too easy, and quickly becomes boring. I love the challenge of conquering a new field. To fill in the gaps in my knowledge, I read lots of accounting, finance, business and computer books."

What has contributed to his success? "First, I tell the truth. Most business people appreciate honesty and find it refreshing. This is particularly true if they've been burned – and I've had many clients burned to the tune of five and six figures. I don't bother with sugar coating or social niceties. This is apparently a rare quality, and those who possess it can collect a premium.

Second, I'm able to totally immerse myself in solving a problem. If need be, I can concentrate on a problem for days, and sit at the computer for 20 hours."

The very qualities that make Scott a good businessman are what make working for someone else difficult. While business clients appreciate honesty, employers are often annoyed, interpreting his blunt and direct approach as rudeness or arrogance.

"I'm thorough, and usually do a much better job than a supervisor would ask for. As the project manager, my recommendations and advice are almost always heeded. As an employee, however, I have issues with authority figures and don't like to take direction from people."

This air of superiority and arrogance is another impediment to regular employment. He's smart, he knows he's smart, and he's not afraid to show he's smart. "I have no tolerance for NTBs (not too brights). In the world of jobs, there are lots of these animals, and they often manage to claw their way into management positions. If you have a job, you're forced to associate with these primitives.

"I've always found social situations awkward. I'm not very good at developing relationships with co-workers. Often, if the conversation isn't particularly interesting, my thoughts wander and I go into my own world. I've learned to compensate by making eye contact and nodding my head. If I have to work around the same people as an employee, I feel I'm missing something and not fitting in; this causes increased anxiety. When I see people lying, taking credit for others' work, ridiculing others, goofing off on the job, doing poor quality work or just meeting minimal standards, I seethe with anger and frustration – and it usually shows. When you're a consultant, you're not considered a worker, which makes things easier."

Since starting his business, Scott has taken formal computer training and earned several certifications. He's currently certified as a Cisco Certified Network Professional (CCNP) and is working on several Cisco security certifications. "Professional classes are expensive, but they deal directly with the subject and are taught by people who work in the field. On the other hand, the professors who often teach university computer classes have little or no experience in the field and a poor understanding of the business context.

"A typical IT class is 40 hours, taught all in one week, and costs about $2500. Since I'm able to hyperfocus, this is a good choice. There are usually 500 to 800 pages of technical material to read, and it takes me 40 to 80 hours of additional study to do well on the test. Since I work in the field, I'm somewhat familiar with the material before I take the course. To keep up with information technology, I try to learn several specific skills or technologies each year, and budget for at least four weeks of in-class training per year."

Organization has been a more difficult challenge to master. "I've taken many classes on organization, and still struggle with it. I carry a Palm Pilot, notebook computer, notebook and pens at all times. I always carry at least one bag to keep all my stuff in. I have developed organization rituals. For example, as soon as I get home, I immediately empty all my pockets into a basket. I have several copies of my keys, and keep a spare set handy at all times. Since I often can't remember what I did yesterday or last week, I keep a journal. Even though I have a photographic memory for certain types of information, I write everything down. I have also read several books on dealing with people you truly despise."

Time management has been another difficult lesson. "I'm often late. One of the ugly truths of life is that you have to show up on time if you have a regular job. I can get so immersed in a project that I forget to show up for work at the designated time. I have learned the necessity of being on time for important business meetings. I try to schedule these in the afternoon. Fortunately, once a project is under way, there aren't too many of these. If it's not a meeting, only work, I'll tell a client it will be done on a certain day."

Scott has accepted his shortcomings and peculiarities as well as his strengths. "There is no better self-esteem builder than true accomplishment. If you can't do it one way, try another approach. Most successful people in the arts will tell you that their success is based on 10 percent talent and 90 percent hard work. I believe this. I also believe there's no such thing as a learning disability. Some people are just wired differently. If you're reading this, you or someone close to you is in possession of an exceptional mind as well as exceptional genetic material. Rather than trying to become normal, learn to use the tools and strengths you were given. Don't rely on doctors, teachers, mental health professionals or government programs. They're not interested in helping you become you. They want to make you like everyone else. Find your skills and talents, then work hard to make them better. Set goals and achieve them. There are probably some things you'll never be able to do; accept them. But there are other things you can do exceptionally well. You have a unique mind, a unique perspective, unique talents and skills. You're not disabled, but you certainly will be if you allow yourself (in the words of Pearl Jam) 'to be diagnosed by some stupid fuck'."

PART II
Career Strategies

Planning for a Career
Finding a Job
Maintaining a Career

Planning for a Career

19 Career Planning for the AS/NLD Individual

Gabrielle describes her first job this way: "First jobs are exciting, scary, exhausting and fun. There are lots of new people to meet and you will always remember what you did. A first job can be a great foundation for other jobs and a big learning experience for the future. If you take care, learn well and try your hardest it will serve you well.

"My first job was much of the above and more. I worked behind the counter in a restaurant that served food and ice cream. Serving the food, waiting on customers, making change and remembering instructions all turned out to be more of a challenge than I had thought it would be. I had particular difficulty with quick thinking and short term memory. It was also hard to assemble the ice cream concoctions correctly.

"After three days, I was told to improve or I would be fired. I quit with a very heavy heart and a looming question in my mind: What happened? What had gone wrong, and what to do next? Those answers would be a long time coming. I can now share with you what I would have done differently.

"From my perspective today, the answer would have been research and self-knowledge. I chose a typical job for a teen that I wasn't particularly suited for. I knew nothing about my NLD, and that caused problems. As I was growing up I had some hint of what my disabilities were, but I didn't have the whole story. Had I known about my disability I would have found something that didn't demand as much quick thinking in a noisy and chaotic environment.

"Self-knowledge is very important, especially for those with NLD or AS. Our disabilities are so subtle to everyone (even ourselves!), making it difficult to understand how to get around them. Often we don't get much feedback until something goes wrong, and we often don't know what happened until it's too late. It's like the saying goes – There are three types of people in this world: those that make things happen; those that watch things happen; and those that wonder what happened. The NLD/AS individual is often left wondering what happened."

Gabrielle illustrates the importance of career planning. A little knowledge of one's skills and abilities, along with some research of various career possibilities before starting a new job, can go a long way towards making it a better experience. Deciding on a career involves extensive self-knowledge, obtaining information about the world of work, and the ability to make realistic decisions. In the self-knowledge phase, you must first identify your interests, abilities, talents, and skills. Build on your assets. Consider your temperament, personality, and values. Think about where these can be esteemed in today's world.

Next, recognize your challenge areas. What do your weaknesses say about you? No two people experience their disability in exactly the same way. Accept what can't be changed, and acquire the tools to change what you can. There are strategies, modifications, accommodations and sometimes medications that can help your strengths to shine above your weaknesses. You may need to try several strategies until you find the ones that work best for you. It's a lifelong process that requires patience and hard work, but does get easier with time. The more you learn about yourself, the easier it becomes.

You will also need to research various jobs. Become familiar with these occupations by reading about them, talking with people working in those fields, going on information interviews, perhaps doing job shadowing. Your goal is to get to know the occupation.

Last, you must match these vocations with the skills you have identified in the first step. It may be helpful to make a list of your strengths and weaknesses in various areas, such as verbal ability, numerical aptitude, spatial skills, motor coordination, speed, multi-tasking, organizational ability, social savvy – and rate the requirements of each occupation according to this list. This will enable you to see how your particular abilities/disabilities match those required in the particular job. For example, though I can drive, I would not want a job as a driver. It is too much of a challenge for my spatial skills and would be too stressful. Though I love to cook at home, I don't feel I would be able to perform well on the job, where speed is essential.

One of the difficulties NLDers and ASers face in this area has to do with the executive function deficit. Executive function does for the brain what a conductor does for an orchestra. Executive skills are those needed to organize one's thoughts, tasks, things, and time. These are the abilities that allow you to plan, prioritize, and organize, or to grasp a problem area and come up with feasible solutions. Coming up with goals is very hard for folks with an executive function deficit.

Career planning is difficult because it requires dealing with many inferences and unknowns. Even when we find an occupation we think might be suitable, we must consider how our disability will impact it. Books like *What Color is Your Parachute? (Bolles 2003)* assume that their audience can do the planning tasks the book recommends.

A related issue is the NLDer's/ASer's trouble with seeing the big picture. Often, we see the trees but not the forest. We can't see how the various steps add up to the end result. For example, when using a book such as *What Color is Your Parachute?*, it can be difficult to see what all the steps add up to. In reading trade journals to glean career information, poor visual memory combined with executive function issues make it hard to organize the information in a meaningful way.

Due to our lack of flexibility and tendency to perseverate, NLDers and ASers easily get stuck on one track and have problems seeing other possibilities. These questions can help you with the decisions of the career planning process:

- What is the problem or task? (Answer: To find a suitable career for me.)

- What is my goal? What do I need to accomplish?

- How easy or difficult will it be to accomplish the goal?

- What plan is needed to accomplish the goal? (What materials do I need, who will do what?)

- What steps do I need to take?

- In what order do I need to do these things?

- How long will it take?

- If a problem arises, what new ways should I think of to solve it?
- Should I ask for assistance? Who can assist me?
- When I'm finished, let's review my goal, plan, and accomplishments.

Remember that the goal of all this is for NLD/AS individuals to find a suitable work environment. Finding that good fit for people with NLD and AS can be very difficult. We may be qualified, but that doesn't mean it will be a good fit. We need to maximize the probability of workplace success and minimize the possibility of failure.

Self-assessment

Because AS/NLD is neurological, rather than physical or even psychological, it's not a cookie-cutter diagnosis. It affects everyone differently, in different areas and to different degrees. Self-assessment means finding a balance between knowing about your limitations, learning what to do about them, and not letting them run you into the ground. Aptitude tests can help you recognize your strengths and your areas of weakness as well as the degree of impairments in those areas. It's imperative that the NLD/AS adult finds a vocation that suits his or her interests and personality style. It is best to avoid jobs that emphasize your weaknesses and find those that focus on your strengths.

In order to achieve success in employment, it's crucial to have a good grasp of individual strengths and weaknesses. This knowledge is vital to choosing an appropriate career direction, and is the first step in developing strategies for success in the workplace and knowing what accommodations will facilitate success. A thorough psycho-vocational assessment is an important step towards self-awareness.

We can create a stereotype of an NLD/AS individual that describes our common characteristics. However, not all NLD/AS adults exhibit the same attributes. Not all have problems with social interaction to the same extent. Not all have the same degree of executive function impairment. Not all have the same degree of clumsiness. Therefore, it's important to know yourself and develop a personal profile. Here's an example of such a profile (Table 19.1).

Table 19.1 Sample personal profile of one NLD individual

Cognitive Strengths	Cognitive Weaknesses
Bright	Visual puzzles (pictorials)
Academic achievement	Problem-solving with pictures (long time to translate into words)
Articulate, eloquent (verbal skills, written skills)	Multi-tasking
Multi-lingual	Whole picture – integrating details into coherent whole (pieces of story)
Sequential processing; step-by-step problem solving and decision making; if–then	Difficulty generalizing information; simultaneous processing of info
Logical	Sticks with one strategy when problem solving
Analytical	
Good memory (verbal)	Visualization; thinks in words, not pictures
Memory for details; attention to detail	Difficulties with spatial perceptions and spatial relations
Processing words and symbols	Visual memory
Verbal memory and concentration	Abstract reasoning
Problem solving (verbal)	Novel or complex tasks
Familiar and structured tasks	Slow processing speed (thinks slowly; takes longer to complete an activity; poor on timed tests)
Creative	
Computer literacy	
Follows instructions (written, verbal, step by step)	Difficulty improvising or "winging it"
	Inability to make quick judgments/think on my feet
	Difficulty following diagrammatic instructions

Emotional Strengths	Emotional Weaknesses
Mature	Chronic depressive tendency
Persistent	Insecure
Dependable, responsible, honest	Taken advantage of
Able to learn and willing to change	Feeling helpless
Helpful and serving others	Anxious
Motivated	Angry
Enthusiastic	Disorganized
Thorough	Team skills
Conscientious	Inability to switch gears
Diligent, hard worker	
Dedicated	
Versatile	
Able to work independently; self-starter	
Sense of humor	
Patient	
Social Strengths	Social Weaknesses
Friendly	Does not perceive/respond appropriately to non-verbal cues
Dependable	Talks too much/asks too many questions
Conscientious	
Caring	Slow to react
Giving	Deficits in social judgment and interaction
Loyal	
Trustworthy	

Physical Strengths	Physical Weaknesses
Individual sports, like walking or swimming Bend, twist, lift, reach Can work out energy/anger	Motor skills – dexterity, clumsiness Uncoordinated; klutz; spills things Visual/spatial/perceptual Orientation difficulties; "directionally challenged" (gets lost easily); disorientation to time and place Peripheral vision Depth perception Restless/distractible (due to anxiety /frustration) Team sports and ball skills Slow to react

Most of us have some idea of what we're good at and not so good at. Parents, guidance and vocational counselors, and individuals with NLD or AS need to keep in mind both the classic strengths, like speaking (channeled into teaching or public speaking professions) or writing, as well as individual strengths. Same goes for weaknesses. NLD makes some things very hard or even impossible. I'll never be a ballerina or a professional athlete. I'm too uncoordinated and slow. But that's OK. The important thing to remember is that we are all individuals with a unique set of interests, skills, talents, abilities, and disabilities. So the most important thing you can do is to dig deep for information about yourself before going out into the world of work.

If a goal is important enough, with time, patience, compensations, and remedial help, it can be achieved. We can learn things that are difficult for us, although they often take us much longer – sometimes ten times as long. So we must save that energy for things that really matter and forget about the rest. Sometimes, however, the effort isn't worth the output. It can be a tough decision, because it feels like you're giving up. Gabrielle writes:

> Before you get your first job there is a lot of work to do. You have some thinking to do before you set out on a job hunt. What do you like to do? There are many different types of jobs and you'll want one that fits

you! Think about what you liked and didn't like in school, what you did well and what was difficult. What did people compliment you on?

Next, think about your learning style. How does your NLD or AS affect you? Many of us need more time to learn. Do you work and learn better in a quiet environment? I know I do. Having instructions written down was very important for me. You may have similar requirements or you may need something different, but it's important to know what you need so that you can ask for the proper accommodations.

When changing careers, ask yourself:

- What types of jobs have I had in the past?
- What worked out and what didn't?
- Why?
- What job functions did I like doing?
- What was I good at – what did I get recognition for?
- What positions allowed me to best utilize my strengths?

As you begin to do this, you can also delve into personal issues:

- What do I want out of a new career?
- What types of careers match my personality?

Dig deep and find the answers.

The problem faced by many ASers/NLDers is that our weaknesses are more pervasive than our strengths. Writing is my strength, but not every job allows me to use this skill. The fact that I have social problems on the job, however, crosses all career fields. I can try to find jobs where I'm more likely to work independently. Yet within every company there are organizational politics that I must deal with. The same is true when I think and work slower than others. I can avoid jobs where my motor slowness will be an issue, like factory labor. But every job requires one to handle some objects. File folders. Make copies. Send faxes. It all requires handling papers, picking them up, laying them down. Those lost seconds add up to minutes and sometimes hours, until I find I simply can't do the expected amount of work in the allotted time.

Remember, we're not all alike. We all have personalities, interests, and abilities in addition to our disability. It's really important to look at all of those things in choosing a job.

Career exploration

Rather than asking "What are the best careers for an adult with AS or NLD?" we should instead ask "What are the best career options for a wonderfully unique individual with special challenges?" The answers are as unique as the individual.

A good job is one you find interesting. It should rely on your areas of strength and minimize your weaknesses. It's a job in which you will be able to find both a measure of success and enjoyment of your work. It's a work environment where people are understanding, flexible, and encouraging rather than rigid and nit-picky.

Most people first learn about various jobs from family and friends. They may pursue their interest by reading about different careers, studying job descriptions with the goal of finding work that matches their strengths and personality. There are indeed many books, websites, and other resources describing careers. While researching these can increase our understanding of different professions, help us analyze industry trends, and give an overview of the general employment trends, it won't tell us what we need to know.

That is because the person with AS or NLD has a totally different set of needs. Despite the fact that we work harder than most, the things that come naturally to others are difficult for us. Although we are hardworking, honest, and conscientious, we fall short. No matter how hard we try, it's not quite good enough or fast enough to compete with those around us.

The job descriptions found in career books don't go far enough. They don't address the types of issues we face in the workplace. For example, Monster's Career Profiles at http://content.monster.com/jobprofiles/ has this to say about librarians:

> Librarians oversee the selection and organization of library materials. They assist people in finding a wide variety of scholarly and public information from a number of resources. Librarians manage staff and develop and direct information programs and systems for the public so all the information is organized to meet users' needs.

They listed the following skills that librarians need:

Prospective librarians should have excellent computer skills such as word processing, database management and Internet research. They need strong organizational skills to efficiently index and categorize library resources. Writing and public speaking skills are critical as librarians often provide training and presentations both in and outside the library.

From the above description I should have been successful in this career. Nothing was said of the necessity for thinking on your feet in a very busy, high-pressure, customer-driven reference desk environment found in a large public library. Nothing was said about the social savvy required of library directors to work with the board, community, and staff in a small town environment, where the library director is the sole librarian. Such brief descriptions, found in many career guides, don't go far enough and don't provide the type of information we need to determine whether the job or the work environment will be NLD or AS friendly.

Two websites that are a little more realistic and detailed are www.review.com and ONet www.online.onetcenter.org/. In its library description, ONet mentioned that needing to work with external customers is at the top of the list. Thus, an inference could be made that work could be hectic. But such inferences are difficult for many NLDers and ASers. More explicit advice is needed, such as this from www.review.com: "You've got to be polite even when you want to break someone's neck." Now, that's explicit.

The run-of-the-mill descriptions found at such sites aren't detailed enough. Career videos are slightly better. Job shadowing programs allow the job seeker to see firsthand whether they would be a good fit for that career, and experience what potential issues might arise. Even these, however, may not be ideal for the NLDer who can't learn by observation. This is why it's essential to find a career counselor who is familiar with AS/NLD and who would have the needed objectivity to help the individual find potential problem areas and work out possible compensatory strategies.

Many NLDers/ASers, due to deficiencies in executive function, have trouble figuring out which jobs match up with the skills and interests they have written down. Often, the area of interest doesn't match the area of skill. For instance, someone might enjoy art but lack artistic talent due to visual-spatial and motor impairments. While Kim has great interest in medicine and has always wanted to be a doctor, she found that NLD impaired her ability to master some of the needed subjects. So we have to ask instead: "What are my top interests and skills which are realistic and could translate into a job?"

Another way to explore careers is to look for environments that are AS/NLD friendly and in which you feel you could be most productive. For example, someone with AS might find it hard to work as a sales clerk in a major department store. The large amount of sensory stimulation and numerous social interactions needed in this environment can be overwhelming, which can make it difficult to stay calm, to concentrate, and not to misinterpret information. Most of us need some measure of autonomy and control, where creativity is valued, rather than working in an environment with many distractions where everyone is competing. It's important to ask yourself these questions:

- Do you work better with people or things?

- How does the job or work environment mesh with your values and beliefs?

- Do you like work with repetition or do you prefer novelty?

- Will this environment enhance or thwart your intelligence, capability, skills, and talents?

The type of work environment is often more important than salary or even the specific type of work. The experience you've had and the places you've worked will help you to know what to look for in your next job. You can create a description of a work setting where you can thrive by discussing your needs with others. For example, tell them that you want to work where you can rely on your research skills, your computer knowledge, your writing ability, and your desire to help others. Explain that you want to work with people who will appreciate your dependability, integrity, and creativity. In response, they might say: "Oh, you should see if there are any openings at the college; it's a great place to work." Or they might tell you to avoid ABC company, that it's the sleaziest, nastiest place to work in town. Instead of narrowing your job search down to "research assistant" or "librarian", look for openings in environments you find stimulating and comfortable.

By describing your skills and abilities, rather than asking about positions in a specific career, you will find more options. Unless someone is a librarian or is on a library board, they may not be aware of library openings. But using this approach and keeping an open mind, they might begin thinking outside the box and may come up with some ideas and leads.

Following this advice, the type of library environment that would work best for me is in a one-person library in a friendly and well-defined setting, like a corporate, hospital, or small school, where I can work independently, planning my own work, without anyone looking over my shoulder. However, this can be difficult to find. Most often, such jobs go unadvertised and get filled because someone knows someone. People keep these jobs for life. You can't apply cold calling for a position that is not open and that there is only one of. You have to know someone, or find out through the grapevine that a certain person is retiring.

As the process evolves and you narrow career choices down, make a choice and dedicate yourself to it. Once you've narrowed the selection, you can meet with people, join professional organizations, subscribe to email lists, do informational interviews, and involve yourself as much as possible in the field you are interested in.

At this point, career exploration can include on-site visits, information interviews, and job shadowing. A day spent on the job with an employee can offer insights into job duties, interactions, frustrations and satisfactions that you wouldn't otherwise know about. Volunteering opportunities or internships can also provide insights into what the work involves.

A little networking goes a long way

Simply put, networking involves interactions and exchanges of information with other people. We share information and resources and develop supportive relationships. We network every day. It's part of how we make decisions – from what movies to see to what doctor to choose. We talk to people, gather information and opinions, and work these into our own decisions. When it comes to selecting a career, the information we collect about the job, the career field, and the working environment helps us to make sound choices.

Because they tend to be introverts, and often don't have a large group of contacts, individuals with AS or NLD can find this task daunting. Building relationships takes time, and it is difficult for folks who don't mix well at parties or other social events.

If you're not comfortable in large social gatherings, that's OK. Talk with everyone you know: friends, relatives, aunts and uncles. Tell them your situation. Discuss the roadblocks you face. Brainstorm ideas on whether and how they can be overcome. There are many ways to meet people: churches and synagogues, alumni groups, sports clubs and other interest groups, from a book club to a chess club. Because other job seekers don't dominate these groups, they have a definite advantage in making contacts that can help in your job search.

If you have areas of special interest, join clubs that share them – such as cooking, community chorus, or social service projects. Talk with the people you meet in these activities, and ask how they use their skills on the job. You can also take classes in the subjects that interest you. Ask the teacher about possible job opportunities using these skills. Find out how others in the class plan to utilize what they're learning.

Often, local career centers will have workshops or groups where people looking for work or changing careers meet with others to motivate each other, think through career decisions, build contacts, and generate job leads. When meeting new people, focus on building mutual relationships rather than obtaining information or getting job leads. Think of what you have to give, and how you can help others. Don't concentrate on what you know or whom you know. Instead, think about who knows you, and what they know about you.

Find someone who likes you, who thinks you're interesting and fun to be around. Ask them to make a list that will remind you why you're good company. This will help you feel less self-conscious when you're out with the group. When you're about to venture out to a meeting, reception, or other event, look at it and remind yourself that, even though public connections are not your favorite game, you have lots to offer people.

Email lists are another way to make friends and contacts without face-to-face interaction. Join mail and email lists and groups that reflect your interests, and talk to folks there. This is a good way to make contacts without the stress, as well as an opportunity to learn from others. When possible, give answers and help to others in the group. They'll remember you when their boss is hiring. If you get to know them better, you can mention you're job hunting.

Find a professional society that's related to the field you want information about, and go to a meeting of the local chapter. Before going to the event, jot down some topics that might come up, and prepare a list of questions, or a script. Once there, scope things out. Come with a business card, and hand it out. Select one or two people to talk with, and bring up your scripted topics. Once you're talking with someone face to face, it might be easier to ask if they would be willing to meet with you and tell you more about their job. Or, if it's less threatening, talk to them on the phone rather than in person. That way, you can have notes to read from.

Make a list of people you know in your profession or the field that interests you. Include their contact information – address, phone, and email. Go through these cards from time to time. Once a month, or once a week, call someone on your list. Have questions ready you want to ask them. If possible, set up a lunch date. Keep a file of the people you've contacted, the dates, and what you discussed.

Accept your disability. Don't fight it. Learn to work within it. Understand what you can achieve, but know your limitations. Talking with others and sharing information is challenging, but it can help you plan strategies to avoid or surmount the obstacles created by your disability.

As you talk to people, share about your condition. Discuss both the qualities you bring to an employment setting and the obstacles you expect to encounter. Networking is about building relationships. You don't know where it's going to lead, but meantime you're making contact with other people. Networking as a concept can be intimidating but, simply put, it's just talking to everyone you know about your situation, sharing your qualities, helping each other and expressing your needs. When I told friends I took a grant writing workshop, two people offered to put me in touch with grant writers at the place they worked. One of these led to an information interview, which resulted in a job interview for a marketing assistant position at a non-profit agency.

A networking coach can help you polish these skills and build a group of talented people to think and grow with. Many companies offer virtual online networking as an essential professional activity. Do a search for "corporate relationship builders". There are companies that teach entrepreneurs, executives and other corporate leaders how to connect effectively.

Find a career counselor or coach

It's in negotiating the final step of career planning, putting the two together and deciding on possible career choices which match one's interests, abilities, and skills, that a good career counselor is essential. Because our needs are so different, general career counseling strategies may not work. For the NLD/AS individual, a typical career evaluation is often not very helpful. Most career counselors use general tools like the General Aptitude Test Battery (GATB) and Myers Briggs Temperament Inventory (MBTI) to evaluate a client's strengths and weaknesses. For the person with NLD or AS, however, such general assessments do not go far enough.

Poor experiences

Many AS/NLD adults have had bad experiences with counselors who weren't knowledgeable about the disorder. Most career planners, job counselors and vocational rehabilitation personnel have never even heard of NLD or AS. These government offices are used to dealing with people with reading and writing difficulties, and so they tend to put all people with learning disabilities in jobs that are difficult for the NLD/AS individual. Because people with neurological impairments like AS and NLD are in the minority, our problems receive less attention.

Al went to a career counselor in the mid-1990s, and that is how he chose speech language pathology. The counselor administered the Myers Briggs inventory, and at the top of the list for his MBTI personality type was Internal Revenue Service (IRS) agent. Since he only got a D in accounting, he ruled that one out quickly. Speech pathology was also high on the list. Since Al enjoys speech and language, has excellent verbal abilities, had majored in speech communications in college, and wanted to go into a helping profession, it seemed to be the ideal choice. However, he wasn't aware of NLD at the time, and couldn't fathom the difficulties that lay ahead in this field. The time pressure, motor skills, and quick thinking required were challenges that caused problems in doing the job. Because of these difficulties, this did not turn out to be a good career choice for him.

A good counselor

What would an ideal career counselor be like? Here are some thoughts. Many people with AS/NLD have numerous past failures dragging them down. There are gaps between intelligence and performance, between expectations and achievements. Feelings of "If I'm so smart, why am I so incompetent?" are common.

A good counselor, therefore, will begin with an attitude of acceptance. She will listen, understand, and empathize. She will take into account your specific needs. She will recognize that your past failures are not due to laziness or stupidity, but result from the neurological impairment. Realizing this will help her to bring you from the negative identity caused by constant failure to a positive identity of a person with potential to succeed. She will endeavor to break the past pattern of poor performance, which instills guilt and leads to poor self-esteem and depression. She will help you to confront your past and use it as a jumping-off point to make changes and plan for success in the future. The AS/NLD client is struggling with a disorder which is neurological in origin and therefore beyond his control. She will help you focus on the present possibilities of success rather than past failures. She will guide you to determine what areas you can and can't change, help you take control of the things you can change, and to accept your neurological limitations. This will help to raise your self-concept and reduce feelings of anxiety and helplessness.

A good counselor will help to clarify your goals by offering concrete, objective, practical suggestions. Sometimes, career goals may not be realistic, or a life dream may not be achievable. It's important to find out where the dream came from in order to help the individual come up with alternatives and arrive at a compromise. If lack of musical talent prevents someone from becoming a musician, he may still be able to enter a field where music is involved – such as working at a music store, a radio station, or in a theater. Someone may have a love for medicine but not the physical coordination or skill to become a doctor or nurse. There are other medical occupations – medical records, medical writing, or medical librarianship. The ASer/NLDer needs guidance that is explicit, positive, realistic, directive and interactive.

A good counselor will help you create a profile of strengths and weaknesses that starts with a career vision and ends with an employment goal. This profile will list your intellectual, emotional, and interpersonal strengths, as well as work skills. She will use a variety of tools to assess your strengths and limitations. A good evaluation for the person with AS/NLD must go beyond general tests of interest and aptitude, like the GATB or MBTI. The counselor must consider your neuropsychological evaluation and understand how the disorder affects you on the job. She will help you discover hidden strengths and limitations and arrive at a total picture that includes your personality, interests, abilities, and problem areas. While presenting the results of the assessments, she will also need to address the effects of the disability. Unfortunately, because work issues are highly personal, emotional, and "learn as you go", matching a person's abstracted traits with the abstract demands of an occupation is only partly successful.

Next, a good counselor will analyze various jobs. This includes identifying job duties the person can perform as well as work tasks that are difficult or need accommodations. She will look beyond the job duties to examine the sensory, visual-spatial, motor, organizational, and interpersonal dimensions of the job. She will explore elements like the pace of work, sequential versus simultaneous execution (multi-tasking), type and amount of deadlines, interruptions or distractions, independent work versus teamwork, time flexibility for dividing large tasks into small segments, the amount of feedback from supervisors, and how easy it is to obtain clarification on an assignment.

Then she will help you to come up with a list of careers that match your skills to corresponding jobs and work settings. The AS/NLD individual requires maximum specificity in order to fit their strengths and limitations to an appropriate career choice. Generalizations just won't do. Job descriptions need to be very specific. A good counselor will be able to figure out exactly where your breakdowns are and, as a result, advise you on work environments which best fit you and resources available to help you to accommodate these disabilities.

Finding a counselor

So how do you find a good career counselor? The National Board of Certified Counselors lists names of nationally certified career counselors. There may be a non-profit career center close to you. Look it up in the phonebook and find out what they have to offer. Local disabilities organizations, like a local Learning Disabilities Association (LDA) chapter, may be able to offer referrals.

Meet the counselor and interview them. Do you feel at ease? Does he/she have the knowledge and expertise to help you? Is s/he familiar with AS, NLD and LDs? Any counselor worth her/his salt should at least be willing to educate herself about AS or NLD and read information you share with her, such as the results of your testing. You must make sure she understands the disability and its impact. If she refuses to do that, you're wasting your time and money.

Consider your counselor a partner in your career planning process. Discuss various aspects of your background, share about your AS or NLD, and acknowledge the accomplishments and challenges in your career path thus far. Be open to her ideas, methods, and advice, but make sure she listens to your ideas and is understanding of your special needs. The career counselor should understand your personality as it fits within the diagnosis. This will enable her/him to provide the framework in which to collect data, test career choices, and offer support for navigating the career planning maze.

After the counselor administers the traditional career tests, let her know that, due to your disorder, she needs to be specific and explicit in her advice. Just giving you the information isn't enough. You need to know how to use the information she gives you. Remember that the counselor's area of expertise is career counseling, not your specific area of interest. Although your counselor may not have worked in your chosen field, she should be able to guide you to resources that will help you explore it. He or she probably knows people who have done what you want to do. Find out if he/she has had clients in situations similar to yours.

Once several occupations have been chosen, you need to set a goal and outline the steps for reaching it. What qualifications are needed for this job? Do you have them? If not, what steps do you need to take to get them? Do you need more education? Are there specific skills you will need? How can you get these? Networking and information interviews will help you to get this information and to narrow your search.

A good counselor will help you find the answers to these essential questions:

- What are your passions?

- What makes you tick?

- What have been your major accomplishments?

- What personality factors and values are important to you?

- What makes you happiest?

- What are you good at?

- What don't you do well?

- What is your energy pattern during the day, week, month? Do you work best in the morning? At night? What are your most productive times?

- What are your dreams? How do they relate to the real world of work?

- How realistic are the options that you feel will be best in terms of today's job market needs?

- How can these options be tested out, rather than tried with the possibility of failure?

- What special challenges does your AS or NLD present? Do you have other challenges as well? How do they impact you? What issues do they create at work?

- What are some strategies and interventions that would help you to work around or overcome these challenges?

- How good is the match between you and the career you chose?

- What can you do to find out how well suited you are to this career field?

- How can you enter this field?

- What is the work environment like?

- What will you need to be successful in the work environment chosen?

- What supports can be in place to ensure your long-term success?

The final decision on a career choice is up to you. While it's important not to focus entirely on the disability, the disability must be taken into account, because the discrepancy between strengths and weaknesses is bigger for those with NLD/AS. There are many careers that seem like a good fit, but may not be due to factors caused by NLD or AS. Jobs like contractor, plumber or mechanic, for example, require the ability to visualize, which is a weak area for many NLDers and some Aspies. Though well-paid, unionized manual labor jobs aren't a good fit for most NLDers/ASers because of the small-motor and perceptual deficits. Most would be better off in fields that require verbal or analytical skills.

It's important to remain realistic. You have to figure out how all of those factors play into the general equation. You may need help to do this, but those attempting to help you must know you and understand the disability. They have to understand what you're talking about.

20 Career Counseling for the NLD/AS World

Marcia Brown Rubinstien

Career counseling: a short history

Until the industrial revolution, there were very few job options not related to agriculture. Class distinctions were rigid, and there was little fluctuation in the job market. Few people were given the luxury of exploring the desires of their souls where occupational satisfaction was concerned. From the seventeenth to the mid-twentieth century, most people started working in late adolescence and either died on the job or retired with a gold watch after 50 years of service at the same position. The gold watch was probably the greatest benefit given for most of those years, since pension plans and health insurance are relative newcomers to the scene.

By the middle of the twentieth century, access to education and the blurring of social class demarcations broadened professional possibilities. People could choose what they wanted to do, and began thinking about what they wanted to be. Career theorists began to develop ideas about the interacting variables of career choice.

In 1951, Dr Eli Ginzberg proposed a three-pronged theory of occupational choice which still holds true more than half a century later. Ginzberg and his colleagues at Columbia suggested that, first, vocational development is a process which starts in childhood and stabilizes as the young adult solidifies values, interests and qualifications, and measures them against both personal and environmental limitations. Second, once the individual has made serious self-assessment and has begun to follow a plan, such as graduate school or training, the choice is largely irreversible. The third component in Ginzberg's theory is compromise. Every person, he suggests, must weigh the opportunities and limitations and then assess the extent to which a maximum degree of satisfaction in work and life can be secured. Although he allows people to re-enter the career planning process to make life changes, the fact that career choice involves compromise is a fundamental doctrine of his theory.

By the end of the twentieth century, countless career planning theorists had jumped on the bandwagon. For every theorist, there were practitioners in geometric proportion. All of them promised the hapless job seeker total professional satisfaction if they followed the path suggested by the course, book, or program they touted. But the goals of career planning have remained essentially unchanged. We all want to use our favorite skills in a job which allows us to work on what's important to us, under working conditions that please us, with people that we like, at a salary that we can deal with.

There is no magic plan which will make the perfect job appear without determination, motivation, and hard work. First, every job seeker must undertake an honest and thorough self-examination. Then, it is necessary to take everything you know about yourself, warts and all, and follow the immutable steps of a successful career search:

1. Assess your skills and values.

2. Know the steps of a career search.

3. Understand and employ decision-making skills.

4. Develop and use your résumé.

The NLD/AS world and career counseling

If you are an adult with Non-Verbal Learning Disability (NLD) or Asperger Syndrome (AS), you have probably noticed that you're a minority in a world of neurotypical thinkers and doers. Most people do things, see things and understand things in ways that are sometimes difficult for you to comprehend. The reverse is also true – neurotypicals have a hard time understanding you. If you were applying for a job at the Non-Verbal Learning Disorders Association or at the Asperger's Association, you might not have to be so careful about learning the rules of the neurotypical world. But for any other type of job, it is your responsibility to fit in with the existing setting, rather than have the setting learn to fit in with you.

If you consider each element of the career search from both your unique perspective and the neurotypical view, you will be well prepared to deal with the rigors of a career search in the real world.

Know yourself

This means that you must have a thorough understanding of your capabilities and skills, your values, your non-negotiable areas, and the situations in which you might be willing to compromise. Make sure you are expressing values which are easily understood and acceptable in the neurotypical world.

It also means that you must be keenly aware of your limitations. Sometimes it's difficult to know what you don't do well. Don't try to assess your skills and values yourself; rather, find someone you trust to help you go over what you've done in a realistic and objective manner. Ask what they think might limit you in the world of work. Listen with an open mind. This is not criticism; it's reality. Learn, and move on. Sometimes the obstacle only applies to certain work areas. For example, if you're terrible at math, don't look for work as an actuary. But there are many jobs which don't require mathematical skill beyond cashing your paycheck.

If a friend tells you that your wardrobe is not suitable for the corporate world, get help. If your phone voice is flat, practice with a tape recorder. If you have trouble remembering names, take notes. But most important, decide what compensations you want to make. If it sounds like too much of a compromise, don't do it. No one would expect you to pretend to be someone else all day long. The stress would be unbearable.

Know the steps of a career search

Don't walk around moaning that you can't find a job if you haven't systematically researched the way to find one. Sometimes a career search can be more work than the actual job. And it's disheartening, too, because there's no paycheck! People with NLD or AS may tend towards negativity. When one thing goes wrong, they want to abandon the whole project, or they think they're useless.

It's very simple to tell people that they should develop and pursue realistic alternatives. Sometimes, however, it seems that there are simply no alternatives available. The reality here depends on the word "seems". Although sometimes people aren't willing to consider them, there are always alternatives. The way to find them is to have a relentless positive attitude, to utilize persistence and motivation, and to engage every shred of optimism you can muster. Persistence is a primary strength in people with NLD or AS, but a common drawback is the tendency to become negative and hostile. These attitudes are counterproductive, and will undermine your search for realistic alternatives. Remember – if you think you can't, you can't!

Understand and employ decision-making skills

When making important decisions about your work values, your skills, where you would like to work, whether or not you would like to return to school, or even if you should accept a job offer, get help from someone you trust. Know what decisions should take a lot of time, and what decisions are less important. For example, it's not critical if name badges are red or blue, but deciding who should sit at the head table at a corporate banquet might offend someone if you don't consider all the players and their positions carefully.

Develop and use your résumé

A well-organized résumé can speak for you even in places to which you are not granted access. Make sure your résumé contains only relevant adult work experience. It's wonderful that you got the prize for best chocolate chip cookies in fifth grade, but unless you want to be a pastry chef, leave it off your résumé. If you have a concise, scannable résumé, you can send it to many places that will consider your credentials. This saves both the time of visiting offices as well as the stress of interviewing in person only to learn that there are no openings or that the position isn't suited to your credentials. Although you must ultimately have a personal interview before being hired, a résumé can do a lot of pre-screening for you.

Compensating for NLD/AS deficits in the career search and the world of work

Since the defining criteria for both NLD and Asperger Syndrome are still in flux, it is difficult to define a group of deficits which consistently characterize either or both of these neuropsychological syndromes. Additionally, individuals can be affected by either disorder with a range of deficits classified from moderate to severe. In order to learn how to compensate for the deficits which affect your particular career search, it will be necessary once again to employ one of the cardinal rules of career planning: *Know yourself.*

The deficits associated with NLD are generally grouped into three categories, which include neuropsychological, academic, and social/adaptational. Dorothy Vacca (2001), in her article "Confronting the Puzzle of

Nonverbal Learning Disabilities", has expanded these categories into concepts that have greater relevance to the world of work. She too stresses the fact that these impairments may be profound or quite mild, so that different people show different characteristics. Vacca's categories follow:

1. *Visual-spatial:* difficulty with visual-spatial organization, perception, and imaging.

2. *Cognitive processing:* difficulty understanding connections between and among independent factors and relating these to the whole; difficulty understanding the "big picture".

3. *Language:* flat tone of voice; difficulty understanding humor, multiple meanings of words, and nuances of language.

4. *Motor:* lack of coordination and small-motor skills related to handwriting.

5. *Social:* deficits in social understanding.

6. *Behavioral:* rigid behavior; difficulty with novelty and transition.

7. *Emotional:* at high risk for anxiety disorder, panic attack, obsessive-compulsive disorder and, in some cases, suicide.

By examining Vacca's categories, we can begin to understand what characteristics might impair a search for success in the neurotypical world and look for compensatory strategies.

Visual-spatial difficulties

A successful graphic artist and painter with learning disabilities once described the NLD visual-spatial disorder as seeing everything in the world one-sixteenth of an inch off, without knowing it. That slight distortion makes everything seem difficult. However, if you are aware of your visual-spatial difficulties, you can learn to adjust for them.

Cognitive processing difficulties

One of the most problematic areas of cognitive functioning in some individuals with NLD/AS is the difficulty in seeing the gestalt, or whole picture. A tendency to get lost in the details often takes away the focus from the main idea. In the career search process, it's important to recognize, identify, and discriminate main ideas from supporting details and supplementary material. Outlining software may be helpful with this.

Language difficulties

Since the diagnosis of either NLD or AS covers such a wide range of function and dysfunction, it's important to get honest, direct and specific feedback on how your presentation of self may be affecting your career search. Ideally, each job seeker should undergo a thorough assessment by a speech and language pathologist sensitive to issues of language prosody and fluency. When such an evaluation isn't possible, ask friends or family members for honest feedback about your interpersonal communication styles. Although it is neither possible nor desirable to change who you are, there are certain elements of interpersonal communication, such as tone of voice or fluency, which can be enhanced by attentive practice.

Motor difficulties

Awareness and determination may help you improve your performance. An occupational therapy assessment can often uncover your weaknesses and show you how to improve them. As an adult, you can avoid some situations by planning ahead. For example, if you have poor handwriting, bring a typed résumé so you won't need to fill out the employment forms that some offices distribute. Simply attach your résumé with a paper clip and write on the form: See attached résumé. Since you are probably not applying for a job as a handwriting specialist, this should be sufficient. If the job you are looking at requires a lot of paperwork that must be completed by hand and you have serous graphomotor disturbances, perhaps the job is not right for you. Likewise, if you have poor balance and are prone to spilling things, don't apply for a job as a waiter.

Social difficulties

All of us have different levels of social awareness. You probably know how comfortable you feel in situations requiring social interaction. Once again, we revert to the primary rule of the career search process: Know yourself. Do not apply for situations that will make you uncomfortable. On the other hand, do not underestimate your abilities and apply only for jobs such as: Hermit required to operate remote lighthouse. If you would like to develop your confidence and fluency in social situations, find a friend or therapist who can help you develop your abilities.

Behavioral difficulties

It has been suggested that the most troublesome aspect of NLD/AS is the difficulty in adapting to novel situations. This makes the entire career search theory, a dynamic process based on adaptability and change, a difficult philosophy to embrace. But the fact is not that people with NLD/AS are unable to change, rather that change is a difficult process which must be supported and explained at every juncture in order to be successful. It is even more difficult when they must be the initiators, facilitators and supervisors of the very change that they find difficult to accept. But people with NLD or AS have been known to do incredible things when they have a goal in mind. If the career search and ultimate transition are important enough, the ability to adapt will follow.

Emotional difficulties

Ironically, the same people who are accused of flat affect are also accused of being highly emotional. Actually, the two are not inconsistent, especially when the emotionality, as it is with most NLDers or ASers, is left to fester internally until it erupts. If you know that you have a tendency to worry, brood, or become unduly anxious, or if you have ritualized behaviors that you can't stop even though you know they are inappropriate, seek the help of a professional mental health worker. Many of these problems can be handled with medication and/or cognitive behavioral therapy.

Depression, on the other hand, is a term that is often misused in our society. There are times when it's appropriate to be depressed or sad. Many people with NLD or AS become frustrated by the extra work they must do in order to make things work for them, and some simply give up. If the depression lasts more than two weeks, and interferes with your work, social life, or daily functioning, you should see a doctor.

Assets of people with NLD or AS in the career search and the world of work

Fortunately for those who bear the diagnoses, many of the syndromes of right hemisphere dysfunction are characterized not only by deficits but by distinct assets as well. In *Syndrome of Nonverbal Learning Disabilities,* Dr Byron Rourke (1995) mentions the following assets:

- abilities for simple, repetitive motoric skills
- well-developed auditory perception capacities
- deployment of selective and sustained attention
- rote verbal memory
- memory for material that is readily coded in a rote verbal fashion
- well-developed receptive language skills and rote verbal capacities
- high volume of speech output (becoming more prominent with age)
- verbatim memory for oral and written verbal material
- dictation skills.

Since the publication of Rourke's original study, we have learned much more about the varied population associated with these diagnoses. We have discovered other characteristics which, although sometimes seen as limitations, could also be considered assets when put to appropriate use in the world of work. For example, since people with NLD or AS tend to be extremely literal and to believe information that is given to them verbally, they are often quite gullible. However, the reverse side of this is that they are generally guileless. Although there are some whose perceptions of truth are distorted by other issues, most people with right hemisphere dysfunction are scrupulously honest, a trait quite prized by prospective employers. They are also very likely to respond to the teaching and attention of a charismatic mentor, making them exceptionally good candidates for professions which are introduced and supported by mentoring programs. When respected and appreciated, they can be incredibly loyal and productive members of the workplace team.

When people with right brain disorders understand the scope of their gifts and the situations in which they can activate them appropriately, they will achieve not only professional productivity, but also a personal sense of self-worth and value. Individuals with NLD or AS are often endowed with astonishing perseverance and determination. By combining these qualities with their assets, they will be able to overcome a significant portion of the difficulties they may face in the world of work.

Personalizing the career search for people with NLD and AS

The market is filled with publications about successful career searches and job development. So many books and programs have been created from so many different angles that career development has become a whole sector of the economy in itself. People can now actually get a job in the business of getting a job. But no matter what components are thrown into the mix, the elements of a successful career remain the same. We are all hoping to use our favorite skills in a job which allows us to work on what's important to us, under working conditions that please us, with people we like, and at a salary we can deal with. If you sell out on any of your non-negotiables concerning the world of work, whether it be ethical principles, working conditions, or salary, it is almost a guarantee that you will ultimately become unhappy enough to quit. Therefore, it's important to know your bottom line and never to cross it. Start with a thorough knowledge of yourself, including your strengths and weaknesses. Have a clear awareness of your personal priorities. Inject a little imagination into the mix, and most of all keep your job search infused with hope. There's nothing more certain to take you out of the running than a dejected outlook and an air of melancholy.

Very few people get a positive response at the first interview. Most career searchers knock on a lot of doors before they find a place where they would like to work which at the same time would like to hire them. But remember, you need only one yes in order to have a successful career search.

Searching for a career is not a science, although it has elements of research and investigation which border on the scientific. It is not an art, although it engenders elements of inventiveness which surely approach the realm of creative talent. It is as unique as the individual who is searching, as strong as his greatest attribute, as weak as her most vulnerable deficit. But it is also exciting in its endless possibilities, for it is only limited by your imagination.

Marcia Brown Rubinstien is an educational consultant. She travels extensively visiting schools throughout the US to understand which learning environments are best suited to which students. She also publishes prolifically on a range of topics related to education and learning differences.

21 Transitioning from School to Work

James Emmett, Karen Steffan and Yvona Fast

Many AS/NLD individuals look back on their college years as the happiest time in their life. They thrive in the structured college setting, enjoying the mental energy and intellectual stimulation. Some become lifelong learners and perpetual scholars. College is a sheltered environment where housing, food, and other needs are met. You're paying for this privilege of education, and the companies providing that privilege try to cater to your needs.

In an academic environment, it is easier to feel that sense of accomplishment. Everyone understands what the objectives are, and how to achieve them. Life has a structure built around the academic requirements, class schedules, and dining hall meals. There are many choices, not only as to the subjects you study, but also the class format: lecture, small group, independent study. This provides an element of control. In the university setting, alternative ways of thinking and behaving are not uncommon, and, in a certain sense, even welcomed.

The work world is completely different. Here, you are not paying; they are paying you. You're not in control; the employer holds the reins. You have to fit into the corporate culture of whatever company you work for. They don't have to adjust to your needs; rather, they expect you to adapt to theirs. The goal of the employer is to get as much work from you as possible, while offering you as little as they can get away with. If they need to train you but someone else can catch right on, they'll hire the other person rather than providing you with the training. Where school offers choices and imposes a certain built-in structure, at most jobs the employee must be able to structure his or her own work. Many individuals with NLD or AS find the transition from school to work difficult. Chris Marsh, an AS adult, writes:

> My disability made my job transition difficult and financially/emotionally painful. Asperger's Syndrome is an excellent example of a disability that poses an occupational handicap but not an academic one…even with college credentials, many may fail in the work world…Career mistakes…are preventable. Students need to know what lies ahead, what's at stake, so they can ask for advice. (Prince-Hughes 2002, pp.82–83)

The transition from school to work is not a magical process, nor is it a mystical process. It's not an event, meeting or sheet of paper containing a transition plan. Rather, it's a practical, logical process that forces us to look beyond the present. It starts with a vision and moves toward that vision. The goal of the transition process is to look at strategies and supports that will make transition seamless as a student prepares, moves forward, moves through and beyond school life.

Transition planning

It is critical for students with NLD or AS to plan for the short- and long-term future beyond school. A useful way to start the planning process is to create a vision of where the student will be living, working, and playing six months, two years, and five years beyond graduation. Specific goals and objectives can then follow from this vision. It is important to plan around the three life areas of Live, Work, and Play because each has a large impact on the other and generally long-term success in one life area is dependent on some degree of satisfaction with the other life areas. A good transition planning process consists of the following:

1. *Determining desired outcomes:* define the long-term vision of where the individual with NLD or AS dreams of living, working, and playing. The desired outcomes in the three life areas should be the focus of the rest of the plan.

2. *Defining the student's strengths, interests, and needs:* make a list of what the student is good at doing and what he enjoys doing. The critical component is using a person's strengths and interests as the foundation to the future. Employers care most about those skills that the employee with NLD/AS brings to the company.

After the development of a list of strengths and interests is complete, support needs that relate to the desired outcome should be considered.

3. *Deciding what activities, services and supports the student needs:* good transitional, educational, and employment supports for persons with NLD/AS can be difficult to find. It is critical to define as clearly as possible the supports needed for the individual to reach the desired outcomes. Clear definition of the necessary supports will assist the NLDer/ASer in advocating for these supports from local service providers.

4. *Translating this vision into specific goals and objectives:* the last step in the planning process is to define overall goals and specific objectives that lead into the vision. These goals and objectives should drive the action and be written in concrete, measurable terms.

Preparation activities

In many ways, successful transition from high school or college life is dependent upon the activities that the person undertook during their years in school. Job training and preparation involves summer or part-time work, preferably in the occupational field that is in the long-term plan. Employers like to see "real world" knowledge of pertinent issues and summer or part-time employment is a great way to develop that knowledge base. Also, this is a good way to gain contacts in the student's specific vocational area. Ideally, individuals with NLD or AS hope to find a supportive work environment and will attempt to stick with that employer through a large portion of their academic careers.

Other proactive preparation activities are volunteering, tutoring, or participation in extracurricular clubs. Employers tend to like to hire individuals who demonstrate social responsibility, and volunteering is a good way to do this. Students with NLD or AS may wish to seek out volunteer opportunities that tap into their skills while also finding an environment that will help them to practice work-related social skills. Volunteering is a very valuable work-related opportunity. It helps to build your résumé. It helps you to tap into and refine your work skills. It also allows you to practice social skills without employment related pressures. Since volunteers are generally appreciated, this is a good way to build self-esteem and increase confidence.

Tutoring is an excellent way for the student with NLD or AS to demonstrate skill and knowledge in their field of study while reducing some social pressures. Tutoring involves one-to-one contact where the tutor can build initial rapport through knowledge of the subject area. In addition, sharing their knowledge with others, a verbal activity, often helps the NLDer/ASer develop a stronger grasp of the subject. In a similar vein, extracurricular clubs allow for opportunities to tap into a particular interest area while affording a supportive environment to practice specific social skills.

Transition tips

Gradual transition

When possible, try to make the transition from high school to college and college to work progressive rather than abrupt. Anticipate change, and prepare for it. For example, the high school student might find it useful and challenging to take a couple college classes in an area of interest, such as journalism, commercial art or computer programming. This will serve as a refuge from teasing while keeping them motivated (Grandin 1999). The person's area of interest may serve as a future career. Many college professors have found that they can get paid for developing their interest through teaching. It is a good idea to work part time while in college to ease the transition into the work world and establish contacts for future references.

Find a mentor

Most successful people have had mentors. A mentor is a wise and trusted advisor and helper, willing to offer guidance and support to someone who is less experienced. The person with AS or NLD needs a guide to help them navigate the social world of work. A mentor can act as a friend and help with social skills. He can teach social mores, help develop diplomacy and tact, and help the individual learn to conform. The best mentor will be someone with similar interests to the mentee.

It is important to find someone who can help the NLDer/ASer achieve their dream. Many companies have established mentoring programs that an employee with NLD or AS can use to their advantage. If a company does not have an established mentoring program, it is helpful to look for a co-worker with similar interests, as well as knowledge of the job and the politics of the workplace. In this case, the mentor can help the employee with NLD/AS navigate the all-important political landscape in the workplace.

Find a supportive employer

It is important to find someone who will be willing to take the time to understand the special needs of the person with AS/NLD. The employer and employees should understand the person's social limits. Supportive employers are generally those businesses that think outside the box. The individual with AS or NLD, in partnership with support persons, should attempt to let the employer know that they will be gaining a wonderful employee if they make a few reasonable accommodations. These accommodations potentially include setting up a social mentor situation, providing clear and immediate feedback, structuring the job with appropriate supports, and making unwritten rules concrete for the employee with AS/NLD. Often, employers find these accommodations work to support all employees and increase production across the board.

Freelance work

Freelance work is often a good option. It highlights the person's talents while minimizing social interaction and avoids the problems of office politics. If the ASer/NLDer has skills in writing, art, a craft, or computer technology, this may be a possibility. This person may need help finding a mentor or advisor to help get the business off the ground and develop a client base. Self-employment is increasing rapidly within the US economy. It is a good time to develop freelance opportunities to capitalize on unique skills and abilities.

Utilizing resources

The most successful people are not those who are the richest and smartest. They are the people who know how to tap into and manage the resources that are available to them. AS adult Chris Marsh advises: "Any college student with a known disability or special education experience should…contact a career counseling official before making a decision on a college major, and the sooner the better" (Prince-Hughes 2002, p.83).

There are many resources on the college campus to assist you in choosing a major, linking with a mentor, and/or setting up volunteer work or tutoring experiences. Start with your advisor and the student services offices. It is often expedient for the student to link with other community based resources before leaving school. You can look into the services and supports from the state vocational rehabilitation agency, as well as volunteer networks within your community. To become more familiar with agencies and services where you live, you can start by contacting the chamber of commerce and/or your local government offices.

James Emmett is the Director of the Vocational Alliance Autism Project and the Vocational Alliance Busniess Approach to Social Integration and Communication (BASIC) Project. Both of these projects focus on the career development process for individuals with social communication disorders, particularly autism and Asperger Syndrome. James has worked for the past ten years assisting individuals with autism spectrum disorders in finding and maintaining quality employment.

Karen Steffan, MS.CRC is a Transition Specialist. Over the past 30 years, Karen has worked with both adults and high school students with disabilities in all phases of career development, job placement and training.

Finding a Job

22 A Short Intro to Job Hunting

Most people seek work by responding to help wanted ads. Whether in the newspaper or on the internet, these ads advertise the jobs that are there. It's the course of least resistance. However, about three-quarters of all job opportunities are never advertised, but are filled informally through the hiring manager's network of contacts. The person responsible for filling the position will ask people in his network about possible candidates. The job seeker should do the same: use his or her network of acquaintances to uncover hidden job opportunities. Because NLDers/ASers have difficulty with social skills, this is a daunting task.

One way to compensate is to create a job-hunting strategy to meet your particular needs. Rather than looking for the perfect job, look for the perfect company. Through research, find organizations and companies whose mission and culture appeals to you. If you believe in a company's mission and like its culture, there's a good chance that the company may have a job that would fit you.

This approach requires more work, but in the long run it will increase your chances of attaining career success and satisfaction. Begin where you are now – by examining yourself and your current situation. Ask yourself what's good about your situation, what you'd like to change, what are your options, and which of those are feasible. What are your preferences? Identify your positive qualities as well as your challenges.

Your job search is like a sales campaign. You must know your assets, and be able to persuade the buyer that you're the best fit for the job they're trying to fill. Develop a personal marketing plan to sell your skills and abilities. This will be your outline as you look for work. It will direct you to your ideal choices of location, industry, company, and profession.

First, identify what you bring to the table. Skills describe what you're able to do, and determine the ways in which you can contribute to an organization. What are the qualities you're offering to the employer? Are you articulate? Do you have computer skills? Are you responsible? Diligent? Honest? Be very specific about the skills and abilities you bring to the company.

Next, find some industries, companies, and job titles within each company that you want to pursue. Match your skills with the place you want to work – the industry, job responsibilities, work environment, and organizational culture.

Finally, list the key contacts and information sources you've gathered in your research. Where will you find the information you need? Check with your library, and do research on the internet. Do you know anyone at the company or in the career you are pursuing who can give you information? Set goals, take steps, and measure your progress. Keep a log of résumés sent, perhaps using a spreadsheet or a database. Use a calendar, palm, or computer to schedule and keep track of your search activities and when to follow up. An outline that shows how all the details relate to each other can also be useful in keeping tabs on the actions you take. For example, the day you plan to follow up on a certain application should be written in your calendar as an appointment or to do.

You don't need to do this alone. Meet with other job hunters to support each other, exchange job leads, and get ideas. Your local Dept of Labor office, community service groups, or library may have information about local support groups. National groups, like the Five O'clock Club, Forty Plus, or Exec-U-Net may have local chapters near you. These require paid membership but provide advice and support.

Find a career counselor to serve as your co-pilot in developing search strategies. Talk to people and get referrals. Look at the schools in your community. Universities often provide career-related services to alumni. Community colleges often have services for the general public as well.

Your ability to describe what you can do for an employer is paramount to finding a job. Your tools for this purpose include your cover letter, résumé, and the interview.

23 Presenting Yourself in Print

The first contact you have with a prospective employer is often through the application form, résumé, and cover letter. These are essential tools to your job search, and come in a variety of formats.

Your résumé is a sales tool; the sales product is you. The purpose of a résumé is to get an interview, not the job. Your résumé should highlight your accomplishments, arousing the interest of the hiring manager to find out more about you. It should make a powerful, quick and lasting impression on the reader. Your qualifications for the position should be immediately apparent. You must hook the reader within the first ten seconds, or your résumé will end up on the slush pile.

All résumés, regardless of format or style, must contain your contact information, work history, and training or education. In addition, some people like to include a summary statement or personal profile, which provides an overview to the rest of the résumé and succinctly describes your accomplishments.

What information you decide to emphasize depends on the type of job you're trying to get. Consider the benefits you bring to a company. Be very descriptive. Don't limit yourself to listing your qualities, but list specific achievements, citing quantitative data whenever possible.

For your paper résumé, state your accomplishments using powerful action verbs. Use short, bulleted statements that pack punch. For example: "Wrote and obtained grants from various international foundations" or "Formulated and drafted policies and procedures". When possible, quantify your accomplishments: "Designed and implemented recruitment strategy for new members, increasing membership by 25 percent". It's best to analyze the job requirements, then create subheadings based on your findings and your work experience. For example, hiring managers in project-based fields like IT, engineering or architecture want a project-based résumé with details and exact dates of all relevant engagements.

You'll also need an electronic résumé in order to use online job sites or email. Employers scan these résumés electronically, searching for specific information. Focus on nouns, rather than verbs, and list credentials liberally. The more you include, the greater the likelihood that the employer's scanning software will find you. For information on developing and posting your online résumé, check out Cyberspace Résumé Kit by Mary B. Nemnich and Fred E. Jandt (Nemnich and Jandt 2000).

Cover letter

A cover letter is your opportunity to present yourself as you want to be remembered. It describes your interest in and enthusiasm for the position. It should stimulate the reader's interest in your résumé, and persuade the employer, in an interesting but concise manner, that you're the ideal candidate whom they should hire.

When writing a cover letter to the ideal company, first let them know you're interested in their product or service. Next, tell them what you can do for them. Tailor this to fit their needs. Last, tell them you'll call them to discuss employment opportunities.

Use the letter to highlight areas that would be of greatest interest to the employer. List several accomplishments and duties, and show how they pertain to the position you're seeking. Mention measurable results wherever possible. Emphasize what you can do for the employer – not the other way around. Use the pronouns "you", "yours", and the organization's name rather than "me", "myself", and "I". Follow up by phone or via email.

Effective letter writing requires good writing skills. It makes use of research and preparation. These are often strengths for the NLDer and ASer. Take the time to present yourself well, and proofread carefully.

There are thousands of books on writing résumés and cover letters. Many college websites and online writing labs offer help for drafting résumés and letters. Use them. The formats and what you should include change with time, so be sure to get current information. See what your library has available. If you want more personalized help, check with a local career center or your local Dept of Labor office. They often offer free job counseling and résumé help.

24 Showcase Your Work

Using a Professional Portfolio to Advance your Career[1]

The employer liked your résumé and you've been selected for an interview. You've gathered information about the company and prepared for common interview questions. But you want to do more. You would like to stand out above the crowd and present your unique talents to the prospective employer. What can you do?

Prepare a career portfolio to showcase your professional achievements. While a résumé outlines your skills and abilities, a portfolio displays the results of your work, offering the prospective employer positive proof of what you can do. As an individual with NLD or AS, this is even more important. You must compensate for impaired social ability by excelling in your field. The portfolio sells your work rather than your personality. It shifts the focus off you to what you have accomplished.

For example, the education heading of your résumé lists your degrees, certificates, and continuing education courses. Your portfolio expands this information by offering course descriptions and certificates, providing evidence for the items listed in your résumé.

Artists and models have been using portfolios for a long time, but almost any profession can do the same. In my library portfolio, I included samples of library brochures, pathfinders, and subject guides that I designed, samples of internet searches, newspaper clippings about the library, and fliers advertising library events. Secretaries can include samples of correspondence, spreadsheets, and other projects. Teachers can include lesson plans, sample tests and student evaluations. Programmers can make a demonstration disk. Blueprints and finished products, such as machine parts, can also be included. Virtually anything you designed, developed or produced can be part of your portfolio. The possibilities are limitless. Be creative. The items you include should illustrate your unique style, ability, talents, and potential.

Creating your portfolio

Step One: Gathering the information

Treat your portfolio as a brag bag. What are you proud of? What have you accomplished? How have your contributions helped others in your organization, school, and community?

Think about your accomplishments. Were you involved in a project or event that was featured in the paper? Cut out the clipping, make lots of copies, and highlight your role and achievements. Did you receive thank you notes complimenting you for a job well done? Include them. Did you help to create a new product or market a new service? Collect samples of the printed materials and document the results. Other examples of work artifacts are reports, technical drawings and before and after photos. Add memos and letters that document your accomplishments. Incorporate company literature which shows what you were involved in. This would include such items as company brochures, organizational charts, and project photos. Anything at all that documents your input to others' lives and relates to your career can and should be included in your portfolio. It may be a good idea to brainstorm with a friend or colleague to help you make a list of your achievements and the items that would support them.

Step Two: Assembling the portfolio

There are many ways to display a portfolio, but it should always be attractive and organized. The physical structure and appearance of the portfolio should complement its purpose. Depending on your career field, you could have the information and artifacts on a computer disk or in a binder. At any rate, you will need some type of case to keep the information together, and a way to organize the materials within this case. You want to make a good first impression, so quality is of utmost importance.

For my own portfolio, I purchased a leather binder in an office supply store. My case had a zipper to protect the contents and a looseleaf binder to organize the materials. Other amenities included extra pockets inside and outside, a section for business cards, a diskette file, and a pencil holder. Because my materials are all paper, I also purchased toploading plastic sheet protectors to shield the main documents, and folders to hold extra copies of the items. If photos are to be included, you may want to add photo sheet holders for vertical and horizontal pictures. Because the sheet protectors are wide, I used extra wide tabbed subject dividers to organize the items by category.

Step Three: Gathering the supplies

Before you get started, assemble the following:

- a computer and printer
- a friend or colleague to help you brainstorm
- a box of work samples and projects to include
- copies of certificates of achievement, diplomas, professional memberships and awards
- an updated résumé
- copies of reference letters.

Step Four: The shopping list

Now, run to your office supply center and buy an appropriate container to showcase your work samples (such as a zippered three-ring binder). Also buy quality paper, an extra ink cartridge for the printer, and other office supplies you may need, such as index tabs for organizing the information, folders, or clear page protectors.

Step Five: Organizing your portfolio

At the beginning of your portfolio, include a section for your résumé and recommendation letters. If you have a functional résumé, use it as a guide to create a table of contents for your portfolio. The descriptive statements from your functional résumé will index and summarize the highlights of your portfolio. Expanding on the objective statement in your résumé, you can develop a mission statement describing your vision, work philosophy, career goals or management style. Now, use the headings from your résumé to create a table of contents for the portfolio.

The next part should contain your educational achievements: copies of diplomas, certificates, degrees and transcripts. For the continuing education section, I include not only the certificate itself but also the class brochure.

The next section is the meat of the portfolio. It contains the work samples you have chosen to showcase your abilities to the employer. A good way to organize it is by skill areas. Think about what you do at work. Ask yourself what skills are required. Brainstorm. Now take the items from your box of work samples and organize them according to skill areas. For example, if your job duties include written communication skills, document them by including samples of reports, letters, memos, or brochures you have created. You may think of additional items to include as you do this – go get them. But remember, you want the samples to show only your very best work.

My library section is organized according to the various library jobs I have held. Included here are brochures advertising the library, library pathfinders, reports of my work, and newspaper articles about me and my job. The writing piece includes copies of articles I have published. There is some overlap because I have created library brochures and pamphlets which are also samples of my writing. I've put these in my library portion because I would be more likely to display them at a library interview. The teaching segment contains teaching certificates, lesson plans, and teaching materials I have created. I also have a community service section displaying the work I have done for literacy volunteers and the certificates I've been awarded for community service, and a technology part with samples of internet searches and other computer-related skills.

Step Six: Using the portfolio

Career portfolios give the job seeker a competitive edge when interviewing for employment opportunities. This is particularly important for the individual with Asperger Syndrome or Non-Verbal Learning Disability. By showing off your work, you take the emphasis off your personality. Remember, the portfolio is a sales tool. Analyze the audience (the company you wish to work for). What do they want? How do your skills and supportive documentation meet the prospective employer's needs?

When applying for a job or a promotion, mention your portfolio in the cover letter. Once you have landed an interview, prepare. Look over your portfolio and decide which items are most appropriate for the company and assignment you are interviewing for.

Bring your portfolio to the interview and have it ready. When the interviewer asks what you have accomplished, smile and say, "Let me show you." This is your cue to get out your portfolio. Use it to answer the interviewer's questions. If they ask about your career goals or future plans, take them to that section in your portfolio. If they want to know about your computer skills, show them computer-generated samples, demonstrating the skills they are seeking (word processing, spreadsheets, etc.). Think of the interview as show and tell. Be selective. You do not need to show everything in your portfolio – only the items most appropriate to the situation.

Brag about your accomplishments. Show them what you have done. Relate it to their needs, and they will see how you can best serve their business.

Note

1   This chapter was published as 'Show and Tell' in 2000 in *Minority Engineer* *21*, 1, 44–46.

25 Presenting Yourself in Person

Often, the candidate who gets the job offer is not the one with the best qualifications, but the one who interviews best. The prospective employer has seen your qualifications on your résumé. Now, he needs to decide whether your manner, attitude, appearance, confidence, personality, conviviality, etc. are a good fit for the company. At the interview, which is designed to screen out those who don't fit into the corporate culture, you're being judged on these qualities. At the same time, you are checking out whether this organization is where you want to use your talents. Does the job fulfill your expectations? Are you compatible with the organization and the other employees?

Many individuals with AS/NLD have trouble with the interview. Because of faulty non-verbal communication, they may have trouble projecting confidence. Their lack of eye contact may set off warning flags in the interviewer's mind. He thinks, "Boy, I can't quite place my finger on it, but that guy is weird."

Lana writes:

> Interviews are killers – especially panel interviews. They're overwhelming for me because of my impaired interpersonal communication ability. I have problems with spontaneous expressive language, maintaining eye contact, controlling body language, and high anxiety, all crucial elements for a successful job interview where special emphasis is placed on a candidate's ability to communicate. Coaching and practicing these interview skills has been of little help. After completing several courses in job search and human resources, I know the dos and don'ts by heart. For the past eight years I have been coaching students and members of the immigrant community in inter-

view techniques. It's not that I don't know what to do or how to do it – rather, I'm unable to handle this process. I catch myself acting against my own advice. I lose control of my hands, which end up all over my hair or in a constant circular motion; I lose my voice; I repeat myself, and can't maintain eye contact. I simply cannot look, listen, think and talk simultaneously. Even memorizing my presentation, career highlights, accomplishments and responses to the most common interview questions doesn't help. My mind goes blank and I watch in horror as I lose yet another job opportunity.

On the other hand, some ASers/NLDers have learned to cope with interviews. At an interview, or for other short periods of time, they're able to act normal, although they find it exhausting. Many find being around people in general tiring. Some NLDers/ASers have learned to become actors for interviews. It takes practice, and it is important to remain focused and calm. For those 30 minutes, however, they can appear outgoing, and if the interviewer asks about something that interests them, it gets even easier.

Again we come to the cardinal rule: Know yourself. Know your skills, talents, abilities, and personal traits. List your professional and personal accomplishments. Ask yourself: "How will these skills and qualities contribute to the organization I want to work for?" Show the employer how the qualities and abilities you bring will solve his or her problems.

The second cardinal interview rule is: Preparation is your best friend. There is much you can do beforehand to make sure you make as good an impression as possible.

Learn interview skills

Take classes and seminars in interpersonal communications, public speaking, and presentation skills. Learn all you can about interview and negotiation skills. The more you know about the process, the more comfortable you'll be, and the more confidence you will exude.

Practice body language

With a friend, teacher, or mentor, practice body language. What's your handshake like? It should be firm but not aggressive. Practice your answers to common interview questions. Taperecord your answers, and listen for what you sound like. Pay special attention to the tone and volume of your voice.

Practice projecting confidence

Talking is one of your best skills. Use it. To increase confidence, talk yourself through the interview. Use self-talk to make yourself feel confident. In your home or car, before you go into an interview, tell yourself – out loud – why you deserve to get this job. This will help you to act with confidence even when you don't feel like it. If you believe it, so will the person you are interviewing with.

Learn to listen

When you're nervous at the interview, you tend to concentrate on answering the interviewer's questions correctly. You need to listen to the interviewer, focusing on what is being said. There are a million questions that the interviewer could ask you, so it's hard to be prepared for everything, but lists of the most common questions abound on the internet and in many interview guides. Prepare for these. If you're asked a question that trips you up, don't be afraid to pause and think about it. You might even use a phrase like "That's an interesting concept. Let me think about that" to give yourself time to digest the question. If you can't think of an answer, it's OK to say so. You can think of ideas and answer in a follow-up letter.

Learn the difference between qualifying questions and those meant to disqualify. The first are open-ended like "Tell me about yourself" or "Why should I hire you?" The latter are meant to exclude you from the position, such as "Are you willing to travel?" or "What are your salary requirements?" If you say you're not willing to travel, they'll automatically disqualify you.

Do your research

Research will help you to prepare for the interviewer's questions by gathering important information about the industry, the company, the salary, and the position. The power of knowledge bestows confidence – something you'll need to succeed in interviews. Find out about their needs and goals. What are they looking for in an ideal employee? Then, present yourself as a problem solver.

Anticipate the interviewer's questions, and study possible answers. For example, by researching the company you're applying to and similar company websites, you can find out what they're looking for, and be better aware of experiences you've had that qualify you for this position. Researching similar positions will also give you salary information. You'll be better informed about the market value of the skills and training that you bring to the table. This will help you maintain a positive attitude and negotiate with confidence.

When looking for industry, company, or salary data, the internet is your best source. It's comprehensive, quick, and free. In addition to company websites, check out professional organizations and the myriad job search resources. You can even search newspapers from various cities for job ads as well as articles about organizations you're interviewing with. Be aware, however, that much web information is biased. For example, while company websites give you much valuable information – the annual report, who the key people are, what public image they're trying to present – they'll only tell you what they want you to know. Always confirm any information you find on the internet. The following tools – available in your public or college library – will help you with industry and company research:

1. *Books:*

    - American Salaries and Wages Survey
    - Dun's Business Rankings
    - Dun & Bradstreet's Million Dollar Directory (print or CD-ROM)
    - Encyclopedia of Associations
    - Hoover's Handbooks (American Business, Emerging Companies, etc.)
    - Moody's Manuals
    - Standard & Poor's Corporations (print or CD-ROM)
    - Standard & Poor's Industry Surveys
    - Thomas Register (print or CD-ROM)
    - US Industrial Outlook
    - US Industry Profiles
    - Ward's Business Directory of Private and Public Companies (also online)

2.   *Websites:*

- Yahoo's special industry site (http://Biz.yahoo.com/industry) can help you track down useful information, and provides links to other sites with specific company information.

- Companies Online (www.companiesonline.com)

- Corporate Information (www.corporateinformation.com)

- Hoover's Online (www.hoovers.com)

The librarians in the business division and the job information center of your public library can help you locate this information. The time you spend in research may be the extra push you need to get to the top of the candidate pool.

Prepare a career commercial

The career commercial is your answer to the most common interview question: "So, tell me about yourself." You want to keep the answer short, taking just a minute to summarize your major career accomplishments. At the same time, you want to pique the interviewer's interest, set the tone, and direct the rest of the conversation.

Prepare your commercial by writing and revising until you get what you want, then memorize it. The repetitive speech patterns of NLDers and ASers will work well for you in this exercise. Practice in front of a mirror, and check your facial expression, gestures, and tone of voice. Of course, you'll have to adapt it to different situations. Tweak it for various interviews, and use a more informal version at professional conferences, business meetings, and networking events.

Prepare stories

In addition to the commercial, have on hand several short stories that illustrate your major achievements and showcase important skills. For example, many employers ask about how one would handle a difficult situation or a difficult customer. Prepare a story of how you handled such a situation. Use these stories to respond to the interviewer's questions. Begin with an overview of a situation, then explain what you did and how you achieved the goal. Like your commercial, these stories can be prepared in advance. They should be clear and concise – usually less than a minute. Write, revise, and rehearse.

A word about body language

For an NLDer/ASer this is often the toughest part of the interview process. Be sure to observe all of the standard job search niceties, from a firm handshake to appropriate attire. Remember to smile. Believe it not, that makes a big difference. Try to greet the interviewer(s) and end the interview with a handshake. You might want to suck on a mint before your interview to make sure your breath is fresh.

Non-verbal cues, like eye contact, show the interviewer you're still on the same page. Look at your interviewer. If you have trouble looking in the eyes, look at his nose. To avoid staring, remember to look away occasionally. Nod your head at appropriate times to show you're listening. Don't interrupt, but listen till the speaker is finished. In this way, you can gather important information that will help you formulate better answers and ask intelligent questions.

Avoid sofas or plush chairs. Sit up straight, and keep your feet flat on the floor. To convey your interest, lean forward slightly towards the person you're addressing. Keep your hands in your lap, unless you're taking notes. Don't fold your arms; this is perceived as defensive or inaccessible. If you take notes, be sure you look attentive. If you have any habits others may find annoying, like rocking or shaking your leg, be aware of them and make sure they don't crop up.

If the interviewer starts shuffling papers or says something like "We have a million other candidates to interview" that is your clue he/she wants to wrap up the interview. Acknowledge that you realize time is about up. If you haven't gotten a chance to ask your questions, do so now, but make them brief. End by asking what part of your background they would like to hear more about.

Follow-up

Always end the interview by asking about the next steps. When you get home, write a follow-up letter. Be meticulous about follow-up with phone calls.

In conclusion, be confident about your abilities and show enthusiasm for the job. Remember that interviewing is about selling. You're selling yourself to the employer. You have to give them reasons to buy by explaining what you can do for them. Your job as a salesperson is to convince them that your product is better than the competition's.

26 How to Survive the Job Interview

Lawrence M. Blim

In my 29-year career I have been on both sides of the interview desk and I can tell you that it's just as hard to interview someone as it is to be interviewed. The ideal interview is one where both parties have an opportunity to find out about the other side: the applicant about the job and the company and interviewer about the applicant's character, skills, and job history. There are five areas in which the applicant with NLD/AS can prepare for a job interview to meet his/her own goals and to help the prospective employer meet his.

1. Appearance.

2. Questions.

3. Answers.

4. Make your case.

5. Follow through.

Appearance

First impressions are crucial. Often the interviewer will make a judgment about the applicant in the first 30 seconds of the interview. To offer a professional, no-nonsense appearance, the job seeker must dress appropriately and be well groomed. Try not to carry a briefcase or large purse to the interview. If you bring a portfolio with work samples, try to find a way to set it down or leave it with the secretary while you greet your interviewer. Make eye contact as soon as you enter the room and immediately offer a hand to be shaken by the interviewer. The handshake must be firm but not painful and made with a dry hand, all the while looking the interviewer in the eye. If this is difficult, stare at the end of his nose, which will look very much like eye contact. Bring a copy of your application or resumé just in case.

Questions

Come prepared with some suitable questions to ask the interviewer about the company, the profession or industry, and the job itself. Your goal is to appear interested and reasonably well informed. This will help you stand out from the majority of applicants who won't bother to do any research about the company before their interviews. Since any research you do is likely to be through reading or surfing the internet, this will probably tap one of your strengths as an NLDer/ASer.

Answers

Here are some tips for impressing an interviewer with your answers to his questions:

1. *Eye contact.* Try to make eye contact as much as possible (or at least stare at the end of his nose).

2. *Be concise.* Rambling can be a sign of nervousness. Use short answers whenever you can. It's hard to stop talking when you know the subject and want to impress the interviewer. It's best to keep the answers short but open ended, and hope the interviewer will ask additional questions that will allow you to elaborate. Watch the interviewer's eyes. If his gaze wavers, you have gone on too long. No interviewer likes long, rambling responses. Don't ramble.

3. *Pause.* Pausing frequently between sentences allows your words to sink in and gives the appearance that you are thoughtful and deliberative, which are sought-after traits. Pausing is often helpful if the interviewer is taking notes on what you're saying.

4. *Smile.* This is essential because interviewers like applicants who appear to be happy, well adjusted, and self-confident. Even if you are shaking in your shoes (which, I can assure you, most applicants are), you can appear self-assured by smiling frequently

at the interviewer. In my experience, a good smile can go a long way toward eliminating any negative effects that your nervousness, or any small mistakes you make in the interview, might have on the person interviewing you. Smile! Show them you're happy to be here!

5. *Take notes.* Taking an occasional note is a sign of interest and may impress the interviewer with your sincerity. Don't overdo this. Bring a small notebook or piece of paper to take notes on and a nice looking pen. Be unobtrusive.

6. *Finish big.* At the end of the interview, stand up, shake hands again (firm and dry, remember), make eye (or eye–nose) contact, and thank the interviewer. Make sure you get the interviewer's specific address (including room number and/or mail stop) before you leave, so you can follow up with a bread-and-butter note. However, don't make a big fuss about getting this information, especially if there are other job applicants around. If there is a secretary, she will be able to give you this information discreetly. If you don't get it while you're there, you can call back later.

Make your case

Most interviewers will give you an opportunity at the end of the interview to make a statement or add anything not already on the application or brought out in the interview. Anticipate this time and prepare for it. Use it to summarize your skills, how good a fit you are with the job requirements, any training or job history (paid or unpaid) you have which fits particularly well with the job's duties, and any other traits or characteristics that make you the ideal candidate. Don't make overblown statements, but don't be afraid of putting your best foot forward. Interviewers like assertive candidates. Don't name drop. Most bosses aren't impressed by who you know; it's who you are and what you know that's important. (Political jobs, or jobs dealing with politicians or political appointees, are an exception.)

What should you say about your NLD or AS? My advice is to say nothing directly. If one or more duties of the job involve activities or tasks which you think might be difficult for you because of some aspect of your NLD/AS, you can tell the interviewer that you have difficulty with this or that activity. For example, if you have trouble with finding your way in big buildings, you might mention that you have no sense of direction and ask for a map. If you have to follow a lot of multi-step directions (a common practice in accounting and information technology organizations), you might ask if someone could help you to make a detailed checklist. If your job skills are strong and you interview well (Pause often! Keep smiling! Be concise!), asking for small accommodations like this should not be a problem. If they are, you probably don't want to work there anyway.

Follow through

Follow up the interview within a day or two with a "bread-and-butter note". This is a brief thank you note which was once commonly sent after one attended a dinner party (hence the name). It's a short letter to the interviewer thanking him for the opportunity as well as summarizing your qualifications. Since not all candidates send such notes, this is another way to help you stand out from the crowd. It is a verbal way of communicating, which is the strength of most NLDers and ASers.

This note is also an excellent opportunity to include any overlooked bits of job history, training, or experience that may be pertinent to the job you've applied for, but which didn't come up in the interview. If there were any questions you couldn't answer well in the interview or for which you later thought of a better answer, now is the time to briefly state it. For example, if the interviewer asked "Why do you particularly want to work for this company?" and you couldn't think of a really good answer at the time, you can include a concise but excellent reason in the bread-and-butter note (e.g., "this company has an outstanding reputation in the industry").

Timed correctly, the note arrives on the hiring official's desk just as he's about to make his hiring decision. For the price of a stamp and a piece of paper, you have the chance of influencing the hiring process a second time. Don't pass this opportunity by.

Lawrence M. Blim is a Certified Public Accountant who has more than 30 years experience in interviewing and hiring professional, managerial, and clerical workers. He's also the father of an NLD teen.

27 Questions to Ask at the Job Interview[1]

The employer liked your résumé and you've been selected for an interview. You're excited, but a bit nervous. You know that during the face-to-face meeting you should actively listen, respond with interest, and ask questions. But just what questions should you ask? Open-ended questions are best. They elicit the information you're seeking, spur the discussion along, and put you in control.

Choose your questions to determine the responsibilities of the position and the needs of the company. Before the interview, learn as much as you can about the firm. If possible, determine the job titles of those who will be interviewing you, and think of questions to ask about what they do in relation to what you will be doing. For example, you could ask "What do you consider to be the five most important day-to-day responsibilities of this job?" or "What personality traits do you consider critical to success in this job?"

It's important to have specific questions for each member of the interview team. Each of these people has a unique perspective about the company and the position. Even asking similar questions of different people enables you to gauge consistency of opinions within the organization.

Inquire about your background. What attracted them? What did they like about your résumé? If you know the answer early, you will be able to tell what they're looking for. Then, you can link your strengths to their priorities.

Ask "Why is the position open?" This will clue you in on the fate of your predecessor. Did she retire? Was she promoted? In the case that the last person was terminated, you will need to ask additional questions to determine whether the company's expectations for the position are realistic. Try to determine where they went wrong and what you would do differently.

Find out whom you will be reporting to. The answer will help you discern the power structure of the company. You can also ask about the duties and responsibilities of the position. To get an idea of their priorities, ask how much time will be spent in each area of responsibility. I also like to learn about communication channels within the organization.

Another way to ascertain their priorities is to find out what are the top three things they would like you to accomplish during the first quarter you're with them. In addition to telling you their expectations, this question can lead to an interesting discussion about various dimensions of the job.

After they ask you to share your strengths and weaknesses, turn the focus back on them by asking "Please describe your management style." The answer will tell you how compatible you are with your supervisor-to-be. If the interviewer will be your boss, ask him/her to define the model working relationship between an employee and supervisor.

You can also ask about training and advancement opportunities. Where will the job take you in five years? What are the opportunities for advancement in this field? Does the company provide ongoing training?

To avoid misunderstanding, ask if there's anything that you could clarify before you leave. Save salary and benefit questions until the end of the interview if you ask them at all. Asking these too early in the game gives the impression that your main interest is dollars, not the challenge or opportunity of serving the company.

At the end of the meeting ask "How soon may I expect to hear from you?" This question makes your interest in the job evident. It also lets you know the time frame they are working with, and allows you to tailor your follow-up strategy.

Most candidates don't realize that they're judged not only by their answers but also by their questions. Smart questions help you get a better feel for the job. They also show your enthusiasm to the employer.

Note

1   This chapter was published as 'Do you have any Questions?' in 2001 in *Equal Opportunity 35*, 1, 46.

Maintaining a Career

28 The Employer's Perspective on Hiring People with NLD/AS

Lawrence M. Blim

Why should an employer hire someone with the neurological, motoric, and social impairments that accompany Asperger or Non-Verbal Learning Disability syndromes? How can someone with NLD or AS get, and keep, a job when competing against neurotypical (NT) job applicants? What, if anything, should someone with NLD/AS tell a prospective, or actual, employer about his/her disability? As a manager who has hired numerous people over the years, including many with technical backgrounds (accountants, systems experts, financial analysts), I will try to answer these questions and offer the person with NLD/AS a set of effective strategies for finding, getting, and keeping a job.

Because people and situations vary, not all strategies will work with all employers or all NLDers/ASers. Part of the NLDer's or ASer's job will be to try to determine which strategies will work best for that individual in a given situation. There is no "recipe" for getting and keeping a job in today's tight job market and therefore there is no foolproof method for getting hired and staying employed. Different employers look for different things, even in individuals who are highly qualified from a technical standpoint for their jobs. This means that the job hunter must be prepared to be flexible in his or her approach. This primer on what most employers look for in a job candidate will give the applicant some tools to use in the job search, but the tools will have to be used selectively and intelligently to be effective.

Basic job requirements

Aside from technical skills, there are certain invariable characteristics that virtually all employers look for in a job applicant. Since most people, including people with NLD/AS, understand and embrace these qualities, I will not dwell on them. But it is important to mention them here since it is the perception that the job applicant or employee has these qualities that is important, as well as the reality, and the presence of certain NLD/AS traits can sometimes adversely affect that perception. Accompanying these characteristics therefore are some tips on how to give the appearance that you do, in fact, embrace these qualities.

Honesty, trustworthiness, and high ethical standards

This means that you won't steal from the company, give away company trade secrets, lie to your boss or the customers, or break any of the company rules or policies. The perception, as well as the reality, that you have these qualities is essential if you plan to keep your job or to rise above the entry level in almost any job.

What you can do

In the interview, all you can do is cite your record of past trustworthiness. If you've had any sort of ethics training, mention it. On the job, it is the unwritten cultural rules of a company, rather than the written policies, that an NLDer/ASer has to take extra care to identify and learn so as to give the appearance of conformance to this standard. Your best bet here is to try to find someone in the company who can explain these informal cultural rules to you and give you some tips on how to comply in a visible, public way. A friendly co-worker can often help you with this; the human resources office may be able to help as well.

Dependability

First, dependability means you will come to work at the time you have agreed to be there and not leave until your shift is over each day. To an NLDer/ASer who, for example, keeps getting lost on the way to work, in the company parking lot, or in the building, getting to work on time can be an issue.

What you can do

In the interview, cite evidence of past dependability, either in a job, at school, or in a volunteer setting. Were you the quartermaster for your scout troop? Did you have responsibility for money or other assets in a former job? Mention any pertinent examples. On the job, either find a way not to get lost or get to work early enough so this isn't a problem. Use watch and computer alarms to get yourself to meetings and back from lunch on time. Find ways to remind yourself about deadlines and due dates; for example, try using a calendar with color-coded dates or deadlines.

Second, dependability means that you will carry out any assignment or complete any task you are given, even if it is not directly related to your normal duties. There can be traps for NLDers/ASers here if instructions are implied or are too complex.

What you can do

In the interview, mention projects that you have completed on time, the more difficult the better. On the job, insist on getting detailed written instructions for complex tasks. Obtain and learn to use checklists for routine tasks; and don't settle for ambiguous or vague descriptions of tasks or outcomes. Missed nuances are the bane of the NLDer/ASer.

Third, dependability means that you will do your work with a consistent degree of quality and that you can complete a certain amount of work in a day. The key here is to reach an explicit understanding with the boss as to what exactly the standards for quality and quantity are. Inferring these things can be risky.

What you can do

In the interview, be sure to mention examples of how productive and effective you were in previous jobs, in school projects, or in volunteer situations. On the job, ask for periodic feedback based on your job standards.

Competence

Obviously your boss expects that you will be able to perform your technical or professional duties as advertised. Because of problems with visual and motor processing speed, NLDers and ASers can be perceived as lazy. NLDers/ASers who have trouble with things like multi-step instructions or cluttered visual displays, or who are disorganized, can appear to lack training or competence.

What you can do

In the interview, mention successes you have had in the past in your chosen field, whether paid or not. On the job, be proactive. Be candid about any specific difficulties you have (such as deciphering cluttered charts) and ask for help or accommodations before you get into trouble. With the speed issue, approach the boss and explain that you want to do a good job. Say something like "I'd like to stay late or take this home because it's taking me longer than it would most people and I don't mind not getting paid overtime."

Attitude

Bosses want a positive attitude, a "can-do" outlook from everyone. Naysayers, pessimists, and constant doubters are not appreciated because these attitudes can hurt productivity and creativity on the job. People who are grumpy all the time put a damper on everyone's energy. Again it is often the perception of negativity that can hurt an applicant or employee who is unaware that s/he is, for example, wearing what appears to be a grim, unhappy, or grumpy facial expression.

What you can do

In the interview, smile and give the appearance of someone with a pleasant personality who will be a "team player". On the job, keep smiling and be friendly. Invest in some "face time" with your co-workers and get to know them, as they get to know you, and smile at them in a friendly way at every opportunity, if you can do so in a sincere way.

Teamwork

In some jobs, people have to work alone and teamwork is not a consideration. But in most jobs, everyone is part of at least one team or work group and often participates in several project teams at one time. Bosses expect everyone in the group not only to get along but also to make positive contributions and help each other be successful. Small group skills are essential to being able to do this, and of course the non-verbal information which makes up two-thirds of human interaction is crucial to communication within the group. NLDers/ASers have to find a way to make sure that they get this information in another way.

What you can do

In the interview, give examples of prior team successes. On the job, ask people to verbalize. Do as much small group work as you can via email or conference calls, which puts everyone on a verbal basis.

What to tell the boss and your fellow employees about your NLD/AS

Nothing. I would only mention specific things you have difficulty doing, like figuring out densely drawn charts or slides which have directly to do with your job. Many people who do not have NLD/AS have such difficulties, and there is no reason to disclose that you have a "syndrome". Such disclosures can't help you and might hurt you. I would tell people about even the specific difficulties you have only on a "need to know" basis.

On the other hand, I would be forthright about any social impairments you have, especially in a small group environment. Telling your fellow work group members that you have trouble understanding facial expressions, tone of voice, and body language is important so as to avoid misunderstandings and the wasting of other people's time. By asking people upfront in a matter-of-fact way to verbalize any important information that they would normally transmit non-verbally, you can actually de-emphasize your disability and signal to the group that you want to focus on the job to be done. At a minimum, you will avoid misunderstandings that can frustrate and delay the work.

Working around the social impairment in the workplace

It is the social impairment of NLD/AS that will probably cause the most grief to job applicants and employees with the disorder. This is because, first, you don't always realize when you have missed some crucial non-verbal information and, second, even when you know this you don't always know what to do about it. There are two strategies you can follow which can ameliorate some of this difficulty.

The first strategy is a very simple but powerful one: smile and be friendly. I have found that if I walk around the office smiling at everyone, greeting them by name if possible, and saying things like "Hi" and "Good morning" and "How was your weekend?" I get a lot more smiles and friendliness back, as well as more understanding and sympathy when I mess up.

What I have found, as both a boss and an employee, is that one can get away with making small mistakes (and we all make them) more readily if one is friendly around the office (this works at home too). People are more willing to make allowances and forgive small unintentional errors if you are on a first-name basis than if you are not. It's that simple. A reasonable amount of small talk at a person's desk or at the office water cooler is also a good investment, but too much can flag a person as non-productive. You want to strike a good balance between "stand-offish" and "office gossip". To maintain that balance, it's good to time yourself. Five minutes is long enough to monopolize someone's attention. Glancing at your watch or computer will remind the other person that you've been talking long enough. Making a half step towards leaving will signal the same message. All these are subtle signs that we've talked long enough. It's quite OK to be calculating about striking this balance so long as the friendliness you do express is genuine.

If you have difficulty remembering faces or names, as I do, just smile and say hello without the name. Try to find a way to remember people's names – this is just common courtesy – but the friendliness is much more important. Tip: this will not work unless you can be reasonably sincere about it. People can detect insincerity. Don't try to fake this. But friendliness is a social skill that can be learned. If you're uncomfortable doing this at first, keep trying. The rewards will be large.

The second strategy builds on the small group strategy of asking people to verbalize their non-verbal communications, i.e., telling people that you have difficulty understanding non-verbal cues and asking them to verbalize for you. You can expand on this strategy by asking people (after you've disclosed your difficulty with things non-verbal) direct questions about, for example, what they're feeling or how they're reacting. If you don't get a positive response from work you've handed in, for example, you can ask "Mr Smith, did I do something wrong? Is that report not what you expected?"

One way to improve your chances of giving the boss the quality and quantity of output that he is looking for is to make sure before you begin a task that you know what he expects the outcome to be. Get explicit instructions; don't settle for ambiguity or uncertainty. If you don't know for sure, ask until you do. If you need an outline, checklist or detailed procedure, ask for one. I would rather annoy my boss upfront by making him pin down exactly what he wants from me before I do the work than annoy him after I've worked long and hard to produce the wrong thing.

Believe it or not, sometimes the boss is not clear in his own mind exactly what he wants, so if you allow him to leave the outcome of your task unclear, there may actually be no way you can succeed. This is called the "bring me a rock" assignment. If the boss doesn't know which rock he wants, the odds of you bringing back the right one are pretty low. Make sure you know exactly which rock he wants before you leave the room with your assignment.

Another useful addition to this strategy is to periodically ask the boss for feedback on how you're doing. Since you've told him that you have difficulty reading non-verbal cues, he should not think it unreasonable for you to ask for occasional input from him on how he gauges your performance. Do not overdo this, however. Some bosses are not comfortable giving feedback to employees, and may get annoyed. Not all bosses have good social skills (ironic, isn't it?). So ask but don't insist if the boss is not forthcoming. If you have performance standards (and you should), you can ask the boss specifically how you're doing on any given standard, such as meeting deadlines, having a low error rate, or keeping the boss informed. (Frankly, this is good advice for all employees.) Tip: keep track of your own performance by keeping a log of deadlines met, projects completed, reports submitted on time, etc. This will help at performance review time whether or not you are getting good feedback from the boss.

There are no certain ways for getting and keeping a job, but by following these tips you will be able to improve your chances considerably. You may have to work harder and prepare more because of your NLD/AS, but in many instances your "disability" will actually prove to be a strength, as in the writing and researching area. Good luck in your job search and your employment, and remember – smile!

29 Your First Hundred Days

So you've got a new job. Now what? Make your work a priority, at least until you get used to it. For the individual with AS/NLD, finding the job is not cause for celebration; it's often only the beginning of a long struggle with an uncertain outcome. It's a big life change, which presents additional difficulties for the NLDer/ASer who often has trouble with adjustments. Thank everyone who helped in your job hunt; they'll be happy to hear of your success. Make sure you get lots of rest, exercise, and nutrition. Give yourself plenty of down time after the workday ends. This will enable you to do your best.

Because you're new, you may be given a bit of slack. That's why the first few months on a new job is called a honeymoon period. You're not expected to know everything. However, you are expected to learn – and in today's fast-paced environment, the quicker you catch on and acclimatize, the better you will be perceived. Your contribution to the department, and your continual improvement, should be evident. When the honeymoon is over, you'll be expected to know the ropes.

It's probably best to keep your NLD/AS hidden at first, if it's not too obvious. Eventually, they'll figure out that you're a bit different. Rather than talking about disability, talk about style, and palliate it by emphasizing your strengths, how well you learn, and how proficient you will become as a result.

Success in the work world has a lot to do with making other people feel comfortable with you. During your first few weeks, your major challenge is fitting in. To accomplish this, you must get to know your colleagues, become familiar with how things are done, and understand the organizational culture, standards, and principles.

What can you do to make the transition smoother?

Take some time before or after work to learn the layout of the office or building. Get a map if possible. Walk the hallways. Try to memorize the layout, and note whose offices are where. If, like many NLDers/ASers, you're "directionally challenged", you may need to give yourself this self-guided tour more than once.

If there's an employee directory, obtain a copy and familiarize yourself with it. If possible, get pictures of various people, especially key people in the organization. Study and memorize them. Try to find out who is important and what the company values are. Learn about the corporate culture – the customs, policies, and procedures of the organization. Some are formal; many are informal, thus difficult for the ASer/NLDer to discern. For example, are headphones considered reasonable? Many ASers/NLDers use these to block out distracting noise. Observe. Ask questions. Seek guidance from your colleagues – people at your level or those slightly higher. Try to obtain their trust.

Your image

Invest in your appearance. The way you look and smell sends a message to others. If you look sloppy, co-workers may assume that your work is sloppy too. Dress and personal hygiene are two things you can control that will enhance your work image.

Personal grooming and cleanliness include body odor, teeth, and breath. Make sure you don't smell, but avoid heavy perfume or cologne. These are often not welcome in the workplace. Make sure your hair and nails are neat and clean.

Look around the office. What do your co-workers wear? Dress to fit in with similar styles. Your clothes send a message; choose them wisely. They tell those around you whether you're earnest or flippant, convivial or reserved, humble or proud, passionate or unemotional. You can find advice on dressing professionally from magazines and books like *Dress for Success (Molloy 1988)*, but make sure it's in line with the environment you're working in.

Attitude is important

Learn to accept change. NLDers/ASers often prefer things to stay the same. In the workaday world, however, things are always changing. In the new job, you don't always know what to expect. Just knowing this is half the battle. Although you prefer structure and predictability, learn how to deal with uncertainty in the workplace. Don't allow unexpected changes to catch you off guard. Try to predict what the day will bring; this will help you meet unexpected challenges.

Maintain a positive outlook. No one likes whiners and complainers. You weren't hired to complicate the lives of your managers by uncovering problems, but to find solutions.

Your reputation

The first hundred days at a new job are vital to developing your reputation and professional image. As the new employee, you're vulnerable. You're being scrutinized. Your employer is observing you to determine if he or she made the right decision. Your colleagues are checking you out. Your subordinates are watching your every move, trying to figure out where they stand and what you're like as a boss.

The people you work with are all making opinions about you. Most of these are one-sided generalizations, but they form the basis of how others view you. This is the time that mutual understanding and respect are established. Your reputation is shaped by the stories they tell about you. These include your abilities, as well as the quirks in your personality, and NLDers/ASers often have lots of personality quirks. Comments about AS/NLD traits might include:

- "Donna is a walking dictionary. If you want to know how to spell a word, just ask her."

- "Wendy gets so hung up on details. She has trouble getting the picture."

- "John is eager to help if you need anything."

- "Susan takes forever to get things done. Everyone else leaves her in the dust."

- "Robert is honest to a fault."

- "Darlene is always here. She tries really hard."

- "You can always depend on James."

Work to create a good impression and learn what others think about you. If you can see yourself the way they see you, you'll be one step ahead in changing behavior that might hurt your career. Inappropriate behavior, rather than a lack of skill or know-how, is what derails most careers. Having a friend or mentor can be a great help here, especially to the NLDer/ASer who tends to be oblivious to signals in the environment and might not perceive what is obvious to everyone else. Ask for feedback, so you can learn from others' advice. Useful feedback includes honest opinions as well as constructive criticism. Use what you learn to develop qualities that will ensure your success at work.

Meet with your supervisor regularly, and keep him or her informed of your progress. If they know what you're dealing with, they may be able to discount any inaccurate information that's being circulated about you before it takes root. For example, they might say, "This just doesn't sound like something Joe would do."

Professional identity

Ask a mentor or trusted colleague what skills would be useful on this job, and how to get the necessary training. In addition to helping you do a great job, this will help you expand your future possibilities. However, beware of perfectionism. Your boss wants you to do good work, but he also wants you to do a lot of work. It can be hard to know where to draw the line between quality work and perfection. When you can see that you've done a good job, it boosts your self-esteem. When others compliment your work, it's an additional boost to morale. When it's the manager who notices, you've earned brownie points. However, when your supervisor wants a task done quickly, not perfectly, this can bring internal conflict for the thorough, precision-minded employee who feels that if the job's worth doing, it's worth doing well. Even if you take a lot of pride in your work, remember that hyper-excellence benefits no one, and can diminish your productivity. Perfectionism on the job is rarely feasible. It can eat up your time, create anxiety, and set you up for disappointment.

Relationships

You're the new kid on the block. As an NLDer/ASer, you'll need to work harder than most during your first few weeks to develop workplace relationships. Because ASers and NLDers tend to need more alone time, they risk hiding in the shadows. Resist the urge to stay apart and just do your work. You can't afford to hide in your cubicle or office. It's important that managers, supervisors, co-workers, and subordinates see you in action. Approach others, ask them about their work, and seek their advice about yours.

Know who the important people are. The "winners" in the company are easy to spot; their achievements are well known. Find out who are the authority figures and leaders.

Attend meetings and try to share your ideas. Being a team player requires communication and collaboration. It may be hard to know when to enter the conversation, because fast-paced, snappy extroverts can dominate meetings. This was Susan's experience:

> I found it very challenging to participate in group meetings. Topics were discussed too fast for me to think of anything useful to say, people volunteered for duties faster than I could evaluate the work involved, and there were many aspects of the organizing work I knew little or nothing about. I felt very much out of the loop and ended up contributing very little. (Prince-Hughes 2002, p.103)

Remember that you bring a unique and valuable perspective, and that your colleagues and supervisors want to know what you think. If you remain quiet, they'll turn to others – and away from you. Beware of the fine line between assertiveness and aggressiveness, however.

While relationships with colleagues are important, the most crucial relationship at your new job is the one with your boss. If he or she doesn't like you, you're sunk. If on the other hand he or she likes you and appreciates your style and contribution, you'll have it much easier.

Think of your relationship as a partnership. Communicate with your supervisor regularly, so he or she is aware of the status of your projects. Try to solve problems and offer solutions. Meet with him/her regularly. You will become familiar with his/her work style and also have opportunities to clarify instructions. Stand behind your ideas, but remain flexible. Recognize his or her authority, and show respect. Remember that the boss always has the final say. Be responsible and accountable for your successes as well as your mistakes. Accept constructive criticism with dignity, and never try to shift the blame onto someone else. Make sure you understand the correction; ask for specific examples to make it clear. It's an opportunity to improve your performance. Learn from your boss's knowledge and experience. He or she wants you to succeed because this will help the department or organization.

Fitting in is a challenge for any new employee, but is especially difficult for someone with AS or NLD. While you need to portray confidence, you must also show respect to those who've been there longer. Observe your colleagues. Watch their interactions. Study their habits, for example:

- Do they work with their doors closed or open?

- What do they talk about?

- How do they dress?

- How do they behave at meetings?

- How is lateness or absence from meetings viewed? Is it seen as rude or inefficient, or as dedication to more important work pursuits?

- How is someone who is often late or absent perceived?

- What about participation in informal events, like birthday parties?

- What are the communication channels?

- Do people use inter-office memos or other written notes, voice mail, email, or personal interaction?

- How do managers communicate with their subordinates?

Your friendliness and helpfulness can help you to fit in, so keep yourself as accessible to co-workers as you can. Ask about their ideas and opinions. Find out how they do things. This will help you gain their confidence. You could ask each one what, in their view, you as a newbie need to know about how things work. Concentrate on things, rather than people. To keep the tone business oriented and not too personal, rather than asking how Sue gets along with Sally, ask about interactions between the two departments. You will gain valuable perspectives, and your co-workers will feel that you trust them and value their opinions. If you ask too many questions, however, you may risk being perceived as a meddler. Be careful not to get too chummy too quickly. Keep the conversations short and business oriented. They're not interested in your hobbies and special interests. Understand the impact of the company you keep. Your reputation will be determined by the reputation of those you associate with.

Inter-office politics are the maneuvers people make to gain favor in the workplace. These are different everywhere. They include things done to impress others, stroking egos, brown nosing, and other such indecent behavior. The political game is tiresome even for the most savvy NT; for the NLDer/ASer, the phoniness is exhausting and demoralizing. Most NLDers and ASers find it arduous to penetrate the hidden agendas behind the demands of others. There's so much writing on the wall and the NLDer/Aser who has trouble reading between the lines finds it hard to know what to look for. Effective office politics depends not only on being able to read it, but also on understanding the significance of each piece. To get this information, you must be a good detective. This intelligence information is often only available through the informal network of contacts that NLDers/ASers often lack. Unfortunately, who you know does matter, sometimes more than what you know. While what you know puts you in the candidate pool, it's often who you know that determines whether you're the one selected for the promotion or job. This is why networking is vital to career advancement.

Office parties are also a difficult time for many ASers/NLDers. At least show up. It's to your advantage that those you work with are aware that you esteem them enough to spend time with them.

The first hundred days are a difficult adjustment period for everyone but the NLDer/ASer faces additional challenges. Remember that once you adjust to your new responsibilities, new surroundings and new colleagues, things will get easier.

3 0 Work Issues

Although NLDers/ASers are intelligent and often have excellent verbal skills, they also have problems with basic life tasks. Sometimes these problems can be awfully subtle; other times, they're painfully obvious.

One of the hardest parts of being NLD is that people don't get it. One individual might have a large vocabulary, be great at trivia, and able to solve difficult math problems, yet be unable to whistle, snap his fingers, or light a match. Another person might be an avid reader, have an excellent vocabulary, and write very well, but have problems folding a letter and putting it neatly in an envelope, pouring a cup of tea, or bumping into furniture. If someone is dyslexic, everyone knows that person has trouble reading, but if you tell people you are LD but good at reading and math they say "If you're intelligent, then you can't be learning disabled." And if you tell people that you can't read body language, they still get mad at you when you don't.

NLDers/ASers have many positive characteristics valued by employers, including honesty, loyalty, dependability, determination and courage. They're intelligent and talented, with a prolific vocabulary, and often excel at tasks that need strong language or logic skills. Many have incredible memories, master facts quickly and easily, have a vast knowledge of specialized fields, and are very attentive to details. These individuals work well independently, have remarkable powers of concentration, and will often focus on a limited number of things for extended periods of time. They're determined, patient, persistent, and purposeful. They're creative, original thinkers with innovative problem-solving approaches. Because they've experienced many hardships, they're kind, compassionate, and caring. They're self-assured, a-political, goal oriented, and practical. They bring a unique perspective, a sense of social justice, and conversation free of hidden meaning. They're motivated, dependable, loyal employees. They're guileless, genuine and straightforward, with a strong work ethic. Since they tend to see things as black and white, right or wrong, they're honest and fair almost to a fault. Often, they'll stand up for principles, ideas or loyalties to the point of their own detriment.

One of the refreshing things about many NLDers/ASers is that they operate with no hidden agenda – ever. It's beyond them. But that also means that they do not see it in others. Because they take what they see and hear at face value, they tend to be very accepting of others, but at the same time very gullible and easily manipulated. Because of this, they're not well equipped to deal with the world of workplace politics, unwritten rules, ambiguity, grapevine gossip, favoritism, nepotism, hostile environments and office bullying. Their naive, trusting, and unassertive ways can cause them to fall prey to exploitation and backstabbing by their co-workers, whom their honesty, dependability, loyalty and commitment sometimes make look bad.

Workplace discrimination and harassment can lead to severe stress, depression, and anxiety, causing diminished work performance and leading to the loss of a job. Prolonged psychological injury inflicted at work can destroy a person's life, health, reputation and career. Such actions are usually carried out in subtle, insidious ways which the ASer or NLDer may have problems detecting. The workplace bullies will, of course, refute accusation and evade responsibility. Unfortunately, the administration may take their side, turning tables on the victim instead of confronting harassing and intimidating behavior.

For the NLDer or ASer, it's very difficult to find the ideal job. Because their brains are wired differently, they may have difficulty communicating in conventional ways and may have problems with work requiring manual dexterity, speed, or judgment. While they often excel at tasks that some find tough, like writing or programming, things that come with little effort to most folks like driving, cleaning up, or tying knots are difficult. They may advance in their professions but fail to get top-level jobs because they can't supervise others, and may run into problems if they're required to make frequent judgments and decisions. Their failure in interpersonal communication only makes these problems worse.

Some folks with NLD or AS have had successful experiences. Jobs with little pressure, few deadlines, and an independent, solitary work style where no one is looking over your shoulder are good. Some have jobs as professors, programmers, or independent consultants or contractors. On the other hand, others have had less success. Inability to read non-verbal communications, lack of eye contact, and strange speech patterns make finding work difficult. While every person who interviews for a job has some weak points, the weak areas of NLD/AS include problems seeing the big picture, a dislike of novel situations, difficulty adjusting to change, difficulty with quick thinking and decision making, and taking much longer than others to learn a new job. Explaining these things to a potential employer results in automatic elimination from the candidate pool, while hiding them causes problems on the job and may lead to job loss. Despite their knowledge and skills, ASers/NLDers often feel misunderstood by most of the NT world and lack the support and validation that they need in order to be happy, productive, contributing members of society. Susan, who worked at the university library, explains:

> I was a rather slow worker, easily spending an hour checking several journals into the Kardex for instance, but this did not bother my boss much. She told me she appreciated my precision, carefulness, and honesty. One of my workmates however took notice of my literal mindedness and found me to be quite amusing, teasing whenever I misunderstood something he said. He told me on several occasions that talking to me was like engaging in a "Who's on First" routine, an allusion to the Abbott and Costello sketch in which an individual misconstrues the names of people as words. (Prince-Hughes 2002, p.99)

Most people associate intelligence with ability. If you can do X about as well or better than most folks, you ought to be able to do Y about as well as most folks too. But when your abilities are so uneven that is not the case. Because the disability is invisible, the individual can appear very capable, bright, and charming. Therefore, when he or she has difficulty with something, others find it hard to believe that there is a real problem. They blame the person for having an attitude, not being a team player, or not trying hard enough. Many seemingly minor deficits, taken together, add up to a major impairment. Disorganization, social difficulties, sequencing problems, difficulty with multi-tasking and trouble taking multiple directions create many workplace challenges. In time, it becomes apparent that the person takes things that are said literally, has difficulty with transitions and changes in routine, can talk a blue streak about his/her area of special interest and not take the cue to stop, can't recognize faces of people he/she has met, is awkward and clumsy, hyperactive and impulsive. He/she may seem rude, selfish, distant, withdrawn, formal, uptight, oppositional, or defiant.

While most NLDers/ASers are intelligent and literate, they may have considerable trouble with organization, math, spatial ability, memory, directions, concentration, speed, efficiency, balance, information processing, comprehension, social judgment, perception, quick thinking, and many other things. If that isn't a disability, what is? People who are in wheelchairs can't walk, but they have most of the other abilities they need to hold down a job. Many NLDers/ASers do not. In addition, they have a constant battle with folks who don't take the time to understand their disabilities, and instead assume a lot of negative things about them that aren't true.

It's difficult for this person to explain that while he/she doesn't mind cooperating with other employees, everything must be spelled out in black and white. How do you explain that you tend to offend people now and then, but it's really unintentional, or that you find it hard to express dissatisfaction without seeming either apathetic or menacing? While there are many things that NLDers/ASers can do very well, there are always some work duties they can't do as well as another employee. They're slower and may make more mistakes. While that may be true for the NT, for people with NLD or AS these things are greater both in number and severity, and so they stick out more in the workplace, appearing deficient.

In former times, ASers and NLDers were able to get and keep jobs in academia or in technical fields where interpersonal communication requirements were few. Research organizations harbored them, accepting and encouraging them as promising brilliant thinkers. During the dot-com boom of the 1990s, the image of the grungy, disheveled, gauche, socially inept tech guy was accepted. Many Aspies have great patience with endless repetition and tedium, along with mathematical skill and a good memory for words, numbers and sequences, which make them good programmers. Computers are logical and non-judgmental – a pleasant environment for introverts who find it easier to interact with machines than people. The current employment market, however, demands much more. Today, even information technology jobs want great social skills so that people can effectively communicate everything to team members and clients. Pure programming jobs have become few and hard to find.

In the workplace of the twenty-first century, the only constant is change. As organizations continue to trim costs and reduce overhead, lower salaried, newly trained young graduates replace older workers. The ability to continuously adapt has become crucial to career success. Companies want individuals who are able to take on many different roles. Workers are required to be multi-talented and perform a variety of tasks. Team skills and interpersonal

communication are important essential elements for virtually any professional position.

For example, when Tony began working in the word processing field, he
did much of the typing for various company departments. Then times
changed. People he had been doing transcription for began getting their
own computers. Reorganization took place, eliminating these jobs, and
everyone did their own typing.

Without an understanding of the disorder, employers see a person who is
extremely capable in some ways and extremely inept in others. They find it
puzzling that some smart employees have trouble neatly stapling a bunch of
papers together or mailing a letter. With proper support and accommodations, however, NLDers and ASers can be productive employees. The trick is
to get the employer to fully recognize the disability while still allowing the
individual to use the strengths and compensations he has developed. Unfortunately, the accommodation requested is often an environmental modifica-
tion (like a high degree of solitude or a very quiet environment) or a change
in procedure or routine. It's not as obvious as a person needing a wheelchair.
Many have found that when they ask for accommodations which require a
simple change in procedures without affecting work quality and don't cost a
cent, employers are resistant. The prevailing attitude is that we have done it a
certain way for many years and we don't see an obvious reason why we
should have to accommodate your needs. Jeff explains:

> I have a sister with severe Autism, who's unable to communicate with
> words. While her Autism is easily recognized by her behavior and
> language difficulties, mine is not. Even though my disability is
> invisible on the surface, its effects upon me are very real and signifi-
> cant. Because those of us who live with this syndrome appear physi-
> cally normal and intelligent, and AS and NLD are not yet accepted as
> valid disabilities, we are often perceived as being intentionally
> anti-social, eccentric or rude. Some of us may be so caught up in our
> own thoughts that we do not notice other people's reactions, while
> others, like me, will be extremely sensitive to how people view us.
>
> I have lived my life feeling like I am looking upon the world of
> normal people through a Plexiglas window. I can observe and imitate,
> but there is no door to enter the room, and the window is unbreakable.
> Now that I have my diagnosis, I am learning to accept myself for who I
> am. I no longer feel compelled to enter the room because I know that
> it is impossible. I simply want to live my life to its fullest potential
> without being persecuted for being different. It is very important for

our future that society learns to recognize and understand neurological disorders like AS and NLD. Many of us have experienced brutal mistreatment since our youth. We have been easy targets for bullies, subjects of teachers' anger, scapegoats, deprived of educational support, and have faced criticism and humiliation throughout our lives.

We need to increase public awareness of AS/NLD as a handicap in the work place. Most people diagnosed with AS/NLD are of normal to above average intelligence, and some are exceptionally gifted. If employers can learn to accept us and accommodate us, they will soon realize the benefits, such as honesty, integrity, and dependability. If employees will learn to tolerate the differences that exist between them and those with AS or NLD, they will find that we will contribute to the success of their company, and the future of their employment.

The elements of Asperger Syndrome or Non-Verbal Learning Disability will translate into the work environment in a variety of ways (Table 30.1).

Table 30.1 NLD/AS characteristics on the job

This NLD/AS characteristic	Is considered a workplace strength when	But could be considered a weakness when
Being intelligent	• the job requires education beyond a high school diploma • the job requires professional certifications • the job requires knowledge of new or novel information • the job changes or grows due to changes in technology, the business environment, or the regulatory environment	• attitude of superiority • the person becomes impatient when they "don't get it" the first time around
Paying attention to detail	• the job needs to be performed in a methodical, systematic, and thorough way • details are needed for problem solving or analysis work • the work requires following processes or procedures • the nature of the work is tactical rather than strategic, that is, it involves completing steps that lead to completion of a larger portion of the work, or completing tasks that contribute to reaching an objective	• a worker gets caught up in "analysis paralysis" • a worker doesn't or isn't able to step back from the work to evaluate the "big picture" • the nature of the work is strategic rather than tactical, that is, it involves setting goals and objectives and then identifying the steps that need to be taken and the resources needed to reach them

Showing enthusiasm for a topic of interest; having an intense, narrow interest	• the work is in a specialized field • the work requires the ability to work on one thing for a long time or to maintain focus for a long time • the worker needs to become immersed in problem solving	• the worker is assigned tasks outside his or her area of specialty, as frequently occurs with downsizing • a one-track mind or tunnel vision • the worker needs to pull up from the details to contribute to other discussions in the workplace
Persevering	• the work requires accuracy • getting the information, resources, and results needed to complete the work requires tenacity • several iterations of an idea or project must be discussed before a final outcome is achieved	• inability to "shift gears" or "let go" of something and move on to the next step • co-workers have a low tolerance for ambiguity or are impatient waiting for decisions to be made • others see the worker as stubborn or obstinate
Having an excellent verbal memory	• the worker needs to recall details of previous meetings or conversations • the work requires accurate meeting notes and minutes	• others perceive that they are being corrected and/or criticized for their recall of conversations or events • arguing about details that aren't important to the overall work
Being articulate	• the worker needs to make oral presentations • the worker needs to communicate clearly and in writing • the worker needs to present him or herself well to others	• others perceive that a worker is "an intellectual" or "above us" and "should be taken down a peg or two" • inability to relate to the "average" person • the worker can't initiate or participate in the "small talk" needed to build rapport with others

Being hyperlexic (Def: the combination of precocious reading, spelling, and vocabulary skills, fascination with letters, numbers, or patterns, and significant problems with learning, interpersonal communication, and social skills)	• the work requires reading and comprehending difficult technical material • the work requires spelling and grammatical accuracy • the work has a specialized vocabulary, such as in computer science, medicine, or law • the work requires using a specific syntax, such as computer programming	• others perceive that the worker is "talking over their heads" • perfectionism – overly concerned about "doing things right" • "nitpicking" instead of focusing on the bigger picture
Being honest and straightforward	• the work requires truthfulness • a lack of flowery language, euphemisms, or "weasel words" would aid clarity in communication • others perceive the worker to be guileless and to be communicating without a hidden agenda	• coming across as blunt or even rude • a worker says things that are considered "politically incorrect" • can't play the corporate political game • the worker isn't able to persuade others to a course of action using emotional proofs (expecting others to buy in to their ideas based on the facts)

Being a hard worker	• the worker is seen as being loyal to their employer • the worker puts in extra effort to do a good job • the worker is seen as "going above and beyond"	• others perceive that the worker could be "working smarter, not harder" • others feel that the worker is trying to "show them up" or get in good with the boss • motives are misunderstood
A "down-to-business" attitude – i.e., being task oriented, sticking to the agenda or project at hand	• the work requires a set schedule or must follow a specific routine • the work must be performed on a timeline or has specific target dates that must be met • the work requires agendas, timelines, and project plans • others perceive the worker to be "down to earth" and "task oriented"	• the worker is inflexible or impersonal • inability to meet the emotional needs of co-workers • others feel that the worker needs to be more "people oriented"
Being friendly and helpful	• the work allows someone to repeat interesting information such as a museum docent or an information booth worker • the work allows experienced workers to help those new to the job or offers formal mentoring programs • the work allows someone to share his or her expertise in a particular area or to help others find specialized information, such as being a library assistant	• others don't need or want help • the "help" given is too factual or pedantic, and others feel that their emotional needs are overlooked • friendliness is misinterpreted by co-workers

Following official standards and procedures	• the work requires following specific rules or rubrics, such as machine maintenance or technical writing • the work is in a regulated industry such as banking, pharmaceuticals, or energy • the work requires following blueprints or using templates • all of the steps in a procedure must be followed to produce a quality product or service	• inflexible adherence to rules or routines • there's a discrepancy between official rules and unofficial practice, for example, start time is 8am, yet most employees show up between 8.15 and 8.30am (in the school environment, this is called the "hidden curriculum") • the worker doesn't know when it's OK to break the rules, or when one rule takes precedence over another
Approaching problems thoughtfully rather than making snap decisions	• reflecting on the details of a problem will result in a higher quality decision • failure to identify all aspects of a problem could cause safety or other concerns • the methods used to solve a particular problem follow a specific rubric	• working with others who have a low tolerance for ambiguity • co-workers prefer to "shoot from the hip" • decisions are needed quickly or the big picture is needed

Source: Charlene A. Derby

31 Major Hurdles
Sociability and Communication

Sociability

In the workplace, office politics and teamwork are paramount. Social relationships with colleagues and bosses are often the biggest area of struggle for the ASer/NLDer. Although these employees may be very qualified and perform exceptionally well, those they work with may not tolerate their idiosyncrasies and anti-social behavior. It's usually social and behavioral issues, rather than lack of technical skills, that derail careers.

NLDers and Aspies who are functioning in the work world invariably hit a glass ceiling, whatever their ability. Although they try hard to be kind, generous, and interesting, it's never enough because they miss most of the social script. While the employee with NLD or AS may have good relationships with co-workers, he/she often doesn't develop the same social networks. We live in a society where success is not based on merit, skill or dedication, but on sociability. Most employers explain that social skills are vital for good work performance. As one climbs up the career ladder, social rules become ever more subtle. Those who are unaware of these subtleties won't be promoted, no matter how good, because they're regarded as not sound, too weird, not one of the club. Despite excellent skills and experience, NLDers and ASers often find themselves passed over for promotion in favor of a competitor with better social awareness, who had got in with the managers.

The difference in thinking between the ASer/NLDer and the NT is another major problem. The Aspie sees the NT as someone who behaves illogically, doesn't say what they mean, and isn't attuned to details. In turn, NTs view ASers/NLDers as odd and not fitting into the corporate organization. They tend to take things at face value, have difficulty meeting peers on an equal level, and may see others in black and white terms. They're unable to read non-verbal cues and have little social intuition. Their concrete, rigid thinking makes it hard to imagine what others think or feel, see another's viewpoint, or respond to colleagues' thoughts and feelings, alienating co-workers. They're simply unaware of standard customs and the social script.

NTs often withhold their feelings and opinions, preferring meaningless, positive small talk instead. While NTs may consider this polite, proper, and considerate, the ASer/NLDer sees it as manipulative, as talking about others behind their backs. If an Aspie has something to say, he will often do so, without considering the person's feelings, but giving him/her an opportunity for counter-argument. The NT, however, regards this as blunt, disrespectful, or arrogant.

Their extremes of behavior may antagonize colleagues and limit their ability to work with them. Their failure to maintain constant eye contact is not deliberate, it's essential. They're unable to listen, look, and concentrate; they need to look away. Looking someone in the eyes is a major effort – too much coming in. In the USA, many people intuitively distrust someone who can't look at them directly. Lack of eye contact is perceived as boredom, inattentiveness, or rudeness, and can cause offense, aggression, and the appearance of dishonesty. In fact, ASers/NLDers often are very honest, and may have great difficulty lying. Darius explains:

> Social communications are difficult for us because they often have as priority not to explain something but "bonding" between conversational partners or taking the emotional temperature of an interaction. You have to be able to use all your senses simultaneously in order to "see" the web of interaction that together makes up a certain pattern of social behavior that has a specific meaning. If you cannot do that you either miss vital information or you take things literally. This is also the reason many of us have difficulty lying. Social skills are at the basis of good lying skills. You need to be able to weave these webs yourself. (Prince-Hughes 2002, p.37)

This inability to identify and follow social protocol causes workplace problems for the ASer/NLDer, whose behavior is strange to the NT and who often seems narcissistic or self-involved. Office politics, social subtleties, and the use of sarcasm by co-workers may be confusing to him. His get-down-to-business attitude, his frankness and his social insensitivity may seem rude and alienate others. Simple activities, like sharing a stapler among two or three co-workers, hold potential for difficulties if the stapler is not returned to its exact location each time it's used.

Because of the neurological nature of these disorders, the degree and type of impairment varies greatly. While some NLDers/ASers are successful in their careers, possess unique qualities and skills that are valued in the workplace, and are very professional and functional, others are more limited in their adaptability or their ability to interact with people. Many have difficulty looking at people's faces or understanding humor and figurative speech. They may need to work alone and be self-isolating during break times, or may engage in self-stimulatory behavior, such as hand flapping or rocking, to cope with environmental anxiety. These differences may lead not only to misinterpretation of their intentions and abilities, but also to many forms of abuse and workplace bullying.

NLDers and ASers may also have trouble managing their emotions. Temper and anger can cause problems at work. They're predisposed to mood swings, and often hold things in until they explode. Misunderstandings with colleagues are common, and they tend to have problems solving interpersonal conflicts.

Another area of difficulty that these issues create is with interpersonal boundaries. Setting boundaries is a matter of not allowing people to enter your space, and conversely, not entering others' space. It requires continual awareness of what is appropriate for you and what you want, as well as understanding others' expectations, and respecting their wishes. Due to the inability to perceive and understand non-verbal cues, combined with their literal mindset, NLDers/ASers often fail to understand what their boss's or colleague's expectations and desires are. If they're around people for any length of time, they will slip up and cross an invisible (to them) boundary, causing offense. They'll probably never know what it was that they did or said that turned the other person off. While friends may in time come to understand that this behavior isn't intentional, and will come to accept this person, this rarely happens at work.

Such social deficits can make it difficult to establish and maintain casual workplace relationships, move comfortably in social settings and work cooperatively in a professional environment. Misinterpretations and misunderstandings can lead to conflicts with co-workers. This inability to fit in creates feelings of stress and isolation, undermining confidence and resulting in poor self-esteem. The shaky hold that the individual has formed in the social setting of the work environment comes loose.

Most NLDers/ASers work well independently, but if they need to work with people they may have problems getting along. They attempt to compensate for their social ineptness with intellectual ability. In time, they may learn how to interact with others, but it takes great effort and never comes naturally. Honesty, integrity, kindness, high professional standards and strong value of competence are the characteristics of folks that NLDers and ASers manage best with, but in our dog-eat-dog world these qualities are rare.

Techniques for functioning in the social world

How much improvement in learning social skills is possible, since an Aspie's brain is wired differently than an NT's brain? On a social skills continuum, most ASers/NLDers are at about a 30, while most NTs are 90 to 100. With lots of work and training, an Aspie or NLDer might reach a 60 or 70.

Will an ASer or NLDer ever be Mr Mixer or Miss Popularity, the life of the party? Ah, no. Would he or she even want to be that? No! He or she would probably be uncomfortable just going to the party. When I was younger, I would sit on the periphery, not knowing how to approach anyone. I was seen as a wallflower. But there is hope. NLDers/ASers can build some skills to use at work and interact with colleagues, though it's often exhausting work. Things learned in therapy are hard to apply in the real workaday world. Because the social problems have different causes in NLD/AS than they do in shyness, withdrawal disorders, or ADHD (Attention Deficit Hyperactivity Disorder), the interventions need to be different. For instance, scripting and rehearsal of social situations and rote, verbal teaching of manners can help an NLDer, but might not particularly help an ADHDer.

While relationships with NTs will probably continue to be exhausting and frustrating for the average NLDer/ASer, it's important not to give up, as you can improve with practice. Here are some tips:

1. Smile, and try to maintain a positive outlook. People are attracted to those who exude happiness, who seem relaxed rather than uptight, and who have a sense of self.

2. Before going out to places where you'll have to interact with others, take a few minutes to visualize yourself being in their company. List what makes you a good friend. Imagine a beautiful bubble in the room and everyone in it, including you, is happy and relaxed. Picture the others there as happy and open to you.

3. Some people simply won't like you. That's OK. But sometimes you'll meet someone who wants to talk to you. Be pleasant, but try not to overwhelm him or her. Let the other person guide the conversation. Focus on the other person, not yourself.

4. Try to be nice to people whether you like them or not.

5. Ask family and friends to point out inappropriate social conduct and discuss ways to effect change.

6. At professional conferences, avoid milling around before meetings. Visit new venues early to become familiar with the set-up. Memorize a script to use when introducing yourself, but remember to adapt it to each situation.

7. Try to notice what is going on with others. What are they working on? Pick up on a comment they made. Follow up with brief, positive comments about them and their experiences. If they answer and walk away, keep a smile on your face. Save face for others who may be watching.

8. To cultivate friendships at work, begin by smiling and saying hello. Look for clues (like pictures) on the person's desk or cube that indicate their interests, and ask questions about them. Talk about work issues that you share such as "Do you have any of those green forms?" Bring in some cookies or flowers for everyone to share. Give the person a small gift – a flower from your garden, a cookie or fruit for their lunch, a friendship card.

9. Try to avoid environments that make you anxious, and remind yourself that every situation is new.

10. Be aware of the personal space of others and learn not to invade it.

Communication

Communication issues include problems in assessing one's impact on others, trouble understanding body language, difficulty with interpreting facial expressions and/or tone of voice, and problems picking up social cues and acting accordingly. The part of the brain responsible for performing simple, subconscious tasks and interpreting social signals, feelings, and motives doesn't work properly. Thus, the NLDer/ASer must consciously think through behaviors that are effortless to the NT. This makes it very difficult for the person to consider the content of a social interaction, such as a conversation, while at the same time reading the countless verbal and non-verbal cues that occur with it. The conscious part of his brain is unable to handle the overload.

This is why NTs use more body language and have greater variation in tone of expression. The exact same words may have several different meanings, depending on the tone and the emphasis given to individual words. ASers/NLDers may miss these nuances during conversations with NTs because their communication style relies heavily on words. Additionally, their inability to separate essentials from details makes it harder to select and pay attention to the important points of a conversation. They may ramble, providing myriad details without making clear points. Since words are their only method of communication, they're much more emotionally loaded than for NTs, making it more difficult to accept criticism without getting upset. Often a person with AS/NLD will keep speaking regardless of the listener's interest, because they're unaware when their incessant talking becomes annoying and can't read the signs of impatience on the listener's face. This can cause undue anxiety. Susan explains:

> The constant mental perspective-shifting that is required in most social contexts is particularly exhausting to me. I also develop a great deal of anxiety when I interact with others, always wondering if I forgot to say or do something or wondering if the other person thinks I'm weird, insensitive, egocentric or ignorant. (Prince-Hughes 2002, p.104)

Due to their literal thinking and inability to understand non-verbal communication, things that seem obvious to most people are overlooked. They have a hard time reading the other person's emotions, as opposed to, or in addition to, what they say. Because all cues are taken from verbal communication, where words convey specific meanings, things that are implied or generally understood rather than directly stated will be misinterpreted. They can't see or visually process what others are doing in terms of maintaining social space, loudness of tone, body language, or facial expressions. They may not notice or may misinterpret the reactions of others, and may be unable to tell from their co-worker's tone or body language whether they're serious or joking. They can't tell when others are flirting, when they're upset, or when they're angry. They don't recognize the more subtle tones and gestures – such as those that might warn them someone is getting mad. They can't tell where the "line" is until they have crossed it, and they often don't learn for next time; it always remains invisible. Sarcasm flies right over their heads. Lies, nuances, or figurative speech elude them. Even a smile can be manipulative or genuine; the NLDer/ASer can't always tell the difference. Since at least 60 percent and sometimes as much as 90 percent of communication is made in these three non-verbal ways (tone of voice, facial expressions and gestures), imagine what it is like to be oblivious to most of it. It's like reading a newspaper and only understanding every fourth word. You get a general idea of what's being said, but you miss the specifics.

For example, personal space can be a problem. Susan writes: "There was the time I stood right up against a stranger at a bus stop in a moment of obliviousness, making him think I was flirting with him when in fact I was hardly aware he was there" (Prince-Hughes 2002, p.195). When I was waiting for a bus in an unfamiliar city, I stared too hard at the woman approaching, because I'd been waiting quite a while, was feeling anxious, and was happy to finally have someone to ask about destinations and fares. She was very hostile. Later, someone explained that she probably thought I was coming on to her.

NLDers/ASers also make mistakes in the signals they send, and sometimes get surprising results. People wonder why they're angry, thinking the person is snapping at them, when in fact that is the furthest from the truth. Since they don't perceive most body language, facial expression, and tone of voice, they're unsure how to use any of it. Their voice may not convey their true feelings, so they appear aggressive or callous when they may actually be very compassionate and sensitive. For example, I'm not always aware of the loudness and tone of my voice, which can come across as yelling or as anger.

Non-compliant behavior and inappropriate verbal responses may be due to misunderstandings. When implications aren't understood, others' expectations become a mystery, and the resulting ambiguity can be scary. The person may seem argumentative because they've misinterpreted something in the conversation. The solution is not to become angry or annoyed, but to reword your request and break complex points into smaller pieces.

Many of my problems at work are with eye contact and reading social cues. It often seems that everyone has the rulebook for this game except me. In performance reviews, my supervisor noticed that I have trouble joining conversations, and tend to dominate them once I get in. I interrupt because I have just thought of something that seems extremely relevant and important. I talk endlessly about things that interest me, my voice is loud, and I may move my hands while speaking. I have a tendency to think out loud, and may say "uhhuh" while somebody else is talking.

NLDers/ASers may have an aversion to small talk and often don't socialize around the water cooler. For example, Tony finds acknowledging, cheerily greeting and saying goodbye to people difficult. It doesn't come naturally. "I normally only say hi when someone speaks to me first," he explains, "but after that I have a hard time thinking of something else to say, since I find small talk difficult, to say the least. The forced chatting seems so unnatural and unnecessary to me. I'm beginning to see how others would consider this rude behavior... Some workplaces no doubt tolerate this sort of thing better than others."

Techniques for effective communication

1. Try to communicate with people via methods that use less body language, such as email or telephone.

2. Tell people that you have difficulty with non-verbal communication. Most people won't get it, but some will.

3. Let them know they must verbalize everything, including their feelings, you just don't "get" it otherwise. This works with people who understand you and know you well.

4. Ask what's going on. This works better with people you know well. For example, you could ask "Do you think I'm angry?" If the reply is yes, answer "I'm not angry at all, but what made you think I was?"

5.   Realize that you're not good at anticipating another's feelings. That way, you can remind yourself to ask follow-up questions in a conversation and to respond with empathy.

6.   Explain that your face doesn't always show your true feelings. For example, say, "I have a tendency to look angry when I am not, so I appreciate you seeking clarification."

7.   Know when it is better to be less candid and honest. In social or employment situations, it's often better to dodge questions about such hot button topics as religion and politics in order to avoid conflict. It's usually best to avoid telling your boss exactly what you think of him or her; otherwise you may expect to suffer the consequences.

8.   Watch and listen to people. For example, if you trust person A but then see that she hangs around with person B, who is definitely a jerk, you may reconsider your decision about putting too much trust in person A. Why is she hanging around with such an idiot? Remember that people you work with often have a hidden agenda. So if you don't know their motives and don't understand their relationships, be cautious.

9.   Small talk is not about content. It's about sharing a smile and a quick laugh. Listen to others' small talk and try to figure out what's appropriate. Stay informed about news and weather, so you can comment on these when they come up. Learn to talk about others' interests and keep quiet about yours.

10.   If everyone is laughing, laugh with them, even if you didn't understand the joke.

Learn about body language

Body language and communication can be improved, though with great effort. NTs learn non-verbal communication as children and teens by instinct or absorption. NLDers/ASers must learn this by making a conscious study of it over many years. Some have used acting classes to improve social skills. Others have made a careful study of good actors in movies, paying close attention to their use of body language. Practicing in front of a full-length mirror is another strategy. It's like learning a foreign language. It's difficult, but worth it.

Some people have learned to recognize certain behaviors and non-verbal signals by thinking about them, organizing them into patterns, and filing them for future recall. For example, they aren't automatically aware that a particular co-worker is upset when she comes stalking into the office after lunch. It never becomes an automatic, subconscious process like it is with NTs; instead, it's a conscious effort. The AS/NLD individual must pay close attention to the co-worker's expression, posture, tone of voice and words, then run them through his/her matrix of patterns and guess what's happening. Years of practice can streamline this process and make it faster and more accurate, but it remains a procedure which must be initiated each time by consciously deciding to find out what's going on with the co-worker.

Due to brain wiring, communication problems will persist, but they can improve with the right training. By becoming aware of problem behaviors it's possible to come up with more appropriate alternatives. Here are some additional tips.

Practice body language

1. Get help in breaking down body language like facial expressions and gestures. Enlist your family or close friends to get a bunch of pictures from magazines having a range of facial expressions with body language (e.g. happy, disappointed, fearful, joyful, annoyed, angry, depressed). Then see if you can identify the still life. *The Artist's Complete Guide to Facial Expression* by Gary Faigin (1990) is an excellent book resource for this.

2. Next try the same idea with a video. Turn off the sound and watch the body language. Try to identify different emotions.

3. Try your own body language. Make a face and walk happily, fearfully, angrily.

4. Use your voice intonations for different emotions. Learn how to communicate subtle meanings through changes in tone of voice and facial muscles. Ask a friend what emotion he thinks you are trying to communicate by using the same sentence and repeating it with different emotions.

5. Watch actors in movies exchange meaningful glances. Notice how they use their eyes. Try to interpret from the context of the situation the meaning of those glances.

6. Classes in interpersonal communication sometimes teach body language.

7. Acting lessons often teach voice modulation and facial expressions.

Practice conversational skills

1. Listen carefully.

2. Learn active listening skills. This will help you with the subtleties of interpersonal communication.

3. Keep tabs on conversations, making sure not to monopolize the discussion.

4. If you've been speaking for a few minutes, it's probably time to stop and give someone else a turn to talk.

5. If the other person doesn't make any comments pertaining to what you're saying, or if he changes the subject, that usually means that he/she is either bored or uncomfortable with the subject. This is a clue to change the subject and move on.

6. A look to the side may also indicate disinterest, and folded arms may indicate boredom.

7. When responding, relate the reply to what the other person said. To change the subject, say something like "What you said reminded me of…"

8. Practice making eye contact during conversations.

9. When the other person is talking, look interested. Look at them, but don't stare. Make short comments, say, "umm, aha," and nod once in a while.

10. When with a group, try to look at each person who's speaking. Also try to look around and notice others' reactions. Note facial expressions, hands, and the rest of their body. Is he or she

showing interest by nodding his head, looking at you, and responding to what you say? Doing this will help you to be aware of how people respond to your reactions.

11. Think twice before speaking to avoid inappropriate comments.

12. Learn to decipher the meanings of idioms and figurative speech through rote memory and context. Some have found keeping a notebook of common idioms helpful.

Learning new tasks

One area where communication is paramount on the job is in learning new tasks. NLDers/ASers may need a more direct approach and more feedback than other employees. They need specificity and concreteness. When supervisors conduct performance reviews, they often use soft phrases that aren't explicit. These can easily be missed, and the ASer/NLDer may not understand the true meaning of the criticism or commendation. Gabrielle describes her problems with job training:

> On the job training was a nightmare because wherever I worked, they didn't really have on the job training. It was more like, "Well, hi, it's your first day, sorry no one has the time to train you. You'll have to learn on your own. Have a good time, bye." Or, on the other extreme, there were several bosses explaining how to do something, and each had a different way the task should be done. Between that and my problems learning amidst noise and chaos, as well as social problems, I didn't get far.

Like Gabrielle, Tony had problems with supervisors who were in a hurry and gave rapid-fire instructions. They would rush through the explanation and leave out steps that seemed obvious to them or that they thought he should already know. In their rush and impatience, they wouldn't give him time to write down these steps.

Multi-step directions are a major problem area because they require efficient speed and recall for the trainee to retain all the parts. If a person's speed of processing information is slow, as is often the case with both AS and NLD, they could still be processing step one, while steps two, three and four are being stated. Many supervisors speak very quickly, and the employee who misses parts of what was said will be accused of not carrying out the instructions. This is why written instructions are so important for the NLDer/ASer.

Inefficient working memory and difficulty visualizing exacerbate the problem with retaining information for the NLDer. When hearing instructions, most people subconsciously form mental images of what they're going to do. These little mental pictures back up the verbal instructions, enabling them to remember what to do, and in what order. Most NLDers, however, rely on just the verbal input, without any mental imagery to back it up. They must memorize the instructions word for word. Unless they have an excellent short-term memory, they're bound to forget some of the instructions. A written structured or itemized list that the trainee can refer to is the best way to accommodate this.

Clear, concise instructions given in an environment with minimal distractions to reduce sensory overload are essential. Casual verbal directions may be misunderstood. They need time to process new information, think things through, put their thoughts in order, and take notes. Many NLDers/ASers are slow learners, and need to proceed very carefully in order to understand every single thing about what they're doing, from various angles. They can't do it until they can make it their own. It isn't a bad attitude; it's an inability. They simply must completely understand something, or they won't understand it at all. This means that in a job where each new task is a learning experience and employees are expected to shoot from the hip, the NLDer or ASer would be substandard. But where things are complex, with variety but also consistency, once mastered, many ASers/NLDers become fast and intuitive. If given time to learn, they can do a great job and employers tend to appreciate them. Darius explains:

> The first few weeks of a new job I have to put so much energy into processing all the new information that it takes an enormous effort to process enough information to know how to do the task one is expected to do. I am generally quicker than others catching up with all sorts of knowledge and skills that require analytical understanding but I need a much longer time to get used to different telephones or copiers or to know where to find what. During the first few weeks I simply don't process my environment beyond the most superficial visual level. Someone who tries to explain something to me in a new environment should take his time, because I can't filter out the relevant from the nonrelevant sensory stimuli when there is too much new visual stuff going on. (Prince-Hughes 2002, pp.33–34)

When training the AS or NLD individual, it's essential to consider the person's learning style. Gross motor deficits mean that these employees will need much practice before they acquire certain skills.

Many Aspies are visual learners but poor on listening skills, and therefore must learn through observation. They like diagrams and visual aids. They have difficulty remembering what was said unless it's repeated several times. They're spatial learners – taking in the scene in its entirety – and cannot learn in a sequential manner.

On the other hand, most NLDers learn through words. These can be verbal or written (if they're verbal, they may need to write them down). Many are auditory learners, and, due to visual processing issues and poor visual memory, simply can't learn by watching. They have difficulty with visual motor tasks. Thus mechanical tasks generally learned by observation – like operating certain types of equipment or machinery – can take a long time to master.

Everything must be explained rather than demonstrated, and NLDers may not understand a concept until it's explained verbally. It's important to give verbal or verbal/written explanations in a linear fashion, and allow the trainee to take copious notes on each of the steps. They often learn sequentially and need several examples in order to understand the concept. Because they learn through verbal mediation, they ask many questions, which can aggravate an impatient supervisor. To ensure understanding, it's important to allow the person to verbalize what he/she is expected to do.

Instructions for both NLDers and ASers should be concrete rather than abstract, without metaphors or multiple meanings. If abstract concepts must be used, they should be explained in words and broken down into their component parts.

The supervisor working with the AS/NLD employee should understand that things that seem simple or uncomplicated to others may not be perceived as such. The supervisor should recognize and accept this individual's social and sensory limitations, and provide clear structure and explanations about work duties and workplace rules. This employee may require more consistent feedback than others, so meeting regularly will help with continual skill building and correcting mistakes. While it may take longer to train an NLD/AS employee, when properly trained, he/she becomes a valuable employee.

32 More Hurdles

While NLDers/ASers have many intellectual strengths, some cognitive processing problems do exist. These include sensory processing difficulties, problems doing several things at once, resistance to change, a slower mental processing speed, a literal mindset, and the inability to see the forest for the trees.

Sensory processing

Since deficits associated with AS/NLD involve neurological processing, it seems logical that sensory processing could be affected as well. Deficits in sensory integration, often a part of NLD/AS, mean that the brain's ability to absorb, interpret, or process information received through the senses is limited. People with deficits in sensory information processing can't use information obtained through the five senses efficiently to learn, solve problems, or carry out work responsibilities. They might be unusually sensitive or over-responsive to certain kinds of sensory experiences, such as touch, pain, temperature, pressure, or where the body is in space. This difficulty results in frequent frustration, which can lead to work failure.

Noisy and crowded settings or fast-paced environments aggravate sensory perceptual issues, causing sensory overload. Too many sights, sounds and smells can overwhelm the person, making them feel anxious. Because of their heightened senses, these people are vulnerable to sensory overload, even in situations that wouldn't bother (or might even entertain) a normal person. Too much emotional or social stimulation compound the problem, so this individual requires extra time to destress away from the stimulation of social interaction. Problems with concentration, feelings of confusion or exhaustion that may show on the person's face, and even loss of emotional control leading to outbursts or emotional shutdown may result. Over- or under-sensitivity to sensory stimuli can make working in some environments, such as an open-plan office setting, very difficult. Many find it hard to work or maintain a conversation in a noisy environment. Screens that minimize distractions may help with visual overload. Auditory overload can be eased with earplugs, white noise, or soft background music.

Auditory issues

The person with an auditory sensory deficit may have trouble following a discussion if people speak too fast or if there are too many distractions. For example, an instructor may have a hard time processing student comments while teaching a large class, especially if students are noisy or rude. Listening to numerous questions asked by several students while others are talking in the background becomes a challenge due to difficulty with auditory figure–ground discrimination. Inability to hear and comprehend simultaneously means that this instructor may need a question repeated so that he/she can listen the first time, and understand the second time.

One coping strategy is to repeat back what you think you heard and ask for clarification. Write down what was said, to jog your memory, in case the subject comes up again.

If noisy co-workers keep you from being able to focus, filter them out with soothing music or white noise. If possible, wear headphones, and inform colleagues you only wear your headphones during "concentration time".

Visual perception

Visual perception, another sensory deficit, creates problems in locating items on a crowded desk. At the computer terminal, it delays the location of relevant items amongst a screen full of information. It interferes with the ability to follow text, so the individual may lose their place within edited text, or enter a phrase twice. It may make it difficult to see an object if it's in an unexpected position or at an unusual angle. Once the information is assimilated and interpreted, this individual can process it and come up with a valid conclusion.

For example, this employee will look for something and then someone else will find it, out in plain view, but in amongst many other items. Her brain can't pick out the shape of the cell phone or keys or stapler from other objects on a crowded desk. None of the other objects has the same shape as the cell phone, but because there are so many of them and because they fill her whole visual field, she can't find the one thing she needs. As a result, she may get strange looks (which she may not notice) from colleagues who don't understand this difficulty in locating objects that are "right there", or her need to ask for supplies that are out in plain view.

Other visual processing issues include difficulty with visual memory and facial recognition. These people get lost easily, because they don't remember what they've seen. They have trouble locating their car in the parking lot or finding their way out of a store or office. They may appear confused and lost, and some have even been asked if they need help or if they can see. Visual memory deficits contribute to this problem, making it difficult to remember or describe places they've been. It helps to get good directions, and write them down, large enough so you can read them without taking your eyes off the road. Verbally labeling where you put things will help you find them later, and an automatic car starter can help to locate the car. By hearing the car start you rely on your hearing rather than your sight.

When navigating around the building, look for landmarks or clues that can help you. For example, if all the cubicles look alike, count them. Find identifying features like numbers or letters. Know what the cubicle right before yours looks like. You can personalize your cube or office with pictures or signs that can help you identify it.

While many NLDers/ASers have prodigious memories, they may have problems with recognizing faces, and don't know people they have seen five, ten, or sometimes twenty or more times. This failure to recognize people who recognize you contributes to the social difficulties of NLDers/ASers.

For example, someone might walk right past a colleague, not noticing them and failing to greet them. Unfortunately, this is viewed as rude, insulting, a lack of interest, or worse – disregard. When NLDers/ASers do recognize others, it's often too late to respond. Many NLDers/ASers identify people by their voices. Others don't directly identify faces so much as they differentiate them within a context.

While most visual patterns are perceived on the left side of the brain, a small part of the brain in the right temporal lobe is dedicated to recognizing faces. Deficits in this area are often part of the NLD/AS neurological glitch. Most people look at someone, ascertain whether the person is an acquaintance or a stranger, and then look away, all in less than a second. Many individuals with AS or NLD need several seconds to tell if someone is a stranger or friend. This can be interpreted as staring, and can be perceived as lewd, shameless 'sizing up'. Darius explains:

> It took me over a year before I could differentiate between the three secretaries of the manager of our department. They were all blond, thirty-ish and about 1.70 meters tall.
>
> I explained my recognition problem to my co-workers, but people simply don't understand until I actually walk by them on the street without recognizing them. My colleague told me that she heard how people thought I was arrogant because I didn't greet them in the street. She had to explain to them all over again that I didn't recognize them and therefore probably didn't realize they were someone I was supposed to know. (Prince-Hughes 2002, p.33)

Here are some things you can do that will help you to recognize and learn your co-workers:

1. If there's a company directory, study it. Look for pictures with names.

2. When possible, communicate by email or phone.

3. Rather then trying to recognize someone in person, call him or her and ask for them to find you.

4. When meeting a colleague, arrive very early, so that they won't be there yet. This places the burden of recognition on the other person.

5. Look into people's offices while walking past on your way to the bathroom, to get coffee, or whatever. Note the nameplate on the door, and then the face (while trying not to be obvious).

6. Watch employees as they pick up their mail, and match the face with the name on the mail slot.

7. Wait for the person to recognize you first. Try to find out who they are by introducing various topics.

8. Learn to recognize people by the topics they talk about.

9. Learn to recognize people by the environment where you're most likely to run into them.

Supervisors and co-workers can help in various ways:

1.   When approaching this person, especially in an environment you usually don't see them in, let them know who you are and where you've met.

2.   Provide new information in a quiet, distraction-free environment.

3.   Speak slowly when providing new information.

4.   Ask the employee to repeat the instructions back, to clarify understanding.

5.   Give directions both orally and in writing, so the employee can refer to them.

6.   Simplify complicated directions and break them down into steps.

Need for structure, adherence to routine and resistance to change

Sensory issues contribute to the problems of NLDers/ASers with changes in routine. The amount of distracting sensory input they can tune out is limited. Just as a blind person would not want the furniture moved, the person with sensory processing difficulties resists change in sensory stimuli.

Another reason for this person's trouble handling novel situations or dealing with new material is poor visual memory. When people can't remember places, directions, or colleagues, they feel anxious. Since even minor changes can throw them off and slow them down, they resist them. In their description of NLD, Myklebust (1975) noted the visual memory deficit, and described the anxiety created by a constantly changing environment.

This resistance to change in work routine, or requests to shift work priority, isn't interpersonally motivated. Rather, the NLDer/ASer may confront individuals making such requests, questioning their reasoning, in order to concretely understand the reason behind the requested change. If he/she remains confused as to the logic behind the change, he/she may have difficulty complying on the basis that it is not a proper request or that such a change is not following an established procedure.

Unfortunately, most people won't understand this rigid adherence to sequence, schedule and procedure, and may even view it as obsessive. Worse, co-workers may interpret the person's need for structure, routine and sameness as insubordination and a challenge to authority. For this reason, the NLDer/ASer is best working in a structured setting with a regular routine of tasks and duties. Advance warning of changes in procedure or routine will help this individual immensely with adjusting to new situations. Work patterns and routines offer constancy amidst the unpredictable work world. He or she is often most comfortable working as a small part of a larger process rather than at the management level, which often requires dealing with the big picture.

Details and gestalt

Another issue for many AS/NLD individuals is a limited ability to generalize. Because of their brain wiring, NLDers/ASers don't think globally. They're so attuned to the details that they miss the whole picture or gestalt. It can be hard to make sense of what you're looking at when you can't see the whole scene. Without understanding the big picture, it's tough to figure out cause and effect, guess what might happen next, draw conclusions, set goals or devise a strategy. This problem leads to difficulty setting priorities, separating the main idea from details, and developing outlines.

This difficulty in seeing the whole picture can lead the NLDer/ASer to become easily overwhelmed by large or complex tasks. Often, the person doesn't know where to begin a project unless they have been given detailed, step-by-step instructions. They have a hard time figuring out these steps themselves, and may need help getting started. The frustrated supervisor might complain "I can't hold your hand all the time, I have other things to do" and job loss may be the unfortunate outcome.

When diagnosing patients in his hospital speech pathology practicum, processing multiple pieces of information was a problem for Al. His supervisor complained that he saw all the details, but couldn't get the big picture.

Literal mindset

NLDers/ASers tend to be very literal in speech and understanding. They often overlook things that seem obvious to others, and may not understand common jokes or idioms. Black and white thinking causes difficulty finding the variations or shades in meaning. This can bring about misunderstandings, contribute to gullibility, and lead co-workers to make them ideal targets for teasing. For example, when Sandy's law partner asked about her wedding plans, she took her literally, not realizing she was just asking to be polite, and gave her a complete rundown.

Speech therapy can help with literal language. Those working with this individual should be familiar with his/her communication style, and communicate accordingly. They should explain any abstract concepts, metaphors, multiple meanings, or anything else that might be misinterpreted. Instructions should be concrete rather than abstract.

Multi-tasking

Individuals with AS and NLD often have significant difficulty with simultaneous processing or multi-tasking. Most people can do many things at once. They'll carry on a conversation, continually paying attention to the mental state of the person they're speaking with, all while cooking, driving, or operating machinery – and they do this with little conscious effort. For the individual with AS or NLD, however, understanding what the other person is saying requires total concentration. Paying attention to several things at once is overwhelming. They need to focus on one thing at a time, and find it hard to rapidly change from one task to another. Their brain can't process all of the incoming information that fast. For example, they would have difficulty working registers at the concession stand because they can't listen to a customer and pour drinks at the same time while working quickly.

This can be a problem at work, where colleagues come up and interrupt, or the boss wants to talk while you're in the middle of a project. Darius explains: "When I am doing something and another person starts talking to me it simply doesn't register. I may hear every word he says but it doesn't sink in. Consequently, I might not react to anything that is being said" (Prince-Hughes 2002, p.34).

Many ASers/NLDers have trouble stopping their intense concentration and switching attention to the person or phone call. If they're working on something with a deadline, they may feel resentful if interrupted, and may have trouble refocusing on what they were doing before the interruption. This is because it may take a few seconds for the brain to focus on the new task. When the new task is done, it takes time for the brain to remember what had been going on prior to the interruption and refocus again. In part it's a working short-term memory issue. It's important to identify all the possible ways this can happen, and discuss them with co-workers and your boss. Understanding each change situation can help minimize the discomfort.

Taking notes helps with keeping track of an array of tasks and deadlines. Tony describes his difficulty with interruptions:

> I sometimes feel resentful if I'm trying to finish and there are a lot of interruptions. I work very hard at not showing this resentment! I realize it's not their fault; they're just doing their job. While I have no trouble switching attention to the person or phone call, once I've finished with the person, if I had begun two or three small tasks (say, info I'd got during a phone call), I may forget to do one of them.

Other ASers/NLDers in office jobs have learned to deal with interruptions. While it can be hard not to get frustrated when one is working to beat a deadline and is interrupted by calls, it helps to realize that the callers didn't set out deliberately to make your life difficult. This awareness makes it easier to handle interruptions.

The first step in coping with several things happening at once is to realize that multi-tasking doesn't really exist; it's impossible to do two things at the same time. All that's needed to do complex tasks is a visual sequence of events, like following a movie in your head. You can turn the AS/NLD detail orientation into an asset by learning to break a task of many steps (or even multiple tasks) into tiny details that you can line up and prioritize into a sequence. This takes practice. Forget about the big picture; just concentrate on the chain of events. By visualizing, making lists, and concentrating on each detail in order, you can learn to deal with multi-tasking.

It's good to avoid jobs that require lots of multi-tasking. For example, receptionists, short order cooks and waitresses have to keep track of many things simultaneously. In contrast, data entry, filing, programming, and some bookkeeping jobs don't require much multi-tasking. Other good choices are a tour guide, landscaping, or a one-on-one aide. Here are a few suggestions for dealing with distractions:

1. To deal with colleagues making ad hoc requests, schedule periods of time when you can control the level of distraction by not accepting interruptions.

2. If you have a project that requires a lot of concentration, schedule a time when you can use your hyper-focusing abilities and work on it without interruptions. Set your phone to voicemail, or ask a co-worker to take your calls.

3. If you have telephone duties, use your voicemail or answering machine to take calls, and return calls at a set time or when you've completed a project.

4. Turn off the new mail notification on your computer. That way, instead of reading and responding to each message as it arrives, you can schedule blocks of time throughout the day for reading and answering email.

Here are some tips for beginning a large project:

1. New tasks may always be a challenge. If you find yourself stuck and unable to start a project, ask for help in breaking the complex task down into its individual parts.

2. Write down these steps for next time. It helps to have the directions written down and spelled out, so you can refer to them.

3. If you have a large task, think of one thing you could do to begin. Don't worry whether it should be the first step, middle step, or last step. Hopefully, just doing something will help you break the logjam.

Strategic and global thinking can be developed with practice. Begin with things that you can do, and gradually build from there. Here are some ideas:

1. Try to think of all the possible situations. When reading, think of what you know about the subject and ask relevant questions. One way to give yourself practice is by reading or watching a movie and at strategic points in the story asking "What do you think will happen next?" Use the keywords "what", "where", "why", "how" and "when" to think of appropriate questions. If you do this in a group, such as a class, you get ideas from other people's suggestions.

2. Analyze the situation, looking for the number of intervening events.

3. Learn to play chess and other strategy games that require you to figure out the strategy and your next move. You won't be good, especially at first, but with practice it does get easier.

Motor issues and processing speed

Perceptual, motor, and sensory deficits, along with problems with multi-tasking, translate into a slower work speed. Many ASers and NLDers are clumsy, and have very poor hand–eye coordination. They are prone to spilling things and have difficulty getting things to look even. Even things that are supposed to be simple, like collating papers or filing folders, can take longer. Stuffing envelopes is slow. Sealing them, as well as cutting or pasting, can be sloppy.

When there are too many competing sensory stimuli, the brain is unable to process them quickly, and the individual's reactions slow down. A related issue is this person's slower thinking or mental processing speed. Some have likened it to being a 386 computer in a world of Pentiums. Those seconds add up, and things take longer, affecting the amount of work output.

For these reasons, NLDers and ASers should stay away from production-oriented jobs, and find work where accuracy is more important than speed. All jobs, however, rely on speed and efficiency to some extent. In addition to doing things well, it's important to complete tasks in the same amount of time as the average person, with or without accommodations. For example, even with a good sense of design, perceptual, spatial and motor impairments can make it more difficult to do document layout or graphics work. Thus, if a person with these impairments worked in a graphics field, it would take them much longer to complete a project than anyone else.

Talking

Many NLDers and some Aspies learn by verbal mediation. Therefore, they must verbalize everything. When learning a new task or completing a complicated project, they use their verbal abilities to talk through the job, muttering to themselves. Unfortunately, many NTs believe that only crazy people talk to themselves, and perceive this individual as crazy.

It is important for this employee's managers and co-workers to realize that this thinking out loud is a coping strategy. It's an integral part of processing information and something this person needs to do in order to absorb the glut of visual and aural information around him, and to sort out what he should be doing. It's a way of running the ideas through the auditory channel. Talking through the steps of the activity reinforces its storage into memory. Hearing someone else talk through the task is easier than learning by reading notes. Since NLDers are usually auditory learners, a small taperecorder can be priceless for meetings.

Sometimes this will make people a bit impatient, but usually an explanation that this is a compensatory strategy for a learning disability stops the negative reaction.

I did it my way

Everyone has a different approach, a different style. Due to problems with motor skills, organization, and processing speed, ASers/NLDers often do things in a slightly unconventional way. They find alternative ways to get the same result. In a work setting, however, bosses may look askance at these strange ways. The NLD way or the AS way may be perceived as being unco-operative, and cause problems for these creative, eccentric employees. Often the employee is unaware in what manner they're being uncooperative.

It's imperative that the supervisor is flexible and understands that there can be equally valid ways of getting to the same conclusion. The supervisor should realize that the person's resistance isn't due to attitude, but rather to inability to follow the expected procedure. The way he or she performs a task may be impossible or very difficult for the person with NLD or AS.

While it's important to understand how the boss wants things done, it's equally essential to find a procedure that works for you. For example, think about the best time of day or week to complete various administrative duties. Remember that this is a framework, and try to stay flexible.

Perseverance or perseveration?

While the NLDer's/ASer's persistence and ability to stick with a project are assets, his or her inability to switch gears can be problematic. For example, when solving a problem, if the first solution doesn't work, this person might react with anger. She'll begin the project thinking she knows what to do. When it doesn't work, she'll get upset. Unsure of how to proceed, she'll keep trying the same strategy over and over again, as if trying harder to do it wrong is going to help. She might blow up, bursting into tears or taking out her frustration on the thing that won't work instead of calmly thinking of other ways to achieve the desired result. Sometimes, after blowing up, she can start to think of other ways. When another approach is found, she's very relieved.

Organization

Many NLDers/ASers have trouble planning and prioritizing. Perceptual, spatial and memory problems, compounded by deficits in executive function, often translate into poor organizational skills. They may have trouble getting started, tracking time, and organizing a routine. Management of time and effort – estimating how long something will take and how difficult the task will be – as well as management of materials, money and workspace are affected. This makes planning and breaking down projects difficult.

There are many adaptations that compensate for deficiencies in executive functioning. Some NLDers/ASers develop routines that can almost be described as compulsive. For example, one nurse uses numerous lists to keep herself organized, has a plan for every day and patient, and categorizes everything by using different colored pens and highlighters. She even color codes her post-it notes to distinguish between a top priority and a lower priority.

Rigid structure and routine, technical organizing tools and freedom from distractions can help you stay focused on the task at hand. Different colored folders make it easier to keep track of things. A planner or electronic organizer can help you stick to deadlines. If you need reminders, there are many gadgets that can do the trick.

Many people use electronic organizers. These gadgets allow you to set reminders for tasks that occur regularly, like weekly meetings, as well as for appointments. Everything is in one place. There's no more losing pieces of paper or flipping through notebooks to find the right page.

Others have found an organizational coach helpful. These are people who specialize in this field and are familiar with executive function issues as well as strategies to combat them. You can find one through your local learning disabilities or ADD (Attention Deficit Disorder) support group.

Organizational strategies

Materials

1. Keep the desk or work area as clear as possible. Try to have only the piece you're currently working on on the desk at any one time.

2. Use organizational tools like colored folders to help you prioritize and organize your work.

3. Highlight important information in a text or on a to-do list.

4. Visual organizers and outlines help organize your thoughts for a presentation or paper. www.Inspiration.com provides software that may be helpful.

Time management

1. Build routine into your workday. Follow a plan or schedule. This will help you deal with interruptions, avoid distractions, and control the tendency to put things off.

2. Write a daily schedule at the beginning of each workday. Create and use to-do lists, and prioritize them. Decide what must be done first, what's urgent, and what can wait.

3. Use your planner not only to record tasks, but also to include the details and task instructions where necessary. This notebook should be organized into headings, e.g. details of task, additional points to remember, deadlines, etc.

4. Schedule a time to work on each task, and write it in your daily planner. Be realistic. Allow more time than is needed for any project. Include time for distractions. A good rule of thumb is to pad the amount of time you think it will take you to complete a task by at least half. If you think a project will take an hour, block an hour and a half. That way, when emergencies and interruptions occur or your boss wants something done right away, you'll still have enough time.

5. Set realistic deadlines, and then work backwards, creating many smaller deadlines. A computer outline is a big help with this.

6. Be flexible. Remember that the schedule is only a blueprint. At the end of the day, take a minute to look over what you've accomplished. If something isn't finished, don't get frustrated. Simply move any unfinished business to the next day.

7. Use calendars. A monthly-to-a-view calendar helps some people be more cognizant of the big picture. If things tend to sneak up on you, you may need to see more at one time and then switch to one day at a time mode.

8. Organizing software and electronic organizers are useful for programming repeating events. Meetings or appointments that take place at the same time each week can be programmed once to repeat at the same day and time each week, reducing the likelihood that they will be forgotten.

9. A multi-alarm programmable wristwatch is another useful time management tool.

10. Record all project deadlines on the calendar or electronic organizer. Break long-term projects into intermediate deadlines and enter these in the planner or calendar.

11. Break large jobs into smaller chunks. Learn how to "chunk" work into meaningful units and time. If you have problems with big projects, don't try to tackle the whole thing, but set smaller clearly defined goals that you can achieve in a reasonable amount of time.

12. Set clocks and watches a few minutes ahead.

13. Don't procrastinate. Do it now, not later.

33 A Few Lists

Fields with higher tolerance of differences tend to be those where the job itself doesn't involve direct contact with outsiders, and where work results are unambiguous and can be measured quantitatively and absolutely. The ideal work environment should be quiet, stable and predictable. The work itself should have clear goals and objectives, routine, and be broken into subtasks with clearly stated specifications and expectations. Projects that allow the employee to use his/her creativity and problem-solving skills are best. Employers should value the individual's laser-like concentration ability and understand and respect these employees' work style and social limitations.

The biggest challenges at work for most NLDers/ASers are social interaction and adjustment to change. A mentor can often help the individual to adapt to workplace demands. Friends, counselors, and teachers can act as mentors. The AS/NLD employee must remember that the boss controls everything about his/her life at a company. If the boss wants you to do something, do it, and do it with a smile – even if you think it's foolish.

In the right job, with the right work environment, an understanding supervisor and needed support, NLDers/ASers can become skilled employees valued for their dependability, honesty, and persistence.

Jobs for NLDers/ASers

Ideal jobs should include the following characteristics:

- quiet, stable and predictable work environments, with few distractions – since everyone is an individual, different aspects of the environment are distracting for different people

- organization should be more laid back and accepting of individual differences and differences in work/learning style

- clear, well-defined goals and objectives

- clearly defined work tasks and expectations

- explicit, written rules and expectations regarding such things as breaks, dress code, telephone use, etc.

- be predictable – variety is good, as long as there is a predictable routine or schedule

- relatively stress free – while including some challenge, reduce things like overtime pressures, productivity orientation, deadlines, and noise

- built-in structure to job duties and/or work environment, or can be adapted to the individual's need for structure

- allow flex time in scheduling

- involve a degree of repetition

- make use of verbal strengths

- capitalize on attention to detail

- take advantage of high-level technical expertise

- employ power of concentration and creativity

- not require manual dexterity

- utilize memory for facts and figures

- logical approach to tasks

- sell your work rather than your personality – use a portfolio!

- free of office politics, without complex social interactions

- make use of calendars, checklists, timers, and/or electronic organizers

- summarize information discussed verbally in writing or via email

- boss should realize your social issues and limits

- employers and co-workers who are receptive to training

- employers and co-workers understand and respect the person's social limitations and are willing to create an environment where an individual is more likely to succeed

- when training employees, make a detailed list of the activities or steps needed to complete a task

- in work team activities, provide a written explanation of the employee's role in the team.

Common accommodations

- hard work

- extra time and effort

- a quiet, distraction-free environment or tools to cut down on distractions like a white noise machine or wearing headphones

- a high degree of solitary work

- an extended training period

- time required to take notes when learning new tasks or responsibilities

- sufficient time to learn new skills and projects

- persistence and perseverance

- clearly stated expectations

- clear-cut procedures

- consistent scheduling

- logical explanations for change

- computer use

- verbal brainstorming

- verbal/written explanation of visual material

- frequent and consistent feedback

- training for co-workers, bosses, vocational counselors, and others involved so that they understand the cognitive, behavioral and social issues unique to NLD/AS

- mentoring.

To what degree are your work skills impacted by:

- short-term memory issues

- clumsiness or slow motor output

- organizational difficulties

- visual-spatial issues

- visual memory

- inability to multi-task?

34 Disclosing
If, When, and How to Do It

There is a lot of debate on whether and when to disclose your disability. Many individuals with AS or NLD have been successful at work despite their difficulties. Others, however, find themselves in a Catch-22 situation. Mr. Wombell says: "If I put on a job application form that I'm suffering from AS, I don't get an interview. If I don't tell people about my disability when I go for the interview, they cannot understand what is wrong with me" (Beaumont 2001, p.10).

Some people feel that one should disclose the disability at the interview or even in the résumé. Lars, a professor with Asperger Syndrome, states in his résumé that he has this condition. He believes that with the disability in the open he doesn't have to worry about how he's perceived or what impression he makes. He explains his oddities and mannerisms, and asks for understanding.

Others advise against disclosing before securing the job. Lana writes:

> The main purpose of the job interview is not to find an applicant with the best skills and longest experience, but to screen out potential trouble. The employer is not trying to zero in on those with the highest skills or greatest experience – he or she already has this information from the resume. Rather, at the interview, he wants to find the candidate who's not simply capable of learning the job, but who has the right attitude. He's looking for the ability to get along with others and be a team player in company politics. He wants to eliminate people who might cause trouble or create a liability for the company.

Lana believes that disclosing a condition that renders you inherently prone to having social difficulties and trouble fitting in as part of a team is not wise. She goes on:

> The employer sees only potential liability. Why should he hire someone who might request ADA accommodations, causing extra costs and hassle for the company? Why should he hire someone who might claim disability discrimination after failing to get along with colleagues? Presenting yourself at the interview as a potential liability is a guarantee to be screened out. Of course, they will never say this to your face, but that's what will and does happen. That's why the law prohibits interviewers from asking prospective candidates whether they have any disabilities or health problems (they only may ask whether the applicant is able to perform all the tasks required by a position). But if you volunteer such information up front, anything you say may be used against you.

Since AS and NLD are poorly understood even by professionals, and you're probably not applying to work for a neuropsychologist, bringing it up at the interview (where your time is usually limited) only sidetracks the conversation, robbing you of precious time to present your qualifications. It all depends on how obvious your quirks and mannerisms are to the interviewer, and how well you're able to hide your AS/NLD traits.

If you think your traits show through, making the interviewer view you as odd, strange, or not quite right, and thus decreasing your chances of being hired, it may be beneficial to mention the condition (not disability). If you do so, you should mention the positive traits – your laser-like concentration and ability to stick with a project, or your wordsmith abilities; for example: "I have a condition which makes it difficult to deal with interruptions and multi-tasking. However, it also gives me great powers of concentration, and I'm able to work on a project or problem for a very long time." You could also explain how you deal with interruptions; for example: "I use voicemail a lot. This helps cut down on interruptions. I schedule a specific time during the day to return calls." You could also address your seeming social inappropriateness; for example: "I may not always make eye contact with you. This is because I find it hard to look and listen at the same time, and I'm very interested in what you have to say. I think this is a great place to work because..." A good time to mention this is when asked about your strengths and weaknesses.

In order to sound informed, it's essential to be familiar with the particulars of your specific diagnosis before disclosing. What are your strengths and weaknesses? What is your work style? What qualities, talents, abilities and skills do you have to offer the employer?

If you're concerned that some aspect of the job will be difficult because of your disability, the interview is a good time to feel things out. Ask for more specifics about what you will be doing, and then discuss anything that might be hard for you. Make it sound like a style preference rather than a problem. Make sure the employer knows how hard you will work to get around these issues and what they can do to help you compensate. For example, if you have problems with oral instructions, you might say "I prefer written directions. I really like to be sure that I understand people, so I like to ask lots of questions and repeat information to verify understanding, because I want to do a great job." Then ask whether such actions are acceptable and appropriate in this position.

If you're able to control your AS/NLD traits for short periods of time, you may not wish to mention your disability, leading the interviewer to assume that you're simply a bit too nervous during the interview, which is common, normal, and expected. You may even reinforce this assumption by saying something like "Please excuse my nervousness, but that's because I'm really interested in working for your company. This is such a great opportunity". As long as you're honest about your skills, qualifications, credentials and background, this is not dishonesty. During the job hunt, you're supposed to sell yourself and present yourself in the most appealing ways, in order to convince the employer to hire you. It is perfectly fine and widely recommended to downplay your weaknesses during the job-hunting process.

If you don't mention AS or NLD at all, you may find that the employer feels betrayed if you later ask for accommodations you didn't disclose you might need when you applied. So, as Mr. Wombell said, it's a Catch-22 situation.

Even after obtaining a position, full disclosure upfront can be risky. In some career fields, the general perception is that if you have a disability, you don't belong there in the first place. When a student brought up issues of a learning disability and the study of computer science, he found that many geeks have the opinion that computer science isn't something people with learning disabilities should pursue. When he asked "If they can do it, why not let them study it?" the geeks responded that if the disabled person couldn't keep up with normally abled programmers, they shouldn't get a job in the field. The student replied that they'd have to accommodate a programmer in a wheelchair, so why not a learning disabled programmer?

A reference librarian was told that due to her poor judgment she didn't belong in the profession. Librarians need to be able to answer questions, think on their feet, and switch gears rapidly from one question to the next. It's really hard for some people to accept that an extraordinarily intelligent person can also be extraordinarily disabled. So, what is Stephen Hawking? Albert Einstein?

It's best not to disclose until the manager has decided that you're competent, capable, and a pretty nice person, even if you are a bit quirky. You can tell them you have trouble with certain things without launching into a long explanation of NLD or AS. My interviews revealed that many people who announced their disability lost their job, or were demoted, allegedly for reasons other than their NLD/AS. One employee realized he couldn't handle the boss's demands and disclosed the disability to the boss, who, in the presence of a union rep, agreed to make any needed accommodations. However, he was fired shortly thereafter. Later an ex-co-worker told him that she had offered to help him, but the boss forbade her to assist him.

The ADA requires employers to make "reasonable accommodations" if you have a disability and are "otherwise qualified to do a job". However, with a social disability like NLD or AS, the term "otherwise qualified" becomes sticky. You have the technical skills and abilities, but social interaction, whether with fellow employees or customers, may be a problem. If you're about to lose your job anyway, declaring your disability may buy you time to look for another job, since employers want to avoid a lawsuit and may need to find more evidence against you.

Many accommodations can be worked out or arranged for without disclosing the NLD or AS. Don't throw problems at the supervisors and expect them to come up with magic solutions. Instead, state a problem and, at the same time, suggest a reasonable accommodation. For example, a simple, straightforward statement like "I have always had trouble figuring out non-verbal signals, like frowns, body language, and tone of voice. So it would help me a lot if you could verbalize those things for me, or at least please don't mind when I seem to have missed them or ask you what you mean by them." Or you might say "I'm really distracted by all of the talking going on around me in my cubicle. I think it would help me if I bring in a white noise machine and/or wear headphones."

Everyone has trouble with something; we can't hear as well, or see as well as others, or we're too short or tone deaf or whatever. It's important to be proactive and to communicate to your supervisor that you are motivated and want to do your best work – so you're looking for solutions. We all know we're really good at some things and very bad at others, and that if we get help with the things we don't do well we can do a better job with the things we do well.

For example, if you have perceptual and spatial issues and are asked to design a document, you may explain that you can do basic page design, but that if they need something more involved they might wish to hire a graphic artist.

If you're traveling on business and someone mentions renting a car, you could mention that you get lost easily and would rather take a cab from the airport so you'll be sure to make it to the hotel.

If asked to do something that requires better coordination than you have, mention that you hate to say it, but you're really clumsy and aren't sure you'd feel safe doing that. It helps if you can do this with a sense of humor, and without taking yourself too seriously. For example, Sandy tells folks giving her directions that she gets lost easily, has trouble finding her way around, and needs explicit directions. If they say "You can't miss it" she laughs and responds "Oh, I certainly can!" She'll explain to co-workers that she sometimes talks too much, and might miss it when people are hinting that they need to end the conversation and get back to work. If that happens, she tells them her feelings won't be hurt if they just say, "I need to get back to work now."

If the accommodations needed are relatively simple, and the reasons seem straightforward to people who don't know anything about LDs, it's easy to simply ask for what you need. One of the problems with all of the glitches and deficits that originate from NLD or AS, however, is that they're often hard to distinguish from intentionally inappropriate behaviors. The individual can be perceived as disruptive, combative, annoying, argumentative, and interrupting. Honesty in answering questions can be viewed as being judgmental, coy, or curt. A direct, honest approach can come across as rudeness. Inflexible adherence to routines can be perceived as insubordination. Slowness learning the ropes on a new project might be misinterpreted as stupidity, laziness, or willful neglect of duty. Along with the problem NLDers/ASers have with interpretation of non-verbal information, such issues often create misunderstandings in workplace situations.

Therefore, it may be necessary to officially disclose, first to your immediate supervisor, and then to the HR department, to receive the accommodations and understanding that you need. When difficulties arise, approach your supervisor with "Next time, this is what I need, so I can do a good job for you". If you decide to disclose, develop an accommodation plan to present to the employer. Assistance is available from the Job Accommodation Network. The current marketplace requires self-reliance from all workers, disabled or not. Learn to ask for what you need.

A young man working as a stock clerk found that when he did disclose the difficulties he was having his employer was patient and understanding. Rather than thinking he was dumb, lazy or slow, his supervisor realized how hard certain tasks were for him, and that it took him a bit longer to finish them and get comfortable with the job. Garry writes:

> After two months the library asked me to stay for a further two months to fill in for a staff member taking a Long Service Leave. They knew of my condition and this was the happiest time of my life. They were wonderful to me and even though I still sat on my own in the canteen I still felt good about myself and felt I was putting in a good effort which was substantiated when I got an excellent reference from them… In wrestling with this "to tell or not to tell," one of my parents telephoned the supervisor at the Parliamentary Library to ask her what she thought and she said, it had helped them to understand why I would get very anxious if I made a mistake, asked many questions to make sure that I had it right, and understood why I did not find it easy to socialize and that it was not because I was standoffish or aloof. (Prince-Hughes 2002, pp.7–8)

In other cases, however, disclosing to your supervisor can backfire. A reference librarian who had trouble noticing when patrons approached the desk asked for a simple accommodation – a sign directing them to please ask for help. This was denied, and eventually, she lost her job.

One woman informed her co-workers that she didn't understand body language well, and that, if they wanted to tell her something, to be straightforward and upfront, and that she would not take offense. She was fired – with no verbal warnings – and told the reason was that she couldn't read body language.

By formally disclosing to the human services department, you make your needs official to the company. The HR representative can serve as your advocate in explaining issues to your supervisor. If, for instance, you get moved to a different department, your disability will be on record. The human services representative can then explain to the new supervisor any issues that arise which are due to the disability, and any accommodations you use that your new boss might think aren't necessary. In conclusion, we need to remember that we're not the customers in this situation, since we're trying to sell our skills to the employer.

35 Some Commandments for an Employer who is Working with an NLD Employee

Jennifer Lerner

This chapter is written from the point of view of the NLD employee, as we basically know that it is what the employer wants that ultimately matters.

1. *Be reliable.* I understand the need to be flexible in our rapidly changing world, but *routine and consistency* help me to do a better job. Please consider this when planning the workday and assigning duties.

2. *Be patient, and know that I am putting forth the best effort I can to get up to speed as quickly as possible.* If I am not able to grasp concepts and tasks quickly, give me more time to learn them, and trust that I am competent and capable. This will help my self-confidence and will make me a better employee. You thought highly enough of my skills to give me the job, right?

3. *Present information to me in written as well as verbal format, so I may review it at my own pace.* Go through the actual process with me, step by step.

4. Because I want to do a great job for you, I need you to *state things precisely and literally* as I have difficulty with assuming anything that is not directly stated. Do not expect me to read between the lines.

5. *Be honest, direct, and sincere in your feedback.* Because I want to correct my mistakes as soon as possible, my feelings will not be hurt if you provide sincere and honest feedback. Share with me how my performance is going, and do not tell me after a few months that I'm not cut out for the job. You cannot offend me by being too straightforward and direct. Feedback is essential because I'm not always aware of my own performance, or of how I appear to others. Remember that I have difficulty with assuming anything that is not directly stated. I can't read between the lines.

6. Because I want to do a great job for you, *I will ask what may seem to you a seemingly endless stream of questions. Please do not get annoyed with me.* This is my only way of making sense of what is going on around me. Take it as an example of my eagerness and ability to analyze my work environment in order to do a better job.

7. Because I understand the importance of teamwork, the above suggestions will help me to be a good team player. In addition, many of these suggestions will benefit other employees and benefit the work efficiency in the company. Never put me down, especially in front of co-workers. I want to feel like I am part of the team, and not any different. If there is a task that is impossible due to my NLD, please help me to find modifications, if possible. Many of these modifications may also benefit other employees.

8. *Please consider me to be a valuable employee, not a disabled employee.* I only aim to please you, my co-workers, and the population being served. I always strive to be the best I can be.

Jennifer Lerner has an MA in Counseling/Learning Disabilities. Her work has included tutoring LD children and adults in writing, academic skills, strategies, and organization; teaching college classes in writing, psychology, and sociology; and working as an Academic Specialist in the Welfare to Careers program for low-income students at Metropolitan College of New York.

36 Strategies for Successful Employment

Debbie Green

1. In many ways, the employee with NLD or AS is the ideal employee. He/she is loyal, dependable, meticulous, and conscientious. His/her goals are the same as your company's goals. There are some specific strategies that you, as an employer, can do to help your NLD/AS employee to succeed and become a valued worker for life. People with NLD have excellent verbal and auditory skills; those with AS are excellent visual thinkers and often have great powers of concentration. Both groups have an excellent rote memory, and will memorize every detail of every operation. This is the most effective way for them to learn new information.

Strategy

Do a new task and explain steps of the new task *verbally* to this employee. Have him/her repeat the task and repeat its steps verbally. Correct mistakes. Allow employee to take notes or taperecord instructions. Allow the employee to do each task under supervision until all the steps are correct.

2. People with NLD and AS thrive on *repetition*. They can become flustered when presented with change, and often have difficulty with new tasks due to the novelty. Change should be introduced gradually and in small increments.

Strategy

Try to avoid change if possible. Don't expect the person with NLD or AS to spontaneously assume new duties. If change is unavoidable, talk to the employee privately. Give him/her a chance to ask questions and process the change. Talk through new expectations step by step. Be patient through the transition.

3. People with NLD or AS may not always know how to ingratiate themselves with co-workers and bosses. Social skill gaffes need to be mentioned discreetly and kindly. This employee wants to get along with others. He/she is not trying to deliberately offend or alienate people. When he/she learns the correct way to act, the inappropriate behaviors will stop.

Strategy

If a co-worker complains about the employee with NLD or AS, write down the concerns, and ask the co-worker to be tolerant. Talk to the employee with NLD/AS privately. Let him/her know that his/her behavior may be offputting, and give him/her suggestions on how to change.

Refuse to take sides. Encourage employees to address problems among themselves, instead of talking to the boss. Encourage events like team lunches and weekend get-togethers.

4. People with NLD often have problems with *visual-spatial perception* and *fine motor issues* like handwriting. Accommodations like a computer and a taperecorder are necessities. Visual-spatial tasks should be avoided whenever possible.

Strategy

Help the employee with NLD/AS create some kind of organizational system. Excuse the employee with NLD/AS from tasks such as formatting, drawing, or anything else involving fine motor control and visual-spatial perception. Realize that when employees with NLD/AS ask for accommodations, these are necessities. They are not excuses to get out of work.

Once the employee with NLD or AS has learned basic tasks, his/her work will be excellent. NLD is a learning disability, not a doing disability. Once the work has been mastered, the NLD/AS employee can do it quickly and accurately. Excellent verbal skills and an eye for detail add to this employee's value.

While it does take a few months to train an employee with NLD/AS, it is well worth the extra effort. A few months of training will lead to a loyal, competent, hard-working, and honest employee for life.

In addition to teaching, **Debbie Green** is a writer. Her poems have been published in a national anthology, and her articles have appeared in Puzzle Pieces and on LDOnline. She is the author of a memoir, *Growing up with NLD*, and is currently working on a children's novel, *Forever Winter*, about the life of a child with NLD and SID.

37 Workplace Bullying and the NLD/AS Individual

Lana Kapchinsky and Gerriann Fox

To Carmen Solom – if not for you, this chapter would have never been written.

Disclaimer: *This information should not be construed as medical, legal or any other professional advice nor is this an endorsement for any resources or publications mentioned below. Please exercise your own judgment in researching information and making decisions about your personal situations.*

At a recent conference on Asperger Syndrome, Carol Gray told a story about a neighbourhood Christmas party. One woman, an obstetrician, described a co-worker, a hematologist, and the strange, funny things the guy did. Recognizing the characteristics of AS, Carol offered to educate this individual about her colleague's idiosyncratic ways, to bring about understanding. But this person didn't want to understand her colleague. Her response was, "No thanks... If we understood him, it would ruin our fun."

What bullying is

The Merriam Webster Dictionary defines bullying as "treating abusively" or "intimidating". Bullying includes having fun at another's expense, saying or writing nasty things about someone, excluding, ostracizing, threatening, or making people uncomfortable. Unfortunately, such behavior is not limited to childhood, classrooms and playgrounds. Many bullies carry their prey drive and predatory behavioral patterns into adulthood. They may see it as a way of making themselves look tough and in charge. Some like to instill fear in others. Others do it out of jealousy. Some try to gain status by belittling others. They gravitate toward positions of power as the means to exercise their unhealthy compulsion to derive pleasure from others' frustration and pain. Harassing those whom they perceive as weak, more capable or simply different is the bullies' way to mask their own deficiencies, shortcomings and insecurities. Grown-up bullies aren't under the control of teachers or parents, and are very adept in getting away with their actions and slipping through the loopholes of existing laws. Adult bullying is immoral, but surprisingly, not illegal, at least at this moment – although there is a growing awareness of the huge socioeconomic costs associated with it. According to some statistics, one in every six workers experiences workplace bullying in any given year (Workplace Bullying and Trauma Institute 2000, p.6). Other sources suggest an even higher incidence.

British researcher Tim Field writes:

> Bullying, especially on a regular basis and for the perpetrator's pleasure, can be regarded as a form of psychological rape because of its intrusive and violational nature.
>
> In addition to abuse of position and power by the bully is the denial of the right of the victim to earn their living through employment. The predictable pattern of a bullying relationship invariably ends with the victim being hounded out of their job, with physical and mental health impaired and professionalism discredited. The iniquity is often compounded by the withholding of a suitable reference, or provision of a deliberately bad one, plus the difficulty of explaining to a prospective employer the circumstances surrounding previous termination of employment. Many then become trapped in the treadmill of repeated job applications knowing how little chance there is of success. Months, perhaps a year or more, of recuperation may be necessary before the challenge of a gainful employment can be faced again. In today's climate, the longer one stays out of the job market, the harder it is to get back – if at all. (Field 1996, pp.4–5)

Why NLDers/ASers are easy, convenient targets

Although bullying can happen to anyone, ASers and NLDers make ideal targets: easy, appealing and safe. We often look and act plain odd and are just fun to make fun of, aren't we? We stand out of the crowd. We usually don't have many (or any) friends who would stand up for us and confront the bullies. Our ramblings are so hard to be taken seriously. We cannot assert ourselves gracefully; under stress, we may act erratically. We have a history of lifelong social difficulties and are regularly crying wolf – what else is new? We're painfully sensitive, apprehensive and anxious. Is our perception of being bullied at work yet another overreaction or figment of our imagination? Last but not least, we bear a label that effectively invalidates us, since our neurological disorders are often misclassified as mental illness. Our dignity and credibility, our feelings and statements are discredited. The signs of psychological injury from bullying are conveniently mistaken and dismissed as symptoms related to our diagnoses – yet another confirmation of the allegation that we are unstable, messed up, or disturbed. Our word isn't taken seriously. This is what the bullies cynically count on, choosing us as easy, risk-free prey.

The chances for NLDers or ASers becoming targets of bullying, therefore, are much higher than average. Dennis Debbaudt, law enforcement professional, advocate and educator on ASD issues, lists among the main risks associated with our condition: "high likelihood of victimization; lack [of] credibility as victim" and "unaddressed or high tolerance for bullying, teasing, taunting and torment...especially for those with higher functioning autism or Asperger's syndrome". He describes AS characteristics as "behaviors that draw attention" and "misrepresentation of those behaviors and characteristics as evidence of...psychosis, defiance or belligerence" (Debbaudt 2002, p.3).

A questionnaire developed by Portland State University's Special Education Program for individuals diagnosed with HFA, PDD, or AS, among other common characteristics typically shared by those individuals of all ages, lists: "Is bullied by others" (Portland 1992). It can and does happen to us anyplace – and the workplace is no exception.

Skills, qualifications and the ability to perform job tasks are not all we need to succeed in the workplace. In any organization – corporate, private or public, large or small – the most crucial survival skills are sociability, ability to understand the balance of power, and navigating the unwritten rules of workplace politics. According to corporate veteran and writer Robert Hochheiser:

> You have to make yourself well aware of how your fellow employees relate to one another, who is on the way up or down, and who is likely to do what under what circumstances. Only when you understand how power is used in an organization, can you rationally decide how to deal with your bosses and peers without being ganged up on, hurt or kicked out. (Hochheiser 1987, pp.126–127)

Due to the nature of our condition, this understanding eludes us. We are physically and biologically unable to master this art.

We just don't seem to fit into organizational hierarchy and culture – whether it's a corporate, private or public entity. Even worse, we come to work with the sole purpose to do work, and find workplace socialization and politics to be a nuisance, a distraction and a formidable challenge. Others consider us difficult. We're oblivious to hierarchy, and might challenge authority. We insist on efficiency prevailing over social considerations. We resent nepotism and favoritism. We are just out of sync. We don't share others' excitement about the latest movies, albums, fashions, TV sitcoms, and popular sports, but are instead fascinated with subjects not considered common hobbies, which we want to endlessly ramble about. We cannot make small talk around the office water cooler. We often don't understand common jokes or idioms, taking every word too literally. We may appear aloof, withdrawn, arrogant, cold, and uptight. On the opposite end, we come across as hyper, immature, and insensitive to others. We often speak too loudly or too monotonously. Our speech is stiff, formal, repetitive, with flowery language and unusual words, and we may appear to imply that others are too stupid to understand. We are clumsy and awkward; our posture and body movements are odd, often with involuntary movements or utterances. We fail to understand, as well as to adequately display, facial expressions and body language. We just don't have a clue. We say and do things regarded as unconventional or just plain strange. We are blunt; we have a hard time with political correctness. When it comes to principles, we're likely to challenge people in positions of authority, if their views or opinions contradict ours, and may even insist that others accept our position.

We set very high standards for others and ourselves. We might persist with certain pieces of work for too long, and may have difficulty setting priorities or cooperating with others. We insist on sameness and have problems coping with change and transitions. Our unique abilities, creativity, high productivity in areas of our interests, and unmatched special talents can trigger backstabbing by colleagues whom we inadvertently make look bad.

Being naive, gullible, easily manipulated, socially clumsy, usually excluded from the organization's informal grapevine, we're out of the loop and lack understanding of the unwritten rules and informal power balance. We're often disenfranchised loners, perceived as odd. Our developmental neurological handicaps are misunderstood and mislabeled as mental illness. All of these traits make NLD/AS workers very vulnerable and virtually doomed to be targeted by bullies at some point in their careers. Highly demanding, fast-paced work environments, along with cut-throat competition, especially during economic downturns, aggravate this problem even more.

Others may not help

Doctor Judith Lewis Herman, an Associate Clinical Professor of Psychiatry at the Harvard Medical School and Director of Training at the Victims of Violence Program at Cambridge Hospital, wrote:

> When the traumatic events are of human design, those who bear witness are caught in the conflict between victim and perpetrator. It is morally impossible to remain neutral in this conflict. The bystander is forced to take sides. It is very tempting to take the side of the perpetrator. All the perpetrator asks is that the bystander do nothing... The victim, on the contrary, asks the bystander to share the burden of pain. The victim demands action, encouragement and remembering. (Herman 1997, p.7)

This is particularly true in cases of workplace bullying, when fellow workers get coerced or intimidated into condoning or even joining the bully out of fear for their own job security – or they risk becoming the bully's next target. This is ten times more applicable in the cases of targeted NLD/AS adults who are not popular among their peers, lack social connections, have no support network, have been naturally isolated and disenfranchised due to their social handicaps, and are defenselessly facing bullies all alone.

A manipulative, glib and smooth-talking bully, especially if (s)he is in a position of authority, has a much higher chance to be believed than his/her distressed target, whose credibility is further undermined by underlying communication difficulties and by the stigma of our disorder. You can bet the bully is going to emphasize those setbacks to maximize this advantage. Dr. Herman writes:

> In order to escape accountability for his crimes, the perpetrator does everything in his power... Secrecy and silence are the perpetrator's first line of defense. If secrecy fails, the perpetrator attacks the credibility of his victim. If he cannot silence her absolutely, he tries to make certain that no one listens... He marshals an impressive array of arguments, from the most blatant denial to the most sophisticated and elegant rationalization... The perpetrator's arguments prove irresist-

ible when the bystander faces them in isolation. Without a supportive
social environment, the bystander usually succumbs to the temptation
to look the other way. (Herman 1997, pp.7–8)

Herman continues: "The perpetrator is…exquisitely sensitive to the realities
of power and to social norms…he seeks out situations where his tyrannical
behavior will be tolerated, condoned or admired. His demeanor provides an
excellent camouflage" (1997, p.75). Bullies do not even have to resort to
physical violence to cause severe trauma: "fear is…increased by inconsistent
and unpredictable outbursts…and by capricious enforcement of petty rules"
(Herman 1997, p.77).

There is no one size fits all advice on how not to become a target of
workplace bullying. So much depends on your immediate environment and
sheer luck. While people with AS/NLD can offer a great deal – punctuality,
reliability, and dedication, for example – informed, understanding, and,
most important, compassionate and well-wishing employers and co-workers
are crucial for workplace survival. Even more depends on the overall culture
and climate of your organization, its internal policies for dealing with such
cases and its willingness to adopt, implement and enforce those policies
(Tables 37.1 and 37.2).

Table 37.1 Assisting targets of workplace bullying: the dos and dont's

DON'T	DO
Don't assume that for an NLD/AS person finding a job is a "happy ending". For us, it's just the beginning of yet another struggle with an uncertain outcome and too many factors beyond our control.	Educate NLD/AS persons about their rights, including employment and civil rights. Inform us about applicable laws, resources, agencies and professionals that provide assistance in case our rights are violated.
Don't dismiss our concerns lightly. Don't suggest that we may be overreacting, imagining things, being oversensitive, paranoid, or crazy. Don't come up with excuses for bullies' behavior. Such wishful thinking will only add insult to injury. By doing so, you are unwittingly acting as the bully's accomplice.	Realize that our failure to communicate coherently and convincingly is caused by severe distress coupled with underlying communication difficulties due to our condition. That's why bullies choose us as safe targets – expecting that we won't be believed and our concerns won't be taken seriously.
Don't be quick to attribute our complaints, symptoms and reactions solely to manifestations or co-morbidities of our condition. By doing so, you're inadvertently helping bullies to push us over the edge. Those reactions and escalation of our difficulties are likely to be symptoms of severe psychological trauma inflicted by bullying or even post-traumatic stress disorder, which according to recent findings, may be caused by severe longtime bullying (Field 1996, p.128).	Acknowledge the situation and its devastating effects. Validate our feelings. Provide emotional support. Make us feel believed, accepted, respected and needed; this may save our lives – literally. Help us restore our self-esteem and self-confidence (which we most likely had low or none to begin with). Try to understand. Do not leave us to face the bully alone. Bullies thrive on isolating their targets. Dr Herb Lovett points out about victims: "Every time they recall their previous maltreatment, unless their panic and rage are recognized as a function of stress, they are likely to be further stigmatized as 'impossible to serve'" (Lovett 1996, p.208).

Don't get fooled by bullies' smooth talk (especially if they are in the position of authority). Don't take bullies' words at face value.	Bullies are adept in covering their tracks and can be very accomplished liars. Don't trust blanket statements. Demand specifics, proof and details (when, where, who, what and how) of every negative allegation. Demand that the bully takes personal responsibility by signing their statements. Be sure to review, explain and counter those allegations.
Don't suggest that we "just ignore" bullies. Workplace bullies, especially in a position of power, are impossible to ignore or avoid. They are usually set to destroy and to drive the target out of the job, and will not stop until that "mission" is accomplished.	Consider meaningful, viable defense strategies. Realize that bullies act with deliberate malicious intent, and attempts to reason with them, appease, educate, or ignore them will not work – they have to be confronted, exposed and combated.
Don't insist that our only option is to give up and leave, instead of defending our dignity and reputation, pursuing justice and holding perpetrators responsible.	Explore all options, their pros, cons and possible consequences, both short term and long term. Provide referrals to professionals. It's our right, life and choice, and it's up to us to bear all the lifelong consequences (emotional, financial, etc.) of whatever course of action is chosen.
Don't expect the administration or the union to resolve the issue. They often choose to get rid of the target and protect the bully, considering this to be easier and less risky.	Intervene personally. Provide referrals to professionals in a position to defend the target. Bring the situation into the light. Exposure is the bully's greatest fear and an effective deterrent.

Don't suggest that all we need in this situation is help from mental health professionals.	Disability discrimination, harassment, and creation of a hostile environment are all illegal, and require consultation with legal experts. Bullying and job loss are social problems, not medical issues. Although psychological injuries may require therapy, counseling, and sometimes medications, this is not all we need. After all, you would not refer persons discriminated for their skin color to seek help from a dermatologist, or people targeted by sexual harassment to seek help from a gynecologist or urologist.
Don't assume and suggest that we would and should find help somewhere else. As a rule, NLD/AS related organizations don't provide assistance or advocacy in employment disputes, and we're often considered not disabled enough by disability serving agencies and lawyers. We fall through the cracks. Due to the nature of our condition, we often lack a support network, contacts, references and finances.	Ask "What can I do to help you out now?" By not helping us, you are helping our bullies. You may be our only and last hope for help. Take it seriously. Intervene. "Nobody made a greater mistake than he who did nothing because he could only do a little" (Edmund Burke). Be our advocate. Find those who can assist us. Recommendations, referrals, references, etc. are an integral part of the support, healing and re-empowerment process.
Don't suggest that we find a professional to assist us via the Yellow Pages, a referral service, etc. At this time, very few professionals are familiar and experienced with NLD/AS in adults. LD/ASD organizations mostly work with pediatric/special education specialists who don't address adult issues. We may not be believed or taken seriously if we just walk in off the street with our stories.	Be proactive. Research and establish contacts with reputable and knowledgeable medical, legal and other professionals and advocates familiar with AS/NLD. Develop and maintain networks and listings of local professionals. Educate them about NLD/AS. Raise public awareness.

Don't suggest "Just go and try to find another job". If we could do this on our own, we wouldn't turn to you for help in the first place. Walking in off the street has already set us up for the situation we are currently in. It can take a long time to recover from psychological trauma caused by workplace bullying. Forcing a person into a similar setting ASAP would be equal to advising a rape victim to start having as much sex as possible.	Facilitate our job search and transition. It's very difficult to ask for help when you expect to be or have been brushed off to seek help somewhere else. Offer and provide your recommendations. Hire us if you are in a position to do so. Utilize your professional contacts and connections. Put in a good word to bypass or offset bad references from vindictive bullies. Help us get on with our lives. Provide practical assistance and intervention. Good words and good thoughts aren't enough.

Table 37.2 If you become a target of workplace bullying: the dos and dont's

DON'T	DO
Do not threaten or attempt to act in a violent, destructive or disruptive manner (including self-destruction). Do not, under any circumstances, say anything that may be interpreted as threats of violence or destruction. That would undermine your position and could land you in trouble, to the bullies' delight and triumph. They may provoke you to elicit such utterances or actions, attempting to discredit you and shift the focus away from them. Don't do them such a favor – they don't deserve it.	Keep your communications professional, unemotional, and to the point, with as many specific facts and details as possible. Contemplate, plan, promise and take only legitimate actions. If you feel that you are "losing it", physically remove yourself from the toxic situation immediately. Stay away for a while. Take a day off, sick leave or vacation. Seek assistance to help you cope with stress and trauma. Speak up about your ordeal. Go public with it.

Do not ever consider self-destruction as a way out of a bullying situation. Bullies aren't worth it.	Give yourself a well-deserved, long overdue break. Focus on your physical and emotional healing and re-empowerment. Try to relax. Do things you used to enjoy. Celebrate yourself – you are something to celebrate.
Don't expect bullies to change and stop on their own, and try to tough it out.	Realize that the longer you suffer in silence, the greater toll it takes on your physical and emotional health, and the further your bully will go to bring you down.
Don't appeal to emotions, mercy, and/or sense of fairness. This life is not guaranteed to be fair, and the bullies don't have any compassion, conscience or mercy. Bullying is not illegal. The administration may find it easier to try to get rid of you instead of dealing with the bully, and will try to build a case against you.	Don't lament it – document it. Keep the paper trail. Keep a detailed journal, write down what's happening. Record all the "when, where, who, what and how". Audiotape meetings, or keep detailed notes. Collect supporting documentation, print out email messages, copy and keep letters and memos (do not store them at work). Describe specific behaviors, statements and incidents that you find unacceptable and unprofessional. Cite relevant laws and policies that have been violated by the bullies' actions. Emphasize negative impact on your workplace productivity and the economic costs of such incidents to the employer, as well as the potential legal liability brought by the bully's misconduct.
Don't ask for permission to audiotape meetings.	File a written notice informing the employer or investigator about your intent to audiotape all the proceedings with your participation. Bring an extra copy of that notice and have it date stamped and initialed by the recipient, for your records.

Don't expect any "independent neutral" investigations conducted by administration or even by outside agencies to be truly independent and truly neutral. Those are often not as unbiased as they are supposed to be. Your interests and getting justice for you may not be their priority.	Be very careful what evidence you give them; make sure it cannot be used against you. These investigations become rehearsals for the employer to see what evidence you have against them, if any, that can be used against you, and prepare to beat it before you sue them. You could tell them you have additional evidence. Lead them to believe you're saving the strongest evidence for legal proceedings. Then they may prefer to settle.
Don't give away to the investigators any original documents or audiotapes, even if pressured to do so.	Keep them in your possession at all times. If needed, make copies for investigators yourself.
Don't try to fight bullies alone.	Seek any assistance and support you can get. Look for and mobilize resources and people in a position to assist you. This search may be long and frustrating, but you're worth the fight.

If your complaint is being investigated

Here are some points to consider when complaints are being investigated by outside agencies:

1. Outside investigators aren't always impartial. They often find in favor of the side paying for their services or with whom they have common industrial relations.

2. Find out whether the employer has used their services. If so, did they "find" in the employer's favor? Can the employer use their services again?

3. Inquire about investigators' credentials and experience in handling similar matters. Beware if qualifications are overly

impressive. They may be used to refute facts of your complaints with "weight" of their expertise.

4.   Obtain their written description of the investigative procedure (process, timeline, etc.). Insist to see the preliminary draft of the report and to correct it as necessary.

5.   Look for signs of foul play. Are the investigators/experts bullying or manipulating you? Beware if:

- investigators don't ask questions and claim they've already got all necessary information from the employer – they don't want to hear and record your story and are trying to protect the employer
- they avoid eye contact with you
- they are too easygoing and friendly, promising you quick and informal resolution – they may be trying to dupe you into coming unprepared and alone for future proceedings, underestimating them
- they discourage you from hiring a lawyer or from filing a lawsuit or a complaint elsewhere
- they insist on phone rather than written communication – they may not want to leave a paper trail
- they say that you shouldn't or that they can't include certain facts into your complaint – that may be your strongest evidence and proof of your employer's fault
- they attempt to elicit statements that may be used against you, such as making you say you refuse to return to your current workplace (which later will be used as proof of your "voluntary resignation")
- they aren't interested in literature about workplace bullying
- they refuse to talk to you in the presence of your attorney or witnesses, or try to talk to you alone with their own witness (co-worker) present
- they don't want you to tape your interviews with them
- they stop communicating with you after obtaining your statements.

If you decide to take legal action against bullies

If you choose to take legal action, you may find helpful these tips, offered by Gerriann Fox, who had spent her entire 30-year professional career doing investigative and legal work:

> If you are being bullied and decide to take any action other than leaving your job, it's best to be as proactive as possible, Follow basic investigative and documenting procedures in order to prove what has happened. Take reasonable steps to address any difficulties. Talk with your boss or management about the bullying and ask for help in stopping it. Expect your complaints to be minimized and misconstrued, so have written proof and witnesses available. To assure your complaint is valid, tie it to violations of your employer's written policies, procedures, rules, mission statement, press releases, etc. Many companies have written procedures regarding employee discipline. Being shouted at, called names or cursed at, or having work labeled inadequate without explanation or corrective guidance, are all likely violations of the company's own promulgated policy.
>
> Creating paper trails is very important; ask the bully to put instructions or complaints in writing. If he refuses, write him a dated memo setting out exactly what happened and any direction given to you. Ask for written clarification of any error in your understanding. If the bully gives feedback only verbally, write that up the same way, asking for the same clarification. If the bully ignores your memo, send another, referencing the first, again asking for confirmation or clarification of your understanding. Keep doing written communication, regardless of how angry the bully becomes. You're building a case for future use, if necessary. If these early efforts fail you might, when applicable, file a grievance through a union or with whoever oversees the one employing you. Obtain the contract between the union and the employer or the policies that apply to your situation. They will set out specific procedures for how to grieve an issue, including timelines, forms, and the like. Be sure you meet all requirements exactly, and have the evidence for the violation and the witnesses ready. It is useless to expect a fact-finder to believe your unsupported statements in the face of the defense your bully will mount. Don't waste your time and energy if you haven't obtained sufficient proof.
>
> If you decide to file a Worker's Compensation or discrimination complaint, hire an attorney. In the US, Workers' Compensation attorneys specialize and work on contingency, while attorneys who specialize in filing complaints about discrimination usually do not. But check with the Bar Association in your area to confirm local law.

An attorney can decide if you have a sustainable case by evaluating the evidence you have collected and weighing it in light of applicable law. What Courts have decided in cases similar to yours is not in the law, but good attorneys follow the precedent being constantly set by Courts. Incidentally, attorneys can be corrupt, lazy, stupid, or themselves bullies so select yours carefully. Check out his/her record with the bar association and Better Business Bureau and speak with previous clients, if possible. Organizations or medical professionals familiar with your condition, or bullying, may provide referrals of attorneys who are familiar with appropriate areas of the law. You will spend a lot of time with this attorney in excruciatingly painful circumstances, perhaps, so put your time into selection. If you're too sick or injured to do all this, get a trusted friend to help. Don't take anything you're told at face value; get numerous opinions.

If you've been bullied, you will likely be claiming some sort of psychiatric injury caused by the bullying; it may well have many physical manifestations. Document your medical and mental problems with your doctor and with a mental health provider. It's best to see a psychiatrist because they carry the most weight with fact finders. In addition, they are medical doctors and can understand and prescribe medication for the entire body, not just the mind. Report all your symptoms and problems; explain all the abuses done to you, all attempts you've made to fix problems, etc. You want your doctors to believe you, and understand your suffering and its cause. If you find your medical doctor won't take the time to listen to you, find another doctor. You must be assertive in demanding appropriate treatment; in the US few professionals know much about bullying and the damage it can wreak.

Workers' Comp or your employer may force you to be evaluated by their own psychiatrist, who might say that you are a sneaking crybaby looking for easy money, or that you've always had the problems you claim were caused by bullying. It's best if your psychiatrist has experience testifying in court and hearings, and is not intimidated by adversarial conditions. Many are not up to the task and will fold if the other psychiatrist or fact finder is aggressive with them. A good attorney should be able to help you find a psychiatrist fit for this duty; being a healer is definitely not enough. He knows exactly what testimony he needs from the psychiatrist to prove your case, and will work with the doctor to assure there will be no surprises at the hearing. Such medical backup is crucial in Workers' Comp, discrimination involving bullying, or Social Security cases, as well as actions involving Disability insurance, so see your doctors regularly.

Finally, although witness statements are embarrassing, painful to collect, and may harm relationships, they can make the difference in winning or losing your legal action. Talk with the person who witnessed your abuse, asking about details and reminding her of what happened, or what she told you previously. Let her know that you are going to write this information because you don't want her or you to forget it. If you have an attorney tell the witness your attorney needs to see what she knows and you'll be giving the attorney a copy. Record the data as soon as possible and show it to the witness, checking for accuracy and making corrections. Then ask her to sign it and give her a copy. If she refuses to sign or to meet with you about the written statement, don't argue, but try to confirm that you got it all correct. Then send the witness a copy by registered mail, with a note that this is the info she gave you on whatever date, and ask her to let you know as soon as possible, in writing, if there's anything not correct in the statement. Keep a copy of your note and the registration receipt for your records. People who have been helped by you through witness statements will practically never claim they don't remember later. They're now afraid of you, your attorney, the fact finder, the subpoena they will receive, and more; this is to the good. Why should the bully win yet more ground through scaring witnesses out of telling the absolute truth? People who are cowards can benefit from a little well-placed persuasion; but do keep your longer-range goals to yourself. While collecting witness statements, you may not know whether there will be a hearing. Most cases have final hour settlements. Your attorney can decide later whether to subpoena witnesses to confront them with their statements at hearing.

Resources

Here are some resources to help you find additional advice.

Online support forums and resources

BullyOnline

(www.bullyonline.org/action/egroups.htm,
www.groups.yahoo.com/group/bullyonline/).
Practical advice, support, insight and information for dealing with and recovering from workplace bullying.

Dana's View: information for AS adults

(www.danasview.net/adultinf.htm).

Dennis Debbaudt

(http://debbaudt.topcities.com/, www.policeandautism.cjb.net/).
Autism and Asperger Syndrome related investigations and consultations for criminal defense and civil plaintiff cases, defense attorneys, prosecutors and law enforcement agencies. (Note: this agency's services are geared mostly toward educating law enforcement professionals and defending AS/autistics in criminal cases, and would primarily help those who ended up provoked into some indiscriminate action.)

Mobbing-USA

(www.mobbing-usa.com/).
This site informs about the mobbing phenomenon. You will find information about the book *MOBBING: Emotional Abuse in the American Workplace* and about services and resources that help targets of mobbing or organizations to deal with the phenomenon in a constructive fashion.

My Toxic Boss

(www.mytoxicboss.com/).
Financial, psychological, legal, and other strategies for moving onward and upward from a verbally abusive or bullying manager.

Nineveh

(www.groups.yahoo.com/group/Nineveh/).
A support group for targets of workplace bullying and/or mobbing and those in toxic work environments, as well as worker's compensation issues. Its purpose is to validate the target and offer practical suggestions and guidance in the fight against work abuse.

Tim Field, BullyOnline

(www.bullyonline.org/, www.successunlimited.co.uk/, www.thefieldfoundation.org/).

Toxic Managers

(www.groups.yahoo.com/group/toxicmanagers/).
Dedicated to providing a forum for research into and discussion of financial, psychological, legal and other strategies for moving onward and upward from a verbally abusive or bullying manager.

The Work Doctor

(www.bullyinginstitute.org/home/workdoctor.pdf).

The Workplace Bullying and Trauma Institute

(www.bullyinginstitute.org/).

Books and publications

Davenport, N. *et al.* (1999) *Mobbing: Emotional Abuse in the American Workplace.* AMES, IA: Civil Society. ISBN 0967180309.

Field, T. (1996) *Bully In Sight: How to Predict, Resist, Challenge and Combat Workplace Bullying.* Didcot: Success Unlimited. ISBN 0952912104.

Futterman, S. (2004) *When You Work for a Bully: Assessing Your Options and Taking Action.* Montvale, NJ: Croce Publishing Group. ISBN 0971953880.

Herman, J.L. (1997) *Trauma and Recovery.* New York: Basic Books. ISBN 0465087302.

Hochheiser, R. (1987) *How to Work for a Jerk: Your Success is the Best Revenge.* New York: Vintage Books. ISBN 0394747771.

Hochheiser, R. (1998) *It's a Job, not a Jail: How to Break your Shackles When You Can't Afford to Quit.* New York: Fireside. ISBN 0684804581.

Job Accommodation Network Publications (www.jan.wvu.edu/media/MR.html).

Kinchin, D. (2001) *Post-Traumatic Stress Disorder: The Invisible Injury.* Didcot: Success Unlimited. ISBN 0952912139.

Lovett, H. (1996) *Learning to Listen: Positive Approaches and People With Difficult Behaviour.* Baltimore: Paul H. Brookes Publishing Co. ISBN 1557661642.

Lundin, W. and Lundin, K. (1999) *When Smart People Work for Dumb Bosses: How to Survive in a Crazy and Dysfunctional Workplace.* Maidenhead: McGraw-Hill. ISBN 0071348085.

Namie, G. and Namie, R. (2000) *The Bully at Work: What You Can Do to Stop the Hurt and Reclaim Your Dignity on the Job*. Naperville, IL: Sourcebooks. ISBN 1570715343.

Nicarthy, G. *et al.* (1993) *You Don't Have to Take It!: A Woman's Guide to Confronting Emotional Abuse at Work*. Seattle, WA: Seal Press. ISBN 1878067354.

NOLO Press: Self-Help Legal Books and Software (www.nolo.com. Phone (800) 728-3555).

Take Charge of Your Worker's Compensation Claim (www.nolo.com/lawstore/products/product.cfm/objectID/FCA8DD0B-A2D1-42E5-8F4E045364F65F6C/authorID/D0231667-CC02-4898-AA0A20A1BB 804983).

Lana Kapchinsky has a BBA magna cum laude and over 20 years of work experience in office environments, customer service, and student/employment assistance services for disadvantaged populations.

Gerriann Fox has over 30 years of experience in professional investigative and legal work.

38 You Have a Bad Attitude

Alice E. Gerard

In 1991, several years after I had earned a bachelor's degree in political science and a master's degree in journalism, I was told that I had a learning disability. It was explained to me that I was to work with counselors who would help me get and keep a job. The counselors were trained to help difficult cases, such as mine.

I was assigned to a vocational counselor named Thor. Before I met him, I envisioned him as some sort of Norse god guiding me toward a career filled with excitement. After all, I had proven from my track record of crash and burn experiences in office-type jobs that I didn't have the attention span for clerical work.

"I am a dash of cold water," a very un-Norse-god-like man informed me. "What is your dream job?"

"Travel writer," I said, blissfully lost in mental images of ancient Inca cities and Egyptian pyramids.

Thor told me that I would get nauseated in airplanes, my luggage would vanish, and the food in foreign countries would be inedible. "How about billing clerk?" I said that I didn't see any connection between journalism and billing clerk. Thor said, "You write letters." I thought, "How about war correspondent?" Instead, I said that billing clerk didn't sound like a very good job for someone who adds on her fingers.

"You have a bad attitude," Thor said.

One day, I went to see Thor, and he was holding the help-wanted section from the Sunday newspaper. He read an advertisement to me for some sort of office job. I told him that I could read the help-wanted ads at home. He said that he had to teach me how to read the help-wanted ads. When I failed to give the proper response, Thor told me that I had a bad attitude.

After I graduated from vocational counselor to job placement counselor, I was placed in a small freelance job doing data entry at a home computer. Once a week, I organized data from fire call logs for two small weekly newspapers. I gained valuable information about car crashes, fires, and ambulance calls. After six years, unfortunately, the job ended when the two weekly newspapers ceased publication.

A number of years and job counselors later, vocational rehabilitation services had entered the internet era. My job placement counselor communicated with me mostly via email, but occasionally on the telephone. The only time that we met in person was during a 20-minute intake interview. The job counselor bombarded me with so many help-wanted ads via email and snail mail that I nicknamed her "Ms Ad Clipper". The ads were for such positions as technical proofreader and technical writer in engineering or pharmacological companies and technical library assistant or advertising sales. She said that the advertising sales job would help me get my foot in the door and that I could work up to a reporter's position. I told her that's not how it works. She said, "You have a bad attitude."

I wondered if she and Thor had gone to the same school, where the instructor said, "Repeat after me: You have a bad attitude."

Ms Ad Clipper wanted a progress report. I indicated discomfort with applying for jobs for which I was clearly unqualified. She told me that I should learn to think outside of the box. "OK," I said. Once, Ms Ad Clipper mailed a truncated, yet familiar looking, help-wanted ad to me. I found the original ad in the Sunday newspaper. Sure enough, she had snipped out the list of qualifications for the job, which included training and experience in "technical library work".

I applied for one of the technical proofreading jobs that Ms Ad Clipper recommended, mainly to pacify her, and I got an interview. I was told about the wonderful salary and benefits and the great, casual working environment. Cash registers started ringing in my head. Maybe Ms Ad Clipper wasn't so crazy after all. I could have a laptop computer, a cell phone, a Palm Pilot, a DVD player. I was given a proofreading test and the warning that the information that I was about to see was "proprietary" and not to share that material with outsiders or risk a dire penalty. My gadget-laden bubble burst as I surveyed all of the incomprehensible mathematical formulas that I was expected to proofread. The company was safe from me. Weeks later, I received a rejection letter. The interviewer said that I was a very good editor but that there were no jobs in that company that were appropriate for a person with my skills.

I decided that I didn't need Ms Ad Clipper's help in finding an inappropriate job. I took a civil service test for employment as a "clerk-typist". I had a variety of interviews, none of which resulted in a job offer. One interviewer at a state college made rapid speech sounds. I asked her to slow down. She described a receptionist's job. It sounded like a great job – for three people. I then heard a high-pitched noise. Fire drill. I ran down the stairs with my fingers firmly planted in my ears, followed by the interviewer. I didn't get the job but I did get the next-best thing – a coupon for a free beverage from the college's coffee shop.

I now have a very good job placement counselor who tells me that I'm smart, talented, and have a great attitude. She asks me to describe the work environment in which I would be comfortable and the kind of work that I would like to do. She drives me to interviews with potential employers. In the car, she gives me an idea of some of the questions that I could be asked. After the interviews, she gives me pointers on how to write effective thank-you letters. She and I work as a team to find me a job. And I read the help-wanted ads on my own at home.

Alice E. Gerard, an adult with learning disabilities, has a master's degree in journalism and works as an Assistant Managing Editor for a small alternative publication (Alt Press) in Buffalo, New York.

3 9 Vocational Rehabilitation Programs and the NLD/AS Individual

When President Bush signed the Americans with Disabilities Act into law on 26th July 1990, he said, "A major goal of this legislation is to demonstrate that disabled Americans want to work to support themselves and maintain independence" (DeVroy 1990). Since then, the ADA has helped those with physical disabilities to achieve this goal by creating user-friendly work environments. Increasingly, the employment needs of individuals with mental impairments are also being met. In addition to sheltered workshops, they're offered community jobs in supermarkets, restaurants, and hotels.

The Division of Vocational Rehabilitation (VR) is designed to help all disabled people become gainfully employed. Vocational rehabilitation counselors are trained to evaluate the individual's vocational strengths and weaknesses and provide training and assistance. However, the special needs of those with neurological or social handicaps aren't well understood by most employers or VR personnel. Because these individuals are intelligent and articulate, their skills and abilities obfuscate their need for supports and services – until they fail. Many ASers and NLDers have sought the assistance of VR services in obtaining and maintaining employment, but found the help available inappropriate to their needs. Susan Moreno, executive director of Maap Services, Inc., explains the dilemma:

> The better they have done in rising to the challenges of their disability – the more able they are to communicate and act in a manner expected of non-handicapped people – the less likely they are to receive vocational rehabilitation services. Yet these rare and wonderful people have

the potential to achieve the most vocationally with comparatively few hours of VR services to help them with those characteristics of their handicap which remain barriers to successful employment. These characteristics include being too honest or blunt with other people; difficulty controlling their tempers; trouble processing information; not knowing how to appropriately seek and/or accept help; difficulty socializing appropriately with co-workers; and problems dealing with the public. Without the help they need, they usually experience failure in the work place.

VR counselors are used to dealing with people with reading and writing difficulties. They frequently work with mentally retarded individuals who can be employed as dishwashers or janitors. They also help people with physical limitations, who work with the aid of accommodations like wheelchair ramps. Most are unfamiliar, however, with neurological conditions like NLD or AS, and often make the VR experience confusing, frustrating, and demeaning for them. Individuals with AS and NLD have been placed in sheltered workshops for the mentally retarded and sent to halfway houses for the mentally ill. But they're neither retarded nor psychotic. They're intelligent, highly skilled, and college educated, yet unable to maintain employment due to difficulties with fast-paced, production oriented, and socially demanding work environments. They need meaningful, satisfying paid employment in the community. When they're not allowed to work and contribute, society is the loser. Even the VR counselors lack understanding of their qualifications and challenges, and don't know how to help them.

While the NLDer/ASer may attempt to fit in and conform, pretending to be normal, society – made up of co-workers and bosses – refuses to accept them. What is really a part of the disability gets blamed on a bad attitude. They find themselves accused of being lazy or rude when in fact most are trying very hard to achieve. People just don't understand how someone who seems so normal or bright has such problems with certain things.

Many AS/NLD adults report that the VR counselors they saw felt their employment problems were due to a poor attitude and other personality characteristics rather than to a disability. Yet, if something cuts down on your ability to work and get by in life, and is involuntary, then it is a disability.

When first approached, most VR counselors seem friendly. However, once the client mentions Asperger Syndrome or NLD, they acknowledge they know little about it. When some individuals described their lifelong troubles working smoothly with others, they were told everyone has those problems. The implications are that such social issues are vague and that they should grow out of them. Some were even told to attend 12-step programs for help with these issues. In fact, most NLDers/ASers have tried to change for years. However, due to the neurological rather than psychological nature of their problems, the differences remain. Most NLDers/ASers coming to vocational rehabilitation aren't looking for excuses; they're at the end of a long road trying to learn coping skills in order to deal with their difficulties. Yet even here they find little help. Instead, they are sent back out into the world and told to get over it. When they try to explain the problems that stem from NLD or AS, they're met with "Oh – everyone has strengths and weaknesses." Yet, if they described issues resulting from having been raped, they would never be told "Oh – lots of people have sex."

Although many NLDers/ASers have demonstrated the ability to do college-level work, many can't keep a job and have a poor work record. Looking for work with the knowledge that job failure is imminent is like chasing illusions; getting your hopes up that the next job will work out, then crashing when you fail again. Unfortunately, most NLDers/ASers I've talked to received little help from the VR agencies. They've found these agencies geared towards placing people in unskilled, entry-level jobs instead of jobs commensurate with the person's educational achievement. The assumption seems to be that if the person is not fit for the entry-level position, they won't be fit for anything else. Not only is this demeaning, but it is often inappropriate. The person can't keep up with the assembly line, pack groceries fast enough, or fold and put away enough clothes in the dress shop. In the kitchen, their clumsiness makes them prone to accidents. They spill food, break dishes, or cut themselves. Due to slow mental and motor processing, these are the very things many ASers/NLDers simply aren't able to do. Laurie explains:

> My experience with Vocational Rehabilitation was not very positive… due to limited funds and even more to the limited number of career options. Everything these people had to offer was dependent on speed, required the ability to multi-task and the ability to think on one's feet. Unfortunately, persons or at least this person with NLD are not too vocational-rehab compatible. (Reed 2001, p.70)

While jobs in supermarkets, the food industry, or cleaning services are plentiful, at professional levels the competition is fierce. Employers aren't willing to hire professionals with invisible handicaps who are clumsy or have poor social skills, even if these employees are capable and talented. They're apt to dismiss the best employee as some kind of idiot savant whose efforts don't really count the way normal individuals' do.

Social demands are part of every workplace. Each job has its own social code. Rules change. People demand adjustment. The new employee must be able to figure out people's various temperaments, who's good to work with, and who isn't. You have to learn how hard to work; hard enough to get the job done, but if you're too good or too quick your co-workers may not be too happy with you. You want to be seen as sharp, but not as a know-it-all. These are fine lines that are very difficult for the AS/NLD individual to master.

Professional work is often easier in one regard. While there are social demands, the work tends to be more intellectual and less manual. Professional work is less likely to be production oriented, so speed is not as big a factor. Often, the individual can fall back on their vast store of knowledge.

Sometimes the VR counselor, who is supposedly an expert in dealing with people with disabilities, assumes that because those NLDers/ASers have certain neurological issues, they are incapable of doing much of anything, least of all holding down a job. What is lacking is the middle ground: acknowledging that NLD and AS are serious disabilities which may require accommodation in the work setting, and providing those accommodations, allowing the person a measure of accomplishment and success in the work world. NLDers/ASers need help finding a work environment where they can succeed, and obtaining leads to jobs in the hidden job market which aren't advertised.

There are supports out there for other individuals with disabilities. The physically disabled have many accommodations. Buses have wheelchair lifts. Public buildings must be wheelchair accessible. The blind person gets readers. The deaf have interpreters. Even individuals with ADD have gained increased acceptance. But NLD/AS? No one knows what these things are, what these individuals need, or how to provide the help that they need. VR counselors are not trained to deal with learning disabilities or with neurological disorders. Their deficient understanding is a function of a numbers-driven system, giving jobs to folks who are more adaptable, easier to accommodate, and provide a less complex challenge.

Supported employment has worked for individuals with other disabilities, and may be an answer for the AS/NLD employee. Specialized employment supports are provided to people with psychiatric disabilities, developmental disabilities, physical disabilities (blindness, hearing impairments, traumatic brain injuries), and substance abuse issues. Supported employment programs help disabled individuals obtain and maintain jobs in the community. The philosophy behind supported employment is that everyone has the right to a meaningful job, should determine their own employment goals and obtain the assistance and supports they need in order to achieve their ambitions. The aim is to place people in community jobs with competitive employers within the local labor market, but provide them with the necessary additional supports that they need to succeed. The keys to successful employment for individuals with AS/NLD are:

- education and training for VR staff about NLD/AS and its effect on the employee
- vocational counseling/career planning, including assessment
- pre-employment skill development, especially interviewing skills
- job development/job placement
- job maintenance support, including long-term follow-up services.

Educating VR staff about NLD/AS

VR personnel, vocational counselors, job coaches, and others working with or helping this population must understand this disability and how it affects the VR client. Information, education, and training about NLD/AS are imperative in order to effectively help NLDers/ASers to succeed in the workplace. VR needs to be educated about the strengths and challenges of individuals with neurological and social disabilities. Only then will they be able to place these valuable, skilled employees in a suitable work setting. If they don't understand the challenges faced by these people, they won't be able to explain the individual's strengths and weaknesses to the employer, ensuring acceptance, understanding, and a good fit.

Approach vocational and rehabilitation counselors with the same type of information you would give the teacher if your NLD/AS child was starting school. The main thing they need to know is that, due to high educational achievement and excellent language skills, NLD or AS often appears a lot better than it is. I can't tell you how many times counselors have looked at me and said "You don't have any disabilities", even though it was very obvious from my job record and medical issues that I do. Most VR counselors don't understand brain-based disabilities.

With no awareness of the issues they face, these individuals are not understood by VR or in the workplace. The challenges they face are not taken seriously. What is in fact part of the disability is falsely attributed to personality. They try hard to be part of the organization, only to be told "Sorry, you just don't fit in here." They attempt to conform, but they're not accepted. They work hard, but are accused of being lazy. They do their best and are told it's not good enough. They're honest, and are accused of being rude. They work very hard to achieve, and are met with frustration due to repeated failure. People – VR counselors, employers, and others – can't understand how someone with a PhD seems so gauche, how someone who seems so bright has such problems with simple things like pouring a cup of coffee, keeping the desk neat, or joining a conversation.

AS and NLD are neurological impairments, and need to be seen as such. They're not mental, psychiatric, or physical disorders. It's essential that the VR counselor has a thorough understanding of these capable, intelligent individuals, a good grasp of the person's capabilities as well as disabilities, and that the person is placed in work appropriate to their level of education and ability and in a supportive, congenial environment. When meeting a VR counselor for the first time, ask the following questions:

1. What do you know about NLD? About AS? (Ask about both, since the work problems are similar.)

2. How many AS/NLD adults have you worked with? What types of educational background did they have, and what types of work are they in? What accommodations do they use/need? What's your success rate in placing these adults in jobs? Are the jobs commensurate with the individual's level of education and training? Do these jobs offer benefits and opportunities for advancement?

3. How do you evaluate the individual employment profile of each candidate? How do you determine what jobs are most suitable? How do you market the client's strengths, skills and talents to prospective employers?

4. How do you plan to educate the employer (communicate with the employer) about AS/NLD issues that may impact the work?

The job challenge for most adults with NLD/AS usually has to do with fitting into and understanding the social rules of the company.

5.   How do you see these folks fitting in? How can you help me to navigate through workplace politics and workplace bullying that derails even NTs' careers?

6.   I'm aware of the jobs that are advertised in the paper and on the internet. How can you help me contact the "hidden job market"? Do you work with employers who hire folks with disabilities?

While the above questions are appropriate, one word of caution is needed. Some VR counselors might feel threatened if their understanding of NLD/AS is limited. They may feel that you're arrogant, become defensive, and not offer you the help you need.

Vocational counseling/career planning

This includes assessment, career exploration, and developing an understanding of how the disability will impact various careers and workplace environments. It's important to use a variety of tools to determine the person's strengths, skills, interests, abilities, and personality type, and balance these against the limitations arising from the disability. Build on the person's strengths rather than emphasizing accommodations for weaknesses, and use those interests and abilities in paid employment.

Identify workplace challenges and impediments to employment, along with their causes. Examples of impediments to successful employment could be noisy buildings, chaotic work settings, too much going on at once, insufficient training period, etc.

The end goal is to find solutions and create strategies, interventions, and accommodations that will reduce the challenges and assist the individual to do a great job. It's important to discover what can be done to accommodate the client's needs and to make the work experience successful for both the client and the employer.

Pre-employment skill development

Most ASers/NLDers will already have a résumé and know how to write a good cover letter. This is the time to discuss and teach interpersonal skills, including interview techniques, how and when to disclose the disability, how to ask for help and request accommodations. Issues that will arise at work, such as office politics, social skills needed to be successful and organizational techniques, can also be brought up. A peer support or discussion group could be useful for this purpose.

The individual should work together with the VR caseworker to determine what accommodations are needed. Consider the report documenting the disability, as well as how the AS or NLD interacts with the work environment. Previous experience is useful for determining what will help the individual to succeed. It's important to remember that no two people have exactly the same needs with regard to accommodating a disability. VR counselors may forget this in their effort to categorize their clients. Anything learned from prior work experience can be valuable.

Combine your experience with the expertise of the vocational rehabilitation counselor assisting you. Together, formulate a plan that works for you, within the guidelines of what they can do. An open mind and a cool head are your most valuable tools, since sometimes dealing with disability offices can seem really frustrating.

Self-advocacy is another important area. It's helpful to be able to tell one's employer "That's not how I work best", and to suggest other ways of handling things that may be more productive and satisfying; for example: "That's not what I do best. Maybe I could work on a different piece of the project where I could make a better contribution." But this is only possible if the employer understands the disability and is willing to make accommodations. Otherwise, the person may come across as having an attitude when they make such requests.

The employee should learn how to state his or her needs. When someone says "I can't handle multi-step instructions, I'm NLD", the other person may write them off (at worst) or won't know how to respond (at best). He will need to be able to say "I'm sorry, could you repeat that for me so I can understand it better?" or "Let me summarize our understanding thus far to see if I've gotten everything". People are more receptive to someone who says "Can you go over that again? I'll need to write those steps down so that I can remember them" or "I learn better when I have written instructions to follow". However, many busy supervisors loathe taking the time to repeat instructions and make sure the trainee understands.

Job development/job placement

As you have read in the previous chapters, those NLD/AS individuals who succeeded did so because the work environment was supportive and friendly. In the right environment, the right job, and with the right supervisor and supports, the NLDer/ASer can succeed. The key to successful work placement is finding the right match between the job and the individual's characteristics. A supportive work setting and friendly, understanding co-workers are other important factors. The job must be a good fit and have components the individual can handle.

The AS/NLD employee can do a fantastic job if the employer is friendly, accommodating, and understanding. James Emmett of the Vocational Alliance says: "Employers must understand that they are gaining a wonderful employee, but they must also realize the importance of structure and clear feedback to help the employee succeed."

The attitude "we've always done it this way, this is how you need to do it" can be deadly. Often, these individuals need to do things a different way in order to work around their disability. The employer needs to understand this and be open to creative ways of accomplishing the same results. It's important that the agency has connections to businesses and employers in the community who will take the extra effort to ensure success for these valuable and skilled employees. VR should have contacts with employers who would be willing to hire individuals with the disparity of strengths and weaknesses, abilities and liabilities, that are part and parcel of NLD/AS, and be willing to work around individual disabilities. VR has contact with employers who are willing to accept individuals with Down Syndrome and other developmental disabilities. Employees with AS and NLD are usually much more highly skilled, though they are somewhat quirky. They need the same employer contact and intervention, but on a more professional level.

Job maintenance and support

The necessary supports and accommodations need to be put in place. Often these accommodations are similar to those used when the person was in school. The issues don't change; the disability doesn't go away. This is why, in addition to an understanding of the disability, ongoing support and guidance are critical for job stability. Peter Gerhardt, who has many years of experience working with AS adults, recommends training for NT co-workers, so that they'll better understand the social and behavioral issues, and look past them to see the individual's strengths. Otherwise, the most well-meaning people – counselors, bosses, and job coaches alike – will say "He's not trying hard enough" or "She needs more confidence". When people see intelligent, skilled individuals, it's hard for them to fathom the problems caused by poor motor skills and motor planning, lack of executive function abilities, and inability to understand non-verbal social cues. The individual's need for detailed written instructions, for extended training time, for organization, for tasks being broken down, is not well understood.

Job coaching

One way that VR can help the individual to maintain employment is by providing on-the-job assistance through a job coach. Even though the coaches are provided free to the employer, many employers aren't willing to work with a job coach, especially in professional positions. Many job coaches aren't comfortable in the role of acting as a go-between and talking to the boss.

A good job coach match depends on many factors, including personality and coaching style. It is crucial for the job coach to be in the know, understand the disability, and have respect for the individual. He should be observant, genuine, and caring. A well-informed job coach can play an important part as a go-between and explain the individual's strengths, weaknesses, and the needed accommodations to the employer. At the same time, he can clarify the unwritten, abstract workplace rules for the AS/NLD employee. If he's aware of the problems, he can anticipate the issues and take proactive measures. This can go a long way towards creating a friendly, accepting work environment.

A job coach can help immensely with social adjustment and teaching social skills. Peter Gerhardt states that "the job challenge for these adults is social based. Either some interaction is misinterpreted, or office politics work against them, or some quirk in behavior is disturbing to an NT co-worker". Therefore, counseling to ensure social adjustment is crucial. It's important for co-workers and supervisors to understand the individual's idiosyncrasies. The boss, the job coach, and the NT co-worker must understand these social and behavioral issues and recognize the individual's strengths. Interacting appropriately with their boss and co-workers is important to fitting into the work environment.

A job coach helps with training the employee, and is aware of the ASers/NLDers learning style, relieving the supervisor to devote his or her time to other things. Many ASers/NLDers have trouble breaking down large projects into their component parts. The job coach can make a list of all the detailed steps needed to complete a task. This is called task analysis, and is a strategy often used to teach a multi-step task.

Developing natural supports on the job site is another important function of the coach. This refers to the time when the individual's co-workers provide the necessary supports. There's great value in assigning a mentor, who can act as an advocate with other employees, to help the disabled employee. This is particularly true with the social aspects of the job. If co-workers are understanding of the individual's communication, learning, and work style, and act accordingly (communicating explicitly, giving specific and step-by-step instructions, etc.), problems can be greatly diminished and reliance on the job coach can be reduced. The goal is to keep the person employed, and intervene when necessary.

We've got a long way to go before companies are willing to accommodate productive employees with neurological disorders like AS, NLD or ADD. Yet, if employers recognized that some people who look, think, or work differently can still be productive employees, they might be more willing to accommodate different work styles or a longer learning curve. The combination of good job coaching, pre-planning, and an employer who gets it are the key components to workplace success.

40 I Have A Dream

I have a dream that I go to a job interview and the interviewer doesn't think I'm strange because I can't make eye contact or don't immediately notice his outstretched hand. He understands that some people listen better when they're not looking at you.

I have a dream that when I take too long to reply to the interviewer's questions, he patiently waits for my reply and is understanding of the fact that some folks take longer to process their thoughts.

I have a dream that when I get lost in the building on my first day of work, my boss and co-workers understand this is due to my lack of spatial skills, and don't wonder what's wrong with me.

I have a dream that one day people won't look at me strangely when I mutter to myself while solving complex problems or learning new tasks. They understand that I need to vocalize everything in order to think and remember.

I have a dream that when I'm engrossed in my work and only see things relating to my task, being oblivious to what's going on around me, my colleagues understand that this is my work style and I'm not deliberately ignoring them.

I have a dream that someday I won't have to worry about people being creeped out by certain subliminal things in the way I look and walk.

I have a dream that when I go to lunch with my co-workers and am a bit messy, they understand this is due to my motor and coordination problems, and don't put me down or think worse of me.

I have a dream that when I fail to greet people because I don't recognize them, they understand this and tell me who they are and where we've met before.

I have a dream that someday people will only look at the positive things and not the negatives.

I have a dream that someday social idiosyncrasies won't matter. People will be valued for their intelligence and skills, and not be seen as weird.

I have a dream that one day people will understand neurological conditions like NLD or AS and won't wonder why someone as intelligent, capable, and articulate as I am seems so clueless.

I have a dream that someday those I work with will accept me just the way I am.

41 Individual Employee Plan
Judy Lewis and Debbie Green

Name: _____

Birthdate: _____

Current date: _____

Age: _____

Address:

_____

_____

_____

Phone Number: _____

Transition

_____Training on how to write a résumé/contact employees/ask for references

_____Training on how to dress for an interview

_____Practice answering and asking interview questions

_____Interview on videotape – discuss strengths and weaknesses

_____Training on how to follow up after the interview

_____Job shadowing

_____Training in flexible thinking skills/brainstorming multiple solutions

_____Career tests/personality inventories

_____Meeting with job counselor to find realistic picture of strengths and deficits

_____Other

Personnel

_____Need peer mentor to explain system and answer questions

_____Need support person outside of work to supervise and offer advice

_____Need regular meetings with supervisor to discuss progress and concerns

_____ Needs someone as a guide from place to place

_____Other

Adaptive equipment

_____ Needs computer with word processor

_____ Needs specific software (list below)

_____ Needs quiet area to work in

_____ Needs clearly defined space with organizational tools in place

_____ Needs written lists of policies and procedures

_____ Other

General accommodations

_____ Needs directions repeated multiple times or written down

_____ Needs as much routine and repetition as possible

_____ Needs direct feedback and direct correction regarding
    problems

_____ Needs to be excused from doing tasks of a purely visual/spatial
    nature like graphs, charts, or graphic presentation

_____ Needs help with organizing possessions and tasks – ideally,
    each new task will be talked through sequentially

_____ Needs to be excused from assignments requiring a high level of
    fine and gross motor control

_____ Needs extra time to process new tasks – do not penalize for
    slow work

_____ All instructions should be written down sequentially

_____ Other

_____

Comments

_____

_____

_____

_____

_____

_____

Employee's signature _____Date_____

Employer's signature _____Date_____

Judy Lewis is Co-Founder and Vice President of the Nonverbal Learning Disorders
Association (NLDA) and the creator and administrator of the NLD Hotline and the
NLDline.com website. She is the owner of NLD Connection and works as an NLD
Coach.

42 Career Choices

Good jobs for NLDers/ASers

Accounting.

Animal trainer or veterinary technician. Work with animals, not people.

Archival or library science. Concentrate on cataloging rather than reference or library management.

Bank teller. Social interactions are routine and stereotypical. Requires accuracy but (in contrast with a busy cashier) minimizes need for short-term memory and quick money handling.

College professor. Specialize in area of interest; information delivery; eccentrics often tolerated.

Computer programming. Can be contractual.

Copy editor. Makes use of detail orientation.

Engineering. Good choice for Aspies who are more visual.

Journalism. Accurate facts, can be done as freelance. May be too high pressure, depending on publication type.

Mathematician. Few jobs, only the most brilliant can get jobs.

Medical information technology (aka medical records). Good detail orientation.

Medical transcription. Solitary, work with tapes and computer.

Physicist. Few jobs, only the most brilliant can get jobs.

Research, e.g. legal, proposal, etc. Makes use of analytical and verbal strengths.

Sales. Although it involves social interaction, this is often one directional. The salesman gets to talk about his area of interest, with little need for understanding of complex social relationships.

Statistician. Work in various fields, such as research, census bureau, industrial quality control, etc.

Technical writing.

Telemarketing. Repeat the same thing over and over. Avoids social problems.

Tour guide. Makes use of the lecturing tone and repetitive speech patterns. Communication is one directional. Can play into the person's special interest.

Tuning pianos and musical instruments. Specialized, can be done as freelance.

Poor job choices for NLDers/ASers

Auto mechanic, small engine repair. Requires physical agility and motor skills.

Building trades. Needs good visual skills and good motor coordination.

Bus driver. Lots of interaction with the public, lots of idiots driving around in cars to cope with, poor sense of direction.

Car salesman. Too much complex social behavior.

Cashier. Making change quickly is difficult on short-term working memory and physical handling of money (motor).

Computer troubleshooter and repair. Needs ability to visualize problems in computers and networks, fine motor skills, manual dexterity and speed.

Customer service. When working with the public, can have difficulties due to inability to read non-verbal signals.

Delivery. Needs good sense of direction.

Factory assembly work. Requires fine motor, speed, and often noisy environment.

Housekeeping, hotel maid. Clumsiness, organization, and time management. "I would spend an hour on the corner of a linoleum floor in order to get it perfect, sort of get into la-la land and lose track of the time. I also was very afraid of breaking valuable collectibles."

Manager. Need to supervise and work with other employees, too much social interaction.

Manual labor. Requires good motor skills, speed, and perceptual ability.

Plumber. Requires ability to visualize, perceptual ability, and fine motor skills.

Police officer. Lots of interaction with the public and colleagues.

Receptionist and switchboard operator. Too much multi-tasking, too many buzzers and bells, too much talking on the phone to people.

Short order cook. Must keep track of many orders and cook many things; multi-tasking demands.

Sports instructor. Indifference to NT sports, poor physical coordination.

Taxi dispatcher, air traffic controller. Information overload, need quick reflexes, high stress, too many things to keep track of.

Taxi driver. Problems with getting lost, poor choice for spatially challenged. Also many NLDers/ASers have problems with the multi-tasking involved in driving a car and paying attention to the road.

Teacher. Classroom behavior can be problematic.

Waiter/waitress. Need to keep track of too many things at once, needs excellent physical coordination.

PART III
Resources

Disability resources
Career resources

Disability Resources

Asperger Syndrome

ASPEN of America, Inc.
(also known as the Asperger Syndrome Coalition)
PO Box 2577
Jacksonville, FL, 32203-2577
USA
Tel: 904-745-6741
Website: www.aspennj.org

Research and Educational Centre
PO Box 351268
Jacksonville, FL 32235-1668
USA
Tel: (866)4-ASPRGR
Email: aspen@cybermax.net
Website: www.asperger.org/
Non-profit organization dealing with Non-Verbal Learning Disabilities (NLD), Asperger Syndrome (AS), and related neurologically based social and communication disorders.

Asperger's Association of New England (for all ages)
Newton Centre, MA
Tel: 617-527-2894
Email: info@aane.org
Website: www.aane.org

Asperger's Disorder Clinician List
Website: www.aspergers.com/asplist.htm
This is a list of clinicians who stated that they are familiar with Asperger Syndrome and willing to evaluate children and/or adults who have this problem.

Center for the Study of Autism
PO Box 4538
Salem, OR 97302
USA
Website: www.autism.org/asperger.html

Families of Adults Afflicted with Asperger's Syndrome
Centerville, MA
USA
Tel: 508-775-1412
Email: faaas@faaas.org
Website: www.faaas.org

Online Asperger Information and Support (OASIS)
Website: www.udel.edu/bkirby/asperger/

On-Line Community
www.asperger_autism-subscriber@onelist.com

Tony Attwood
Website: www.tonyattwood.com.au
This website is a guide for parents, professionals, people with Asperger Syndrome and their partners.

www.aspergerssyndrome.org

Assistive technology

ABLEDATA
Website: www.abledata.com
Provides information and links on assistive technology, including over 30,000 reviews on adaptive equipment.

Assistivetech.net
Website: www.assistivetech.net
Features a database of assistive technology products and a wide variety of links.

Center for an Accessible Society
Website: www.accessiblesociety.org
Disability news items and links to background material.

Tech Connections

Website: www.techconnections.org

Allows users to search a comprehensive resource of applications of assistive technology related to vocational rehabilitation needs.

Employment for People with Disabilities

Accommodating disabilities

Cornell University School of Labor and Industrial Relations Program on Employment and Disability
Ithaca, NY
USA
Tel: (607) 255-7727
Fax: (607) 255-2763
TTY: (607) 255-2981
Website: www.ilr.cornell.edu/ped/hr_tips/home.cfm
Great information for employers and employees.

National Collaborative on Workforce and Disability for Youth (NCWD/Youth)

c/o Institute for Educational Leadership
1001 Connecticut Ave., NW, Suite 310
Washington, DC 20036
USA
Tel: 877-871-0744 (toll free)
Website: www.ncwd-youth.info

Rehabilitation Research and Training Center

Website: www.worksupport.com

The site contains current information, resources and research regarding the employment of people with disabilities.

Disability Info.gov

Website: www.disAbility.gov

The comprehensive federal website of disability-related government sources. Has information on hiring and recruiting workers with disabilities.

Hogan, G. (2003) *The Inclusive Corporation*. Athens, OH: Swallow Press.

General disability and legal information

ADA (Americans with Disabilities Act)
Website: www.adata.org
Voice/TTY: 800-949-4232
The ADA has established ten regional disability and business technical assistance centers in ten regions in order to answer questions about the Americans with Disabilities Act.

ADA: Human Resource Guide
Website: www.hr-guide.com/data/083.htm

Americans with Disabilities Act: Information and Technical Assistance
Website: www.usdoj.gov/crt/ada/adahom1.htm

Job Accommodation Network
Website: www.jan.wvu.edu. http://janweb.icdi.wvu.edu
Voice/TTY: 800-ADA-WORK
The Job Accommodation Network (JAN) is an international toll-free consulting service that provides information about job accommodations and the employability of people with disabilities. JAN also provides information regarding the Americans with Disabilities Act (ADA).

US Department of Justice
950 Pennsylvania Avenue NW
Washington, DC 20530-0001
USA
Website: www.usdoj.gov/crt/ada/adahom1.htm
Voice: 800-514-0301
TTY: 800-514-0383

US Department of Labor – Office of Disability Policy (ODEP)
200 Constitution Ave, NW
Washington, DC 20210
USA
Website: www.dol.gov/odep/
Voice: (202) 376-6200
ODEP's mission is to provide leadership to increase employment opportunities for adults and youth with disabilities. ODEP is a federal agency in the Department of Labor. They also publish a booklet, "Win With Ability", designed to assist employers with hiring the disabled.

US Equal Employment Opportunity Commission (EEOC)
1801 L Street, NW
Washington, DC 20507
USA
Website: www.eeoc.gov
Tel: toll free 1-800-669-4000 (TTY 1-800-669-6820)
Publications/voice: 800-669-EEOC (669-3362)
This is the federal agency that deals with ADA title I issues. The informative article "Enforcement Guidance: Reasonable Accommodation and Undue Hardship Under the Americans with Disabilities Act" is available at www.eeoc.gov/docs/accommodation.html

Learning disabilities

Learning Disabilities Association of America (LD)
4156 Library Road
Pittsburgh, PA 15234
USA
Tel: 412-341-1515/412-341-8077
Fax: 412-344-0224
Website: www.ldanatl.org

LD OnLine
Website: http://janweb.icdi.wvu.edu
An exceptionally comprehensive learning disabilities website servicing parents, teachers, and children. LD OnLine is a service of The Learning Project at WETA, Washington, DC, in association with The Coordinated Campaign for Learning Disabilities.

LD Pride Online
Website: www.ldpride.net
An online information and community resource for adults with invisible disabilities including learning disabilities and attention deficit disorder (ADD). The website is the online home for the Vancouver Island Invisible Disability Association, a non-profit organization supporting adults of all ages with learning disabilities, attention deficit disorder, Asperger Syndrome, mental illness, mild brain injuries and fetal alcohol syndrome.

Non-Verbal Learning Disability

NLD-In-Common
Email: NLD-In-Common-subscribe@yahoogroups.com
NLD-In-Common is a members only listserv for adults with NLD and families of children with NLD. To subscribe, send a blank email.

NLD on the Web
Website: www.nldontheweb.org
You'll find valuable information about NLD, including articles and links to important websites.

NLDline
Website: www.nldline.com
This website is devoted to increasing awareness of NLD among parents and professionals. Included are articles and resource listings, personal stories, and a bulletin board.

Nonverbal Learning Disorders Association
2446 Albany Avenue
West Hartford, CT 06117
USA
Tel: (860) 570-0217
Email: NLDA@nlda.org
Website: www.nlda.org
A non-profit corporation dedicated to research, education, and advocacy for non-verbal learning disorders.

Rush Neurobehavioral Center
1650 W. Harrison St.
Chicago, IL 60612
USA
Tel: (312) 942-5000
Website: www.rush.edu/patients/rnbc/index.html
One of the leading centers for NLD and AS diagnosis, research and intervention. Led by Meryl Lipton, MD, PhD.

Tera's NLD Jumpstation
Website: www.geocities.com/HotSprings/Spa/7262
Tera Kirk, a young college student with NLD, shares her witty and wise perspectives on the disorder and life in general. NLD teens or young adults can benefit from her insight.

Organizations with pilot employment programs for individuals with AS or NLD

Access Unlimited
Website: www.accessunlimited.com/links.html
An impressive cascading index of disability links, although quite commercialized.

AlderCentre
Adult Learning Disabilities Employment Resource Centre
2625 Danforth Avenue
Toronto
Ontario
Canada
Tel: (416) 693-2922
Fax: (416) 698-6453
Email: ld@aldercentre.org
Website: www.aldercentre.org/home.htm

Community Enterprises, Inc.
441 Pleasant Street,
PO Box 598,
Northampton, MA 01060
USA
Tel: 413-584-1460
Website: www.communityenterprises.com

Emory Autism Resource Center (EARC)
Robert Babcock, PhD
Emory Autism Resource Center
1551 Shoup Court
Decatur, GA 30033
USA
Tel: 404-727-3964
Sheila Wagner, M.Ed.

Emory Autism Resource Center
718 Gatewood Rd.
Atlanta, GA 30322
USA
Tel: 404-727-8350
Emory Autism Resource Center (EARC) is a university-based program for children, adolescents and adults with autism and related disorders, their families, and professionals and agencies that serve them.

Maap Services, Inc.
"More Able Autistic People"
Susan J. Moreno
Executive Director
PO Box 524
Crown Point, IN 46308
USA
Tel: 219-662-1311
Email: chart@netnitco.net
Website: www.maapservices.org

Mission Possible
64 Charles St., E.,
Toronto
Ontario
M4Y 1T1
Canada
Tel: 416-466-5498 or 416-466-6135
Email: info@anythingispossible.ca
Website: www.anythingispossible.ca
Helps people with Asperger Syndrome (AS) and more able autism acquire vocational skills and find meaningful work. They report an 85 percent success rate.

Prospects
Prospects London
Studio 8
The Ivories
6–8 Northampton Street
London N1 2HY
Tel: +44 (20) 7704 7450
Fax: +44 (20) 7359 9440
Email: Prospects-London@nas.org.uk

Website: www.nas.org.uk/nas/prospects/index.html
An "Employment Consultancy with a Difference", Prospects is part of the National Autistic Society. The organization addresses the issues that arise in the recruitment and employment of people with Asperger Syndrome. They work intensively with all candidates to get to know their skills and abilities before placing them in a job, and recognize that it's in the interests of both candidates and employers to get the job match right. They also have offices in Manchester, Glasgow and Sheffield.

TEACCH
Gary Mesibov
Director of Division TEACCH
University of South Carolina,
Chapel Hill, SC
USA
Email: Gary_Mesibov@unc.edu
Website: www.teacch.com

Vocational Alliance
1301 W. Cossitt Ave.
LaGrange, IL 60525
USA
Tel: 815-919-9093
Email: Emmettx4@aol.comwww.vocationalalliance.com

Vocational Support Program for Individuals with ASD
Karen Mastriani
Program Coordinator
Ohio State University
1654 Upham Drive
452 Meann Hall
Columbus, OH 43210
USA
Tel: 614-293-5183
Email: mastriani.2@osu.edu

Other Disabilities

Face blindness (Prosopagnosia)

Face blindness is listed as one of the AS-related conditions.
Introduction: www.anything-balloons.com/glenn/prosopagnosia.shtml or try www.choisser.com/faceblind/

LiveJournal Community

Website: www.livejournal.com/userinfo.bml?user=faceblind

Hyperlexia

American Hyperlexia Association
Website: www.hyperlexia.org

Canadian Hyperlexia Association
Website: www.home.ican.net/%7echa/

http://dmoz.org/Health/Mental_Health/Disorders/Child_and_Adolescent/Learning_Disabilities/Hyperlexia/
This page links to many sites and articles on hyperlexia.

Neurological disorders and stroke

National Institute of Neurological Disorders and Stroke (NINDS)
Website: www.ninds.nih.gov
The National Institute of Neurological Disorders and Stroke (NINDS) conducts and supports research on brain and nervous system disorders. Created by the US Congress in 1950, NINDS is one of the more than two dozen research institutes and centers that comprise the National Institutes of Health (NIH). The NIH, located in Bethesda, Maryland, is an agency of the Public Health Service within the US Department of Health and Human Services. NINDS has occupied a central position in the world of neuroscience for 50 years.

Neurosciences on the Internet
Website: www.neuroguide.com
This site has lots of neurological information and many links.

Traumatic brain injury (TBI)

Because of its neurological nature, the effects of TBI can be similar to those of NLD or AS. Here are four sites that can be helpful.

Centre for Communicative and Cognitive Disabilities (CCCD)

Faculty of Education University of Western Ontario
1137 Western Road
London, Ontario N6G 1G7
Canada
Tel: 519-661-2088
Fax: 519-661-3833
Website: www.edu.wo.ca/cccd/_CurrentSite/CCCD/CCCD_home.htm

Centre for Neuro Skills

www.neuroskills.com
This is a commercial site. Included are the "Traumatic Brain Injury Resource Guide", how-to manuals related to TBI rehabilitation, information on cognitive rehabilitation, and online course materials for continuing education in TBI.

Traumatic Brain Injury: A Guide for Employers

Website: www.mayo.edu/model-system/navpos5a.html

Social skills

Connections Center

4120 Bellaire Boulevard
Houston, TX 77025
USA
Tel: 713-838-1362
Fax: 713-838-1447
Email: administrator@connectionscenter.com
Website: www.connectionscenter.com/rdi/index.htm

Relationship Development Intervention (RDI) is a program modeled after the way NT (neurotypical) children learn to relate emotionally. This intervention approach developed at the Connections Center is different from the typical social skills programs currently available elsewhere. The program systematically teaches skills needed for social competence.

Gray Center for Social Learning and Understanding
Jenison Public Schools
2140 Bauer Rd
Jenison, MI 49428
USA
Tel: (616) 457-8955
Website: www.thegraycenter.org
A quarterly newsletter, *The Morning News*, is available from the Gray Center.

Mind Reading
Website: www.human-emotions.com/mindreading/default.asp
The Interactive Guide to Emotions DVD is a unique reference work covering the entire spectrum of human emotions. Using the software you can explore over 400 emotions, seeing and hearing each one performed by six different people. It has been designed with awareness of the special needs of children and adults who have difficulties recognizing emotional expression in others. Go to human-emotions.com for more information. The DVD got a pretty good review (BBC) and is almost certainly worth the £74.95 cost. But the "important" note says if you are a member of a relevant organization, cost is £54.95.

Michele Garcia Winner
Website: www.socialthinking.com
Author Michele Garcia Winner has written two books on social cognition disability and teaching techniques to help students identify and overcome their weaknesses, leading to the acquisition of social skills.

Further reading

Baldrige, L. (1993) *Letitia Baldrige's New Complete Guide to Executive Manners.* New York: Dimensions.

Cohen, D. (1992) *Body Language in Relationships.* London: Sheldon Press.

Csoti, M. (2000) *People Skills for Young Adults.* London: Jessica Kingsley Publishers.

Markham, U. (1998) *How to Deal with Difficult People.* London: Thorsons.

Pease, A. (1984) *Signals: How to Use Body Language for Power, Success and Love.* London: Bantam.

Pease, A. (1999) *Body Language.* Oxford: Butterworth-Heinemann.

Searle, Y. and Streng, I. (1996) *The Social Skills Game.* London: Jessica Kingsley Publishers.

Winner, M.G. (2002) *Inside Out: What Makes A Person with Social Cognitive Deficits Tick?* London: Jessica Kingsley Publishers.

Winner, M.G. (2003) *Thinking About You, Thinking About Me.* London: Jessica Kingsley Publishers.

Visual, spatial, perceptual and motor skills

ARK Foundation: Applied Research Knowledge overcoming obstacles to learning
Allenmore Medical Center
19th and South Union
Tacoma, WA 98405
USA
Tel: (253) 573-0311
Fax: (253) 573-0211
Email: ARKfdn@aol.com
Spatial disability, the least recognized learning problem, is a focus of ARK Foundation.

"The Learning Window" is a possible remediation for the motor and spatial perception problems associated with NLD and AS.
Website: www.newhorizons.org/spneeds/inclusion/learning_window/front_window.html

Givens, D. *The Nonverbal Dictionary of Gestures, Signs and Body Language Cues: From Adam's-Apple-Jump to Zygomatic Smile.* A WWW Virtual Library© "Best" Site (1999, 2000) © 1998–2001 by David B. Givens, PhD, Center for Nonverbal Studies. www.members.aol.com/nonverbal2/diction1.htm.

Held, R. (1972) *Perception: Mechanisms and Models. Readings from Scientific American.* San Francisco: W.H. Freeman.

McKim, R.H. (1980) *Thinking Visually.* Belmont, CA: Lifetime Learning.

Samuels, M. and Samuels, N. (1980) *Seeing With the Mind's Eye.* New York: Random House.

Schone, H. and Strausfield, C. (1984) *Spatial Orientation: The Spatial Control of Behavior In Animals and Man.* Princeton, NJ: Princeton University Press.

Vocational rehabilitation

Association for the Advancement of Rehabilitation Technology (RESNA)
Technical Assistance Project
1700 North Moore Street, Suite 1540
Arlington, VA 22209-1903
USA

Tel: 703-524-6686
Fax: 703-524-6630
TTY: 703-524-6639
Website: www.resna.org

National Association of Rehabilitation Professionals in the Private Sector

1661 Worchester Rd., #203
Farmingham, MA 01701
USA
Tel: 508-820-8889
Fax: 508-820-4337
Website: www.narpps.org
You can search their directory of over 3000 members to find someone in your area.

National Clearing House of Rehabilitation Training Materials (NCHRTM)

Website: www.nchrtm.okstate.edu/resources/state_vr.html
Each US state has a Division of Vocational Rehabilitation that provides vocational rehabilitation services to individuals with disabilities. These services include counseling, advocacy, job training, and job placements. They will work with you to develop an employment goal. You will be evaluated to see if you're eligible for these services. For the Office of Vocational Rehabilitation Services in your state, consult a phone directory or find a state-by-state listing of vocational rehabilitation agencies on the website. www.nchrtm.okstate.edu/rrc lists career opportunities in public vocational rehabilitation programs across the USA.

National Consortium of State-Operated Comprehensive Rehabilitation Centers

Website: www.ncsocrc.org/

National Rehabilitation Association

633 S. Washington St., Suite 300
Alexandria, VA 22314
USA
Tel: 703-836-0850
Fax: 703-836-0848
Website: www.nationalrehab.org

National Rehabilitation Counseling Association
8807 Sudley Rd, #102
Manassas, VA, 20110-4719
USA
Tel: 703-361-2077
Fax: 703-361-2489
Website: http://nrca-net.org

National Rehabilitation Information Center (NARIC)
8455 Colesville Road, Suite 935
Silver Spring, MD 20910
USA
Tel: 301-588-9284
Fax: 301-587-1967
800.346.2742
800.34NARIC
800.227.0216 Abledata Product Database
Website: www.naric.com

Career Resources

Websites

These websites offer guidance on many issues related to work and career planning.

www.acinet.org/acinet/default.asp America's Career Info Net offers career exploration, wage information, and job market outlook.

www.americasemployers.com Includes information on the job search, recruiters, and electronic networking, as well as a résumé bank, job listings, and a company database.

www.asktheemployer.com Ask the Employer gives the employer's perspective on a variety of career management issues.

www.asktheheadhunter.com This site gives the recruiter's view of job hunting.

www.bls.gov/oco/ Occupational Outlook Handbook is the online version of the print standard for occupational information produced by the US Department of Labor. Search for information on working conditions, training, job outlook, and average salaries for hundreds of jobs.

www.careermag.com Career Magazine contains articles on managing your career from Career Magazine.

www.careermosaic.com Features a cross-section of various industries and careers.

www.careerpath.com Career Path allows the user to view classified want ads from newspapers all around the USA.

www.careerpathsonline.com Career Paths Online can help you with self-assessment. Here you will find a ten-step career planning guide and links to many informative articles.

www.careerresource.com This is a career source offering valuable career management information and tools to help you improve your career performance.

www.careers.org Claims to be the web's directory of career directories, and offers guidance and direction for the career planner.

www.cdm.uwaterloo.ca/ This University of Waterloo career site contains self-assessment, career research and decision making (including educational options), networking résumés, cover letters, and interviewing tips, choosing work offers, and life and work planning.

www.cpl.tcu.edu/CareerDec.html This Career Decision Making page from Texas Christian University provides tools for self-assessment as well as exploring various occupations.

www.dbm.com Sponsored by Drake Beam Morin, a large career consulting firm.

www.dice.com Dice is another good career and job-hunting site.

www.doleta.gov/programs/onet Contains a database of occupational titles with job requirements, tasks, and abilities for about 1100 occupations.

www.employmentspot.com A digest of career and employment sites as well as articles on job search strategies.

www.fiveoclockclub.com Kate Wendleton's The Five O'clock Club focuses on implementing effective job search strategies.

www.hotjobs.com Includes advice-filled articles by professional career counselors, as well as doing a job search by industry sector, company, location, or keyword.

www.iccweb.com A comprehensive site that features many career-related categories, and links to other career sites.

http://icdl.uncg.edu/ The International Career Development Library (ICDL) is a free, online collection of full-text resources for counselors, educators, workforce development personnel, and others providing career development services.

www.jobhuntersbible.com The JobHunters Bible is sponsored by Richard Bolles and designed as a supplement to his legendary job hunter's manual, *What Color is your Parachute?* Contains interactive quizzes and directions on how to use the Internet to look for a job.

www.jobs.com Promotes itself as a fast-growing job search resource center.

www.jobstar.org Jobstar offers career guides on a variety of specific careers as well as online career tests, information on résumé writing, and salary information.

www.jobtrak.com Jobtrak features career information and resources.

www.jobweb.org Jobweb features employment information and an e-zine on job choices.

www.keirsey.com Site discussing temperament.

www.monster.com The Monster Board is a comprehensive career management website providing personality and career quizzes, interviewing and résumé advice, and access to career chats.

www.ncna.com The National Career Networking Association provides information and guidance on many topics relating to managing your career, including how to find a career counselor.

www.onetcenter.org O*NET is a web-based version of the Occupational Information Network, allowing consumers to explore employment options and the skills and education needed. Extensive disability resources and job accommodation features are included to assure accessibility to all users.

www.princetonreview.com/cte/default.asp The Princeton Review has a comprehensive site on all aspects of career guidance and job hunting.

www.rileyguide.com The Riley Guide offers advice, strategies and resources from Margaret F. Dikel.

www.self-directed-search.com Gives an explanation of the Holland career system and self-directed search. His theory classifies workplace profiles according to individual interests. You can take the Holland test and also find a career counselor trained in the Holland system here.

www.shrm.org Home to the Society for Human Resource Management. Here you'll find news and resources about important workplace issues.

www.smartbiz.com A resource for managing your small business, but many of their resources apply equally well to managing your career.

www.temperament.com Site discussing temperament.

www.typelogic.com Discusses your personality type (Myers Briggs Type Indicator, MBTI) and personal style as it relates to work and relationships.

www.usnews.com/usnews/work/wohome.htm The US News Career Guide has information on résumés, cover letters, interviewing, benefits, salaries, self-assessment, work and family, and more.

www.wetfeet.com/asp/home.asp Wet Feet has resources on career research, career advice, and finding a job.

Books

Career planning

Allen, J.G. (1994) *Successful Job Search Strategies for the Disabled: Understanding the ADA.* New York: Wiley.

Bronson, P. (2002) *What Should I Do with my Life?* New York: Random House. Fifty essays about real people in the real world searching for their true calling.

Brown, D.S. (2000) *Learning a Living.* Bethesda, MD: Woodbine House. She has some good tips on finding a job, and great ideas on compensating for social skills deficiencies.

Bruzzese, A. (1999) *Take This Job and Thrive.* Manassas Park, VA: Impact. The author offers advice on dealing with office politics, business etiquette, entertaining, and obnoxious co-workers. The book includes many real life examples.

Buckingham, M. and Clifton, D.O. (2001) *Now, Discover Your Strengths*. New York: Free Press. This book is based on the simple but all-too-often overlooked premise that enhancing employees' strengths (already within them) rather than eliminating their weaknesses makes for a more rewarding work environment. Descriptions of each of the 34 strengths, each accompanied by quotes from people who discovered themselves to have that particular strength, and a chapter on how to manage people with each strength are all wonderful.

Casperson, D.M. (1999) *Power Etiquette: What You Don't Know Can Kill Your Career*. New York: AMACOM. This book offers guidance on topics like telephone, email and internet etiquette, table manners, gift giving, making introductions, and more.

Cassidy, G.A. (2000) *Discover Your Passion: An Intuitive Search to Find Your Purpose in Life*. Westfield, NJ: Tomlynn Publications. Provides self-assessment exercises and information in a concise, easy-to-read book style for people seeking personally satisfying work.

Crispin, G. and Mehler, M. (2000) *CareerXroads 2000*. Indianapolis, IN: Jist Works. This reference book reviews and rates job, résumé and career management websites.

Duffy, P.L. and Wannie, T.W. (1995) *Setting your Career and Life Direction*. Indianapolis, IN: Jist Works.

Harvard Business Review (2001) *Harvard Business Review on Finding and Keeping the Best People*. Cambridge, MA: Harvard Business School Press. This is a collection of articles by leading business scholars offering a guide for managers on finding and keeping quality employees.

Jansen, J. (2003) *I Don't Know What I Want, but I Know It's Not This*. Harmondsworth: Penguin. Career coach Julie Jansen addresses work dissatisfaction and presents a guide to implementing positive career change. Using career assessment quizzes and personality exercises, she helps readers understand their present work or career situation, discover the type of work for which they're best suited, and learn how to create the changes they need.

Krannich, R.L. (1999) *Change Your Job, Change Your Life: High Impact Strategies for Finding Great Jobs in the Decade Ahead*. Manassas Park, VA: Impact Publications. The book was featured in *U.S. News and World Report* and covers subjects like skills assessment, researching and identifying the best jobs, understanding the job market, and networking.

Kroeger, O. and Thuessen, J. (1989) *Type Talk*. New York: Delta.

Kummerow, J.M., Berger, N.J. and Kirby, L.K. (1997) *Work Types*. New York: Warner.

Lawson, K. (2000) *KISS Guide to Managing Your Career*. London: Dorling Kindersley.

Rozakis, L. and Rozakis, B. (1998) *The Complete Idiot's Guide to Office Politics.* Indianapolis, IN: Alpha Pearson. A humorous look at getting ahead in corporate America.

Tieger, P.D. and Barron-Tieger, B. (1995) *Do What You Are: Discover the Perfect Career for You Through the Secrets of Personality Type.* New York: Little Brown. This best-selling career guide shows how to determine your personality type and explains which jobs are best suited to each type.

Waldroop, J. and Butler, T. (2000) *Maximum Success: Changing the 12 Behavior Patterns That Keep You from Getting Ahead.* New York: Doubleday. The authors explore attitudes and behaviors that damage careers, and offer specific advice on overcoming them.

Wendleton, K. (1997) *Targeting the Job You Want.* New York: Five O'clock Books.

The job search

Bolles, R. (annual) *What Color is Your Parachute?* Berkeley, CA: Ten Speed Press.

Figler, H. (1999) *The Complete Job Search Handbook.* New York: Henry Holt.

Hacker, C.A. (1999) *Job Hunting in the 21st Century.* Boca Raton, FL: St. Lucie Press.

Hemming, A. (2003) *Work It! How to Get Ahead, Save your Ass, and Land a Job in Any Economy.* New York: Simon and Schuster. The founder of workforce agency The Hired Guns and creator of the world-famous Pink Slip Parties offers valuable advice for finding and keeping a job.

Satterfield, M. (1995) *VGM's Complete Guide to Career Etiquette: From Job Search to Career Advancement.* Lincolnwood, IL: VGM Career Horizons.

Wendleton, K. (1997) *Job Search Secrets.* New York: Five O'clock Books.

Résumés and cover letters

Block, J.A. and Betrus, M. (1999) *101 Best Cover Letters.* New York: McGraw-Hill. This book features sample cover letter/résumé combinations.

Enelow, W. (2003) *Best Keywords for Résumés, Cover Letters and Interviews.* Manassas Park, VA: Impact Books. A comprehensive, authoritative guide for key words and phrases in the language of employers, including more than 500 action verbs, high-impact phrases, and personality descriptors. Great for developing effective résumés and cover letters and for formulating answers to critical interview questions.

Enelow, W. and Kursmark, L.M. (2003) *Expert Résumés for People Returning to Work.* Impact Books. This book highlights 100 résumés for individuals returning to work after an extended absence.

Fein, R. (1999) *101 Quick Tips for a Dynamic Résumé.* Manassos Park, VA: Impact.

Ireland, S. (2000) *The Complete Idiot's Guide to the Perfect Résumé*. Indianapolis, IN: Alpha Books.

Parker, Y. (1996) Rrésumé Catalog: *200 Damn Good Examples*. Berkeley, CA: Ten Speed Press.

Rosenberg, A.D. and Hizer, D.V. (1990) *The Résumé Handbook*. Holbrook, NA: Adams. Samples of both good and bad résumés along with a realistic step-by-step guide to building a résumé.

Whitcomb, S.B. (1999) *Résumé Magic: Trade Secrets of a Professional Résumé Writer*. Indianapolis, IN: Jist Works.

RÉSUMÉ WEBSITES

www.careerlab.com/letters/default.htm Tips on writing cover letters, thank you letters, and more with hundreds of sample letters.

http://owl.english.purdue.edu/handouts/pw/ Professional writing handouts and resources from Purdue University's Career Center, includes good résumé writing tips and tools.

www.provenresumes.com An excellent site with lots of information, including booklets you can download.

http://students.syr.edu/careerservices/index.html Basic information on writing résumés, plus a couple sample résumés. Under "Quick Help", click dropdown arrow and select "Resumes".

http://wrocc.csun.edu/otherproducts/student.html Student handbook that California State University, Northridge puts out for its disabled students. Page 41 begins the section on résumé writing.

RÉSUMÉ SOFTWARE

Several software packages offer guidelines for developing your résumé:

- RésuméMaker (Individual software)
- Résumés that Work (MacMillan)
- WinWay Résumé (WinWay).

Job interviews

Deluca, M.J. (2001) *More Best Answers to the 201 Most Frequently Asked Interview Questions*. New York: McGraw Hill.

Gottesman, D. and Mauro, B. (1999) *The Interview Rehearsal Book*. Winchester: Piccolo Press.

Kennedy, J.L. (2000) *Job Interviews for Dummies*. Foster City, CA: IDG Books.

Morgan, D. (2001) *Interview Fitness Training, A Workout With Carole Martin, The Interview Coach.* Danville, CA: Interview Publishing. An interview coach leads you through 13 powerful preparation exercises to help you present your best skills and abilities.

Porot, D. *et al.* (1999) *101 Toughest Interview Questions: And Answers That Win the Job!* Berkeley, CA: Ten Speed Press.

Yeager, N. and Hough, L. (1998) *Power Interviews.* New York: Wiley.

Networking

Balzano, F.J. and Kelly, M.B. (1999) *Why Should Extroverts Make all the Money?* Chicago: Contemporary Books.

Fisher, D. and Vilas, S. (1992) *Power Networking: 55 Secrets to Personal and Professional Success.* Austin, TX: Mountain Harbor.

Michelli, D. and Straw, A. (1997) *Successful Networking.* Hauppage, NY: Barron's.

Stoodley, M. (1997) *Information Interviewing: What It Is and How to Use It in Your Career.* New York: Ferguson.

Tullier, L.M. (1998) *Networking for Everyone!* Indianapolis, IN: Jist Works.

Research in your job hunt

Freed, M.N. and Diodato, V.P. (1991) *The Business Information Desk Reference: Where to Find Answers to Business Questions.* London: McMillan.

Growther, K.N.T. (1993) *Researching Your Way to a Good Job.* New York: Wiley.

Jandt, F.E. and Nennich, M.B. (1997) *Using the Internet and the World Wide Web in your Job Search.* Indianapolis, IN: Jist Works.

Other useful references:

- *City and State Directories in Print*
- *Encyclopedia of Associations*
- *Encyclopedia of Business Information Sources*
- *Professional Careers Sourcebook*
- *The Job Hunter's Sourcebook.*

INDUSTRY RESEARCH SOURCES

Books

- *American Salaries and Wages Survey*
- *Dun's Business Rankings*

- *Encyclopedia of Associations*
- *Standard & Poor's Industry Surveys*
- *U. S. Industrial Outlook*
- *U. S. Industry Profiles.*

Websites

http://biz.yahoo.com/industry Yahoo's special industry site can help you track down useful information, and provides links to other sites that provide specific company information.

COMPANY RESEARCH SOURCES

Books

- *Dun and Bradstreet's Million Dollar Directory* (print or CD-ROM)
- *Hoover's Handbooks* (American Business, Emerging Companies, etc.)
- *Moody's Manuals*
- *Standard & Poor's Corporations* (print or CD-ROM)
- *Thomas Register* (print or CD-ROM)
- *Ward's Business Directory of Private and Public Companies* (also online).

Websites

www.companiesonline.com Companies Online

www.corporateinformation.com Corporate Information

www.hoovers.com Hoover's Online

Self-employment

www.entrepreneur.com and www.entreworld.com Guidance and a variety of resources including articles, tools, databases and links to other sites.

www.freeagent.com An information hub for freelancers, consultants, and independent contractors.

www.nase.org The National Association for the Self Employed offers news and articles on self-employment.

www.sba.gov The Small Business Association provides information and guidance on starting and maintaining a small business.

www.score.org The Service Core of Retired Executives advice site.

www.tdigest.com The Telecommuter's Digest.

Bibliography

American Psychiatric Association (APA) (1994) *DSM-IV Diagnostic and Statistical Manual of Mental Disorders*, 4th edn. Washington DC: APA.

Archives of General Psychiatry (2002) *59*, 10, 885–891.

Asperger, H. (1944) 'Die satistischen Psychopathenim Kindesalter.' *Archive for Psychiatrice und Nervenkrankheiten 127*, 76–136. Trans. and annotated by U. Frith in U. Frith (ed) (1991) *Autism and Asperger Syndrome*. Cambridge: Cambridge University Press, pp.37–92.

Attwood, T. (1998) *Asperger's Syndrome: A Guide for Parents and Professionals*. London: Jessica Kingsley Publishers.

Barnard, J., Harvey, V., Prior, A. and Potter, D. (2001) *Ignored or Inelligible?* London: National Autistic Society.

Bauer, S. (1996) *Asperger Syndrome: Through the Lifespan*. (www.aspennj.org/bauer.html). (www.udel.edu/bkirby/asperger/as_thru_years.html).

Beaumont, P. (2001) 'Adult victims of autism are left on jobs scrapheap.' *Observer*, 13 May. (http://observer.guardian.co.uk/uk_news/story/0,6903,490062,00.html)

Bolles, R.N. (2003) *What Color is Your Parachute? A Practical Manual for Job Hunters and Career Changers*. Berkeley, CA: Ten Speed Press.

Bonnet, K.A. and Gao, X.K. (1996) 'Asperger's syndrome in Neurologic Perspective.' *Journal of Child Neurology 11*, 483–489.

Brumback, R.A., Harper, C.R. and Weinberg, W.A. (1996) 'Nonverbal learning disabilities, Asperger's syndrome, pervasive developmental disorder – should we care?' *Journal of Child Neurology 11*, 6, 427–429.

Carlowe, J. (2001) 'Signal failure.' *Observer*, 20 May. (http://observer.guardian.co.uk/life/story/0,6903,493180,00.html)

Cullen, I. (2001) 'Adults with Asperger's Syndrome often go undiagnosed.' *Boston Globe*, 18 February.

Debbaudt, D. (2002) 'Police and autism: Avoiding unfortunate situations.' (www.policeandautism.cjb.net/).

DeVroy, A. (1990) 'In Emotion-Filled Ceremony, Bush Signs Rights Law for America's Disabled.' *Washington Post*, 27 July, A-14.

Faigin, G. (1990) *The Artist's Complete Guide to Facial Expression*. New York: Watson-Guptill Publications.

Field, T. (1996) *Bully in Sight: How to Predict, Resist Challenge and Combat Workplace Bullying*. Wantage: Success Unlimited.

Forrest, B. 'The Boundaries between Asperger and Nonverbal Learning Disability Syndromes.' *Pediatric Neuropsychology Interest Group Newsletter 5*, 3, 1–y.

Frith, U. (ed) (1991) *Autism and Asperger Syndrome*. Cambridge: Cambridge University Press.

Gillberg, C. (1989) 'Asperger Syndrome in 23 Swedish Children.' *Developmental Medicine and Child Neurology 31*, 520–531.

Gillberg, C. (2002) *A Guide to Asperger Syndrome.* Cambridge: Cambridge University Press.

Gillberg, I.C. and Gillberg, C. (1989) 'Asperger syndrome – some epidemiological considerations: A research note.' *Journal of Child Psychology and Psychiatry 30*, 631–638.

Gillberg, I.C., Gillberg, C., Rastam, M. and Wentz, E. (2001) 'The Asperger Syndrome (and high-functioning autism) Diagnostic Interview (ASDI): A preliminary study of a new structured clinical interview.' *Autism 5*, 57–66.

Ginzberg, E. (1951) *Occupational Choice.* New York: Columbia University Press.

Grandin, T. (1999) 'Choosing the Right Job for People with Autism or Asperger's Syndrome.' (www.autism.org/temple/jobs.html).

Herman, J. (1997) *Trauma and Recovery.* New York: Basic Books.

Hochheiser, R. (1987) *How to Work for a Jerk.* New York: Vintage Books.

Johnson, D. And Myklebust, H. (1967) *Learning Disabilities: Educational Principles and Practices.* New York: Grune and Strattan

Klin, A., Volkmar, F.R. and Sparrow, S.S. (2000) *Asperger Syndrome.* New York: Guilford Press.

Klin, A., Volkmar, F.R., Sparrow, S.S., Cicchetti, D.V. and Rourke, B.P. (1995) 'Validity and neuropsychological characterization of Asperger Syndrome: Convergence with NVLD Syndrome.' *Journal of Child Psychology and Psychiatry 36*, 7, 1127–1140.

Lovett, H. (1996) *Learning to Listen: Positive Approaches and People who are Difficult to Serve.* London: Taylor and Francis.

Molloy, J.T. (1988) *John T. Molloy's New Dress for Success.* New York: Warner Books

Muir, H. (2003) 'Einstein and Newton Showed Signs of Autism.' *New Scientist*, 3 May, 19–30. April 03 (www.newscientist.com).

Myklebust, H.R. (1975) 'Nonverbal learning disabilities: Assessment and intervention.' In H.R. Myklebust (ed) *Progress in Learning Disabilities*, vol. 3. New York: Grune and Stratton, pp.85–121.

Nemnich, M.B. And Jandt, F.E. (2000) *Cyberspace Résumé Kit 2001: How to Build and Launch an Online Résumé.* Indianapolis, IN: JIST Works.

Portland State University (1992) *Survey: Social Behaviours.* Portland: Portland State University Special Education Department.

Prince-Hughes, D. (ed) (2002) *Aquamarine Blue 5: Personal Stories of College Students with Autism.* Athens, OH: Swallow Press.

Reed, L. (2001) *Unaware: Living with Nonverbal Learning Disabilities.* (www.LaurieReed.com)

Roman, M.A. (1998) 'The Syndrome of Nonverbal Learning Disabilities: Clinical Description and Applied Aspects.' *Current Issues in Education 1*, 1, 1.

Rourke, B.P. (ed) (1995) *Syndrome of Nonverbal Learning Disabilities.* New York: Guilford Press.

Rourke, B.P. (2000) (http://web.archive.org/web/20010406051128/ www.nldontheweb.org/Byron_Rourke_homepage.htm).

Shore, S.M. (2003) *Beyond the Wall: Personal Experiences with Autism and Asperger Syndrome*, 2nd edn. Shawnee Mission, KS: Autism Asperger Publishing Company.

Thompson, S. (1996) 'Nonverbal Learning Disorders (pt. 1).' *The Gram* (LDA-CA newsletter), Fall.

Thompson, S. (1997) *The Source for Nonverbal Learning Disabilities.* East Moline, IL: LinguiSystems.

Vacca, D.M. (2001) 'Confronting the Puzzle of Nonverbal Learning Disabilities.' *Educational Leadership 59*, 3 (www.ascd.org/frameedlead.html).

Subject Index

The abbreviations AS for Asperger Syndrome, NLD for Non-Verbal Learning Disability and NT for neurotypicals, are used throughout

Author Index